SALES
LETTERS
That *SIZZLE*

SALES LETTERS That *SIZZLE*

SECOND EDITION

All the Hooks, Lines, and Sinkers
You'll Ever Need to Close Sales

Herschell Gordon Lewis

NTC Business Books
NTC/Contemporary Publishing Group

Library of Congress Cataloging-in-Publication Data

Lewis, Herschell Gordon, 1926–
    Sales letters that sizzle : all the hooks, lines, and sinkers you'll
ever need to close sales / Herschell Gordon Lewis. — 2nd ed.,
new and rev. ed.
       p.   cm.
    ISBN 0-8442-2348-4
    1. Sales letters.   2. Direct marketing.   I. Title.
HF5730.L48   1999
658.8'1—dc21   98-55946
                                  CIP

Cover design by Scott Rattray
Cover and interior illustration copyright © Barton Stabler/Artville, LLC.
Interior design by City Desktop Productions, Inc.

Published by NTC Business Books
A division of NTC/Contemporary Publishing Group, Inc.
4255 West Touhy Avenue, Lincolnwood (Chicago), Illinois 60646-1975 U.S.A.
International Standard Book Number: 0-8442-2348-4
99 00 01 02 03 04 05 HP 15 14 13 12 11 10 9 8 7 6 5 4 3 2 1

Contents

Preface

This is the second edition of this book.

Has the method of creating sales letters changed enough to warrant a second edition? Wellll . . .

If you've saved some of the letters you've received over the years, because you felt they were either effective or ineffective, you'll probably agree that an evolutionary process exists, even with standard communications.

Handwriting, marginal notes, big display type above the greeting, subheads, multiple colors—these are additions and power-enhancers designed to lift a letter above the clutter . . . to swing an apathetic or even hostile reader into a positive orbit . . . and to create excitement and the ultimate symbol of success: the desire to lift the phone or a pen because of a "Yes!" reaction.

What sometimes happens is that form overcomes substance. Or the writer cares more about impressing associates in the office than about generating the buying impulse. Or the writer just doesn't know how to grab the rhetorical trigger—and fire!

Another circumstance warranting a second edition: The first edition of *Sales Letters That Sizzle* was published early in the last decade of the twentieth century. It made no mention of the World Wide Web and its amazing child, e-mail. How could it? The World Wide Web wasn't even a gleam in anyone's electronic eye.

The twenty-first century is a new, faster-paced, more brutally competitive ball game. We have to throw strikes or our team loses. And this new edition, with new examples and a new awareness of what works and what doesn't work, can be your pitching coach.

So get out there and knock the competitors out of the box.

A Note About Structure

This book is divided into two parts:

- "Rules and Tools: Tricks of the Trade"
- "100 Letter Openings That Will Work Every Time"

Part I features descriptions and examples of the various components and techniques of letter-writing—both mechanical and creative. Included are chapters covering easy-to-follow rules for writing *any* letter, mechanical aspects such as overlines and "Johnson Boxes," the short but mighty P.S., envelopes, and a chapter on the most recent addition to the world of force-communication, e-mail.

Part II offers a menu of one hundred easy ways to start a letter. You know from your own experiences: The impact (or lack of impact) generated by the opening affects your reaction far more powerfully than the rest of the text, even in the case of four-page and six-page epics.

Depending on how many letters you write and how serious a student of the craft you are, the one hundred different openings can be a lifetime supply or just a starter kit. One benefit of having them on hand is their availability as a checklist, or even as a personal test of your own versatility.

To me, the principal value of this book is its ability to prevent the writer from "running on tracks"—repeating the same type of message time after time, regardless of what's being said or to whom. The examples included here aren't contrived samples but actual letters and envelopes; most were mailings to my home or office.

Use this information and use these letter openings with one purpose in mind: to increase both the volume and the intensity of response.

How to Use This Book

The two parts of this book are "in sync" with each other.

Neither section is designed to give you clever phraseology when you're writing a chatty letter to your Aunt Minnie or a thank-you note to your host at a dinner party. This text is solidly aimed at *force-communication*, the noble art of causing a client, a customer, or a prospect to perform a positive act as the direct result of reading your words.

You wouldn't have the book in your hands if you weren't a serious (and, probably, a professional) letter writer. So if you want to sharpen your commercial letter-writing skills, this is the logical way to put this book to work.

It's a three-step process:

1. First, read each chapter of part I twice, but not twice on the same day. Digest it overnight, then reread. You'll pick up nuances that clarify themselves on a second reading.
2. Then, if you're a genuine student of the craft of force-communication, on separate slips of paper write each of the one hundred letter openings from part II. Put the slips of paper in a hat or container.
3. Choose a subject. You're trying to convince Mr. or Ms. X to do what? Without looking at them, take two of the slips out of the container. Write an opening using each.

This stretches and strengthens your communications muscle. It prevents your communications from "running on tracks." It gives you an asset every one of us force-communicators needs—viewpoint.

I'll tell you what else it does: It lifts your letters above the morass of all those "boilerplate" letters that result from picking up the approach of a letter that came to you (which itself was probably written as the result of a letter that came to that writer). It lifts your letters above the morass of all those "boilerplate" letters that result from a CD-ROM loaded with prewritten, fill-in-the-blanks letters. It lifts your letters above the morass of all those letters that don't quite come off because it's obvious the writer is struggling to be clever.

After you've started the exercise, continue it. Throw away the two numbered slips you've used, and next time pick two more. What a terrific creative exercise!

Just one more suggestion: This book includes one hundred ways to begin your sales letter. Once a week, discover a new one, not included here. Over the period of one year, you'll add half as many as are in this text. And believe me, they're out there.

Enjoy the power of words. That power is our edge over all those other folks who do run on tracks. Be glad they're our competition!

Acknowledgments

I'd be derelict if I failed to acknowledge the tremendous influence of the late Henry "Pete" Hoke, who as publisher of the watershed periodical *Direct Marketing* published my rantings for nearly twenty years. Some principles of writing sales letters, codified in this book, were the result of hard cogitation necessitated by the realization that I was writing articles for professionals; lapsing into platitudes and nonspecifics just wouldn't cut it.

Writing the "Better Letters" column for *Selling Newsletter* has forced me to analyze: "Why does this work? Why doesn't that work? What makes this wording strong? What makes that wording weak?" So to Bill Keenan, former editor, and "B" Zaban, current editor, my thanks.

And of course, to Danielle Egan-Miller, that most astute, charming, and incredibly persuasive editor at NTC/Contemporary Publishing Company, I owe a huge debt of gratitude for convincing me that a new edition was necessary at all. How right she was! How slow I was to recognize that she was right!

And to my infinitely patient project editor, Heidi Bresnahan, and to the copyeditor, Deborah Roberts, that brilliant catcher of typos, non sequiturs, and off-the-wall observations, my profound thanks for bringing coherence to the manuscript.

I'm forever indebted to the many marketers who entrusted me with the job of creating sales letters for them. By being able to follow the results of testing and comparisons, I've been able to add to the principles outlined in *Sales Letters That Sizzle*.

The benefit of being on the firing line . . . of having one's sales letters judged by the harshest of all critics—those the letters are trying to influence—is a benefit no amount of theory can match. A sales letter succeeds not because it has perfect grammar or cleverness or gimmickry, but because it convinces a target to respond. So, yes, without that multi-battle-field experience, this book could not exist. Thank you, dear clients.

But one acknowledgment towers over all others. My life partner Margo, whose awareness of reality far exceeds mine, is responsible not only for many of the exhibits and examples in both editions ("Can you believe they mailed this?" . . . "Doesn't this make you want to call?" . . . "What the devil are they trying to say?" . . . "You have to include this one because . . .") but also for my claim of ongoing sanity.

So thanks to all. And to you, for joining me in the search for the perfect letter.

HGL

SALES
LETTERS
That *SIZZLE*

PART I

Rules and Tools:
Tricks of the Trade

How easy it is!

Part I of this book shows you how easy it is—not just to understand all the devices you'll ever need to write sales letters that effectively and persuasively communicate your sales message to your prospects—but to *use* them, starting today.

"Tricks of the Trade" at first glance may seem to be the wrong title for this section. "Trade" implies a craft, and effective, persuasive letters are the private domain of self-called "creatives" who think great thoughts and turn clever phrases. Right?

Nah. There *are* rare individuals who have an innate talent to create truly memorable messages that dazzle us with their inventiveness and salesmanship. But more often than not, the people who call themselves creatives are called other things when their rhetorical pearls turn out to be faux pearls.

If you're reading this book you already know why the adjectives *creative* and *effective* aren't always applicable to the same person: Too many writers concentrate on being creative instead of using rules and tools of effective salesmanship, which in the heartless world of marketing is called *force*-communication. Your targets either respond or they don't. If you keep score any other way, you're kidding yourself. And make no mistake: Accidents happen too seldom to allow any letter writer to claim success without exhibiting credentials. Being able to apply these rules and tools is a craft.

That's what part I is about—the craft of communicating convincingly to a potential customer. The chapters that follow explain how and when to use the devices effective communicators use to sell.

And how about "Tricks"?

We live in the Age of Skepticism. Our best targets are bombarded by hundreds of messages every day, many written by creatives who muddy the water instead of clarifying it.

Our targets have become wary. So we "trick" them into reading our message . . . and responding to it.

Hold it! That doesn't mean tricking them into making a positive decision by overstating or misrepresenting. We're communicators, not cunning thieves. When you misrepresent, you run a double gauntlet:

1. Many of your prime prospects will see through the charade and your message will end up in the garbage.
2. Of those few naïve souls who are duped by false claims and promises, when you make one sale you also eventually make one enemy—for life. That enemy, no longer naïve, despises not only you but your legitimate competitors whom you've tarred with your word-brush. So your competitors rightfully hate you, too.

Ah, but if your trickery results in a prospect's reading and responding to your message instead of a competitor's—*without misrepresentation*—then you're a genuine professional.

And it's easy . . . because the rules and techniques are easy.

That's not just a promise. It's a guarantee. It's what part I will help you do.

1

Everybody Writes Letters!

The most primitive element in direct response is the letter. The most sophisticated element in direct response is the letter. Everybody—*everybody*—writes letters. And a handful of people who recognize and respect the potential power they have at their fingertips when they sit down at the keyboard . . . just a handful . . . know how to write effective letters.

Are you in the force-communication (read advertising, marketing, or public relations) business? You should take your direct-mail letters *very* seriously. As so many letters say, frankly, I'm puzzled. I'm puzzled to see so many writers and art directors fussing over inconsequential details of brochures, or insisting on die-cuts and six-color printing, while paying no attention to the message. They pay attention to production, not message—form, not substance—and they pay *no* attention to the letter.

I'm puzzled to see so many e-mail messages that pay so much attention to form they lose their substance. I'm puzzled by the prevalence of cleverness for the sake of cleverness instead of cleverness for the sake of salesmanship by the deadly "That which is different = that which is good" cult.

If you're in business or government or the brutally competitive fundraising profession, your problem is compounded. You have to compete with letters written by those who have made a semi-scientific study of communication. Yet many, whose incomes depend on their ability to convince others to act, in their letters lapse into clichés and grammatical stupidities . . . and paint themselves into rhetorical corners.

Is a puzzlement. As I said, everybody writes letters. Everybody. From the day we write our first job-hunting letter to the day we write our retirement valedictory, we create letters.

Ads may be written by a committee; various sets of hands tinker and alter, so a finished ad or brochure may be a hybrid product the writer who started it doesn't even recognize. Not so with letters. They're one person's statement.

THE WALL STREET JOURNAL.

World Financial Center, 200 Liberty Street, New York, NY 10281

Dear Reader:

On a beautiful late spring afternoon, twenty-five years ago, two young men graduated from the same college. They were very much alike, these two young men. Both had been better than average students, both were personable and both—as young college graduates are—were filled with ambitious dreams for the future.

Recently, these men returned to their college for their 25th reunion.

They were still very much alike. Both were happily married. Both had three children. And both, it turned out, had gone to work for the same Midwestern manufacturing company after graduation, and were still there.

But there was a difference. One of the men was manager of a small department of that company. The other was its president.

What Made The Difference

Have you ever wondered, as I have, what makes this kind of difference in people's lives? It isn't a native intelligence or talent or dedication. It isn't that one person wants success and the other doesn't.

The difference lies in what each person knows and how he or she makes use of that knowledge.

And that is why I am writing to you and to people like you about The Wall Street Journal. For that is the whole purpose of The Journal: to give its readers knowledge— knowledge that they can use in business.

A Publication Unlike Any Other

You see, The Wall Street Journal is a unique publication. It's the country's only national business daily. Each business day, it is put together by the world's largest staff of business-news experts.

Each business day, The Journal's pages include a broad range of information of interest and significance to business-minded people, no matter where it comes from. Not just stocks and finance, but anything and everything in the whole, fast-moving world of business. . .The Wall Street Journal gives you all the business news you need—when you need it.

Knowledge Is Power

Right now, I am looking at page one of The Journal, the best-read front page in America. It combines all the important news of the day with in-depth feature report- ing. Every phase of business news is covered. I see articles on new taxes, inflation, business forecasts, gas prices, politics. I see major stories from Washington, Berlin, Tokyo, the Middle East. I see item after item that can affect you, your job, your future.

(over, please)

Fig. 1.1　This surely is one of the longest-running and most famous subscription letters of all time. Over the years the *Wall Street Journal* has mailed it to me a dozen times or more. The one niggling question: Isn't this letter, whose point is that a subscription to this publication can make a profound career difference, inadvertently aimed at junior executives?

And there is page after page inside The Journal, filled with fascinating and significant information that's useful to you. The <u>Marketplace</u> section gives you insights into how consumers are thinking and spending. How companies compete for market share. There is daily coverage of law, technology, media and marketing. Plus daily features on the challenges of managing smaller companies.

The Journal is also the single best source for news and statistics about your money. In the <u>Money & Investing</u> section there are helpful charts, easy-to-scan market quotations, plus "Abreast of the Market," "Heard on the Street" and "Your Money Matters," three of America's most influential and carefully read investment columns.

If you have never read The Wall Street Journal, you cannot imagine how useful it can be to you.

A Money-Saving Subscription

Put our statements to the proof by subscribing for the next 13 weeks for <u>just</u> $44. This is among the shortest subscription terms we offer—and a perfect way to get acquainted with The Journal.

Or you may prefer to take advantage of our <u>better buy</u>—one year for $149. You save over $40 off the cover price of The Journal.

Simply fill out the enclosed order card and mail it in the postage-paid envelope provided. And here's The Journal's guarantee: should The Journal not measure up to your expectations, you may cancel this arrangement at any point and receive a refund for the undelivered portion of your subscription.

If you feel as we do that this is a fair and reasonable proposition, then you will want to find out without delay if The Wall Street Journal can do for you what it is doing for millions of readers. So please mail the enclosed order card now, and we will start serving you immediately.

About those two college classmates I mention at the beginning of this letter: they were graduated from college together and together got started in the business world. So what made their <u>lives</u> in business different?

Knowledge. Useful knowledge. And its application.

An Investment In Success

I cannot promise you that success will be instantly yours if you start reading The Wall Street Journal. But I can guarantee that you will find The Journal always interesting, always reliable, and always useful.

Sincerely,

Peter R. Kann
Publisher

PRK: id
Encs.

P.S. It's important to note that The Journal's subscription price may be tax deductible. Ask your tax advisor.

Fig. 1.1 Continued

KI-058

****
Get the Quarterly Report
Forbes Columnist Ken Fisher
Sends His Private Clients FREE
****
Please respond by July 31

FISHER
INVESTMENTS
13100 Skyline Boulevard,
Woodside, CA 94062
1-800-851-8845
E-mail: info@fi.com
Website: www.fi.com

Kenneth Fisher
Chairman and Chief
Investment Officer

Dear Investor:

On a beautiful spring afternoon, 15 years ago, two men returned to their 25th college reunion. They were very much alike, those two men. Both had been better-than-average students, both had a remarkable record of achievement up to then and much to look forward to.

Recently, the two men, along with their wives, went on an extended Caribbean cruise vacation.

They were both still very much alike. Both were happily married. Both had two grown children. And both, it turned out, had retired a few years ago with a significant payout at the end of their time at work.

One's medical practice partners took over his share. The other sold his firm to a much larger rival. The results of these asset sales left both in a position to retire comfortably.

But on the cruise, the difference between these men emerged. One was constantly phoning and faxing the mainland to stay on top of his portfolio. The other spent no time even thinking, let alone worrying, about his investments.

What Finally Made the Difference

Have you ever wondered, as I have, what makes this kind of difference in people's lives? It isn't, within limits, the size of one's investments or a willingness or need to relax. It isn't that one person wants to enjoy his or her success and the other doesn't.

The difference lies in how people approach the management of their assets.

And that is why I am writing to you about Fisher Investments. That is the whole purpose of Fisher Investments: to give you the comfort and secure feeling to relax and enjoy your investments.

Fig. 1.2 If imitation is the sincerest form of flattery, this is the most sincere letter ever written. The letter says, "They were very much alike, those two men." And they were very much alike, those two letters. Copying a successful idea is a venerable marketing ploy. It makes sense … when the people to whom you send the communication aren't familiar with the original.

This tends to be true not only of two-paragraph notes but of four-page and eight-page direct-mail epics. Why? Because a letter is—or at least should be—a single, coherent statement. A supervisor or "copy chief" might say, "Rewrite this section," but the writer who starts it usually is the writer who finishes it.

Are you an ongoing student of letter-writing? If so, you ask yourself as you read, "What about this sentence or paragraph bothers me?" Your analysis leads you to formulate rules; since you formulate them from mistakes other letter writers make, you're less likely to make them yourself.

Three Reasons Some Letters Succeed When Others Fail

I can name three principal reasons some letters succeed while others fail. By "succeed" I mean *pull response*. That's how we keep score. Remember the following three points and you can sleep-read through the rest of this book, because if you can write a letter that doesn't violate these three little elements, you're home free:

1. The letter should be a single coherent statement.
2. The letter should get to the point.
3. The letter should tell the reader what to do.

The first reason will make sense to you if you have any sense of salesmanship:

> ✎ The letter should be a single coherent statement.

Don't misinterpret this. By "a single coherent statement" I don't mean mindlessly repeating the same words over and over. I do mean thinking, before sitting down to write. Ask yourself, "What am I trying to convince the reader to do?"

Write down the specific imperative as a note on the side. Then build your sales argument around that core, that nucleus, that essence. Weave your pattern. *Don't* rush at the reader like a bowling ball, unless your offer is implicitly so attractive, so terrific, that just announcing it is the best salesmanship.

When you think in terms of a single coherent statement, you force yourself to be specific. This can make a gigantic difference in the pulling power of your message, and I'll tell you why: specifics outpull generalizations.

The difference between the world of specific communication and the communication formula espoused by a typical advertising counselor is that

AMERICAN EXPRESS
TRAVEL RELATED SERVICES COMPANY, INC.

Phillip Riese
Executive Vice President

Ms. Margo E. Lewis
340 N. Fig Tree Ln.
Fort Lauderdl, FL 33317-2561

Dear Ms. Lewis:

The road to financial success has many milestones
marking how far you've come. Becoming an American
Express® Cardmember is one such milestone.

You are now cordially invited to apply for the American
Express Card.

As you may know, Cardmembership is accorded only to
those who have achieved a certain measure of financial
success. That's because -- unlike credit cards -- <u>we do
not set a spending limit in advance</u>. Instead, your
purchases with the American Express Card are approved
based on your ability to pay as demonstrated by your
personal resources and your past spending and payment
patterns.

<u>Now, you can easily apply for the Card by completing
this short form and signing your name</u>. Simply reply by
the date on the enclosed application form and if you
qualify, all the benefits of Cardmembership may be
yours.

For example, you pay no interest with the American
Express Card. None. <u>That's because the American
Express Card is a charge card, not a credit card</u>.
Since you pay your bill in full each month, all you pay
is the $55 annual fee. With most credit cards, if you
carry over an unpaid balance from one month to the next
-- even one dollar -- you pay interest on that balance
as well as on any new purchases. Even purchases you pay
for in full. Result: The American Express Card could
easily save you hundreds of dollars a year in credit
card interest.

Cardmembership also signifies that you merit an
unrivaled level of personal service. We're here for you

                                        (over, please)

Fig. 1.3   This is another famous letter that has become part of American folklore. Many people know and recite the line, "As you may know, Cardmembership is accorded only to those who have achieved a certain measure of financial success." (My wife and I both have had American Express cards for years. Each of us gets this letter once or twice every year, which suggests a serious deficiency in the company's database.)

24 hours a day, 365 days a year. From a simple question about a bill to obtaining medical or legal referrals when you're away from home, you'll find the Card to be an invaluable asset.

<u>We've even made it easy for you to apply</u>. Just return the enclosed short application form, and provided that you meet all the necessary requirements, and as long as any account you may have with us remains in good standing, the Card will arrive in just a few weeks.

I greatly look forward to welcoming you as a Cardmember.

Sincerely,

Phillip Ross

P.S. Understandably, how fast we are able to process your application depends on how quickly you return it to us. Please respond by the date on the enclosed form.

Fig. 1.3 Continued

a letter can't claim success if the recipient recalls it; a letter can claim success only if the recipient performs a positive act as the result of having read it.

Specifics sell. Generalities don't. And regardless of what you may have heard from some of the philosophers who *don't* earn their living matching wits with the great unwashed public, the purpose of *any* direct-response message is to convince the reader, viewer, or listener to perform a positive act as the direct result of having absorbed the message.

So if you want that phone to ring . . . if you want that mail to come through the door . . . if you want those people out there to say, "I want that" . . .

> ✏ Get to the point!

Get to the point. Don't dawdle. Don't try to be subtle, because subtlety will cost you some response. Subtlety suppresses response. Cleverness for the sake of cleverness suppresses response. In-jokes suppress response. Starting in super-low gear suppresses response. So—*Get to the point!*

And how, you ask, can you be sure you're getting to the point?

Here's a little help for you—four short opening phrases whose benefit will be obvious when you start using them. They force you to get to the point. No professional communicator can write one of these and then not follow up with specifics that get to the point.

1. *For example . . .*

When you say, "For example" after making a statement, you force yourself to give an example. You force yourself to get to the point, no matter how loose and nonspecific your argument may have been before that.

2. *Why? Because . . .*

This technique has the advantage of dismantling the skepticism your target may be erecting. Internally or externally, that person may be asking, "Why?" By asking the question on his or her behalf, you seem to place yourself in the position of your target individual. You establish that wonderful word, *rapport*—and you force yourself to be specific. This construction has terrific power.

3. *The reason is . . .*

Once again you force yourself to be specific by going a step beyond trying to make a point without offering evidence. Evidence is by its very nature specific. Evidence by its very nature gets to the point.

SIXTY YEARS
I.C.SYSTEM

August 24

Margot E. Lewis
President
COMMUNICOMP
340 North Fig Tree Lane
Plantation, FL 33317

Dear Ms. Lewis:

In the direct marketing industry, there is a constant battle being waged. A battle for potential customer's attention, dollars, and most of all—their loyalty. This is a battle that requires careful planning, perfectly timed and executed maneuvers, and the desire to come out on top when the dust settles.

For over 30 years, I.C. System has been providing intelligent solutions to direct marketing problems. We have the resources to help you fortify your current markets and attack new ones, by focusing on the strengths <u>you</u> bring to the marketplace.

I. C. System is a privately held company that places a high priority on teamwork and a higher priority on customer satisfaction. We believe in long-term relationships with our customers. I.C. System has the ability to cover every aspect of your direct marketing needs. From database analysis and file enhancement, to printing and mailing, we provide marketing weapons that work.

If you are ready to do combat on the direct marketing battlefield, and need a partner with the talent and technology to produce long-term results, give I.C. System a call today. Please contact me at 651-481-6369 or simply return the business reply card as soon as possible.

Sincerely,

Mark Christiansen
Associate Vice President

I.C. SYSTEM, INC.
444 Highway 96 East • P.O. Box 64226 • St. Paul, Minnesota 55164-0226 • 612/483-0585 • 800/245-8875 • Fax: 612/481-6363
#6103 12/97

Fig. 1.4　A basic tenet of effective letter-writing: *Get to the point!* What point does this letter make? In the second paragraph, the writer says his company "has been providing intelligent solutions to direct marketing problems." The recipient asks, "What problems?" ... and the answer to that question would have been a more effective opening.

4. *I have something you want.*

This is the easiest of all. If I say to you, "I have something you want," what is your immediate reaction? Right! Your immediate reaction is, "What is it?" I've grabbed your interest by involving you, and while I have your interest I force myself to get to the point.

Do you run the risk of the individual saying, "No, that isn't what I want"? Certainly not. We're dealing in *force*-communication. We take the reader by the hand and lead him or her through the maze. We're in command. Any reader who resists our command—who mutinies—deserves to be left behind while the smarter, more astute readers are enjoying the benefits of whatever we've convinced them to do. Serves them right.

And anyway, we're writing for our best targets. In theory, if the mass-mailing list selection is decent, or we've done even a modicum of homework for a one-to-one mailing, when we say, "I have something you want," it *is* something the recipient should want.

Now the third element:

> ✐ **Tell the reader what to do.**

You can see how easy the three elements are. You can see how logical the three elements are. You can see how basic the three elements are. So why, oh why, do so many writers ignore all three?

My answer is: Too many writers don't understand what our function is. We're salespeople. Yes, I know that hurts. We'd rather be called "creatives" or "executives." (I'll settle for "creative salespeople," but that's my final offer.)

Who Are We?

In the second half of this book is a cold-blooded analysis of one hundred different ways to begin a sales letter. Number 91: "Who are we?"

Who, indeed? Who are *you*?

No, not your actual person, the *persona* you project in a letter. Are you casual or severe? Are you pedantic or a plain ol' country boy or gal? You're in command because you're the one writing the letter.

In a multi-part business mailing, the letter is the identifying component. Who are you? P. T. Barnum? Dale Carnegie? Zeus? Uriah Heep? Good Sam? Florence Nightingale? J. P. Morgan? Lucrezia Borgia? Albert Einstein? The Emperor Tiberius? Socrates? Nostradamus?

Who are you?

```
* * * * * * * * * * * * * * * * * * * * * * * * * * * * *
*                                                       *
*      I want you back.                                 *
*                                                       *
*      .I want you to try BOTTOM LINE again.            *
*                                                       *
*      .So I am going to send you SIX FREE ISSUES.      *
*                                                       *
*      .As each free issue arrives, will you do me a favor? *
*                                                       *
*         Just settle into a comfortable chair and take only 3 *
*      minutes to skim each one.  I'm betting you find BOTTOM *
*      LINE better than ever, and that you'll pick up lots of *
*      valuable ideas.                                  *
*                                                       *
*         However, if you decide after 3 minutes that BOTTOM *
*      LINE isn't for you, just toss it out.  I lose my bet. *
*      So be it. You don't lose anything. The risk is all mine. *
*                                                       *
*         Fair enough?                                  *
*                                                       *
*         BUT.  Maybe...just maybe...an idea here or another *
*      there will grab you, and you'll find yourself reading *
*      beyond the 3 minutes.  That's okay.  Take your time. *
*      No harm done.  You've got everything to gain, and *
*      nothing to lose.                                 *
*                                                       *
* * * * * * * * * * * * * * * * * * * * * * * * * * * * *
```

Dear Friend:

I REALLY want you back as a BOTTOM LINE reader, and to prove it...

...I'll send you a gift with your free issues -- and it is also ABSOLUTELY FREE if you return the enclosed certificate with the good-luck stamp above.

This is no ordinary gift. In fact, it contains information that can make a big difference in your life, because it concerns your money ...how you spend it, save it, make it grow and protect it -- or waste it and lose it, if you're not careful.

No, I'm not touting some new financial fad, "get-rich-quick" scheme, or pipe dream of fabulous wealth with no risk.

Rather, the gift I want to send you is a super-valuable source of inside information that will give you the know-how and power to get what you need and want when you're dealing with banks, insurance companies, stockbrokers, accountants, credit card companies, real estate agents... all those people and organizations that affect you and your money -- and who wish you didn't know their secrets!

You're going to find literally hundreds of the smartest, savviest, best money ideas and strategies in Money Confidential: Secrets of Financial Security in Tricky Times -- the gift I'm going to send you

over

Fig. 1.5　This letter gets right to the point: "I want you back." It then adds muscle—a free gift and free issues of the publication. The Johnson Box at the top succeeds because it really isn't a Johnson Box. (See chapter 3 for more on Johnson Boxes.) It is actually the beginning of the letter.

-2-

when you return the enclosed certificate.

For example:

. How to spot the signs that your bank is sweeping problems under the rug.

. Beat the penalty for taking money out of an IRA before age 59 1/2.

. Term insurance is always cheaper than whole life, right? Wrong. Now you can take advantage of the exceptions.

. Cut your credit card interest rate with one simple phone call.

. What money market funds don't want you to know about how their money is invested. What they leave out of their financial reports. What not to take at face value even if they do disclose it.

. Income that doesn't affect your Social Security benefits. You can earn all you want.

. Insurance companies that are allowed to sell you a policy but may not be good for the money.

. Questions you should be asking right now about how your pension money is invested, and what the answers should be.

. Three kinds of life insurance never to buy.

. How to get a discount from a nondiscount stockbroker ...proven strategy saves 20% to 30%.

. How to pick the perfect financial planner: 5 crucial questions you must ask.

. When not to leave everything to your spouse. Spouses may not like the sound of this at first, but they will really appreciate it once they understand. And so will your children.

. Investments that make money in a recession.

. Ten $1,000 CDs are much smarter than one $10,000 CD with same maturity. (Don't expect your bank to explain this.)

. How to sell your house fast! Here's an unconventional, off-the-wall approach that gets results...and quick.

Fig. 1.5   Continued

-3-

. How to read a financial statement and where to look for
the bad news they're trying to bury.

. Hidden risks in 401(k) plans. They're not as safe as you
might think.

...and much, much more. This book is chock-full of money secrets
you never would expect to see in print, from authentic financial
insiders and experts...all in plain English. And, I repeat, it's all
yours FREE with six FREE issues of BOTTOM LINE.

Don't forget...

...the deal is that you look at BOTTOM LINE again. Although
you've had a subscription before, I hope you give it a fresh reading to
see how it concerns you now, today -- how it can benefit you in your
work, your personal finances, your health, your leisure...practically
every aspect of your life.

* * * *

These are very tricky times, indeed. Managing your money is a
formidable challenge, as opportunities -- and danger -- may appear
around the next corner. The value of the dollar fluctuates. Inflation
is always a threat. Changing interest rates affect everyone's life.

New technologies appear so fast, a person may not grasp their
meaning. Medical, nutritional, and scientific knowledge seems to
change just as rapidly.

How do you protect yourself and your family?

How do you take advantage of the real moneymaking opportunities
that do exist -- and avoid the traps and pitfalls?

What should you do?

One thing is clear -- the more you know, the safer you'll be. And
your position will be strongest if you have the benefit and advantage
of real inside information...the kind of information that is normally
kept secret from the average American.

That's where BOTTOM LINE comes in. There are inside angles to
everything, and our readers learn dozens of them in each twice-monthly
issue, from our staff of editors, writers and researchers...plus an
Advisory Board of 165 leading experts and professionals nationally
renowned in their fields.

Their mission is to show you how to do everything right: Taxes.
Investments. Budgeting. Travel. Health. Fitness. Insurance.

over

Fig. 1.5   Continued

-4-

Banking. Estate planning. Managing your finances...your household
...your career.

Of course, not every item may apply to you, but you'll find plenty
of nuggets relating directly to your job, your income, your health,
your life. And you can put those nuggets to work for you.

* * * * *

See for yourself. Please return the FREE ISSUES CERTIFICATE in
the enclosed reply envelope. No stamp is needed. We'll pay the
postage at this end.

If you find BOTTOM LINE helpful, I invite you to get a 1 year (24
issue) trial subscription at a substantial discount. Or, if you wish,
simply mark our bill "cancel" and return it. Pay nothing.

You have so much to gain...and nothing to lose.

Please reply now, while this special offer is still in effect.

Sincerely yours,

Martin Edelston
Publisher

ME:xnw

P.S. Remember, to get your FREE gift -- Money Confidential: Secrets of
Financial Security in Tricky Times -- paste the GOOD-LUCK stamp
on your FREE ISSUES CERTIFICATE.

Bottom Line
PERSONAL
55 Railroad Avenue, Greenwich, Connecticut 06830

Fig. 1.5 Continued

SPT0898/D

balance

Expanding your mind ... nourishing your body ... nurturing your spirit
Get 4 Books, Cassettes, CDs, or Videos for Only $1 Each

Dear Friend,

　Maybe you began your journey with meditation ... or by exploring eastern religious traditions ... or by investigating homeopathic remedies ... or maybe you simply decided to reassess what's important to you.

　When you're seeking balance in your life, you can choose your own path. There's no one right way to cultivate your entire being: spirit, mind, and body.

　And, as you probably know, there are more resources for balanced, holistic living available than ever before. But how do you stay on top of them all? How do you separate the gimmicks and quick-fixes from the works with real, lasting value?

　　　　You'll find what you need
　　　　to light your way at One Spirit:
　　　　Join today and get 4 books, cassettes,
　　　　CDs, or videos for only $1 each.

　One Spirit is dedicated to bringing you a wide range of products that we have found to be informative, useful, nourishing, inspiring. You'll find these tools in a wide variety of formats: books, audiotapes, compact discs, videocassettes, and merchandise.

　<u>And there's never any risk</u>: We stand behind all of our selections. If you're ever unsatisfied with anything you order from One Spirit — including the items you choose today — simply return it for a full refund. No questions asked.

Fig. 1.6　Do you find this letter hard to read? Probably it's the spacing. Do you find it hard to penetrate? Maybe it's the multisyllabic rhetoric. Do you find it hard to find a benefit? Maybe it's because instead of a hard description following up the offer (the centered paragraph on page 1) is the nondescript, nonspecific, and nonstimulating sentence, "One Spirit is dedicated to bringing you a wide range of products that we have found to be informative, useful, nourishing, inspiring."

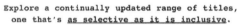

Explore a continually updated range of titles, one that's <u>as selective as it is inclusive</u>.

After you've received the selections you choose today, we'll start sending your free resource guide, the <u>One Spirit Review</u>. Because there is no single path to achieving balance in your life, every issue includes offerings on a wide array of topics, presented through book excerpts, interviews, paintings and drawings, and in-depth descriptions.

You'll find philosophy and mythology. Homeopathy and ayurveda. Nutrition and yoga. Meditation and prayer. Simplicity and healing energy. Contemporary teachings and ancient texts. Sacred music and how-to videos. Creativity and erotica. Psychology and self-discovery. Western, Eastern, African, and Native American spiritual traditions.

One Spirit allows room for a diversity of beliefs and practices. We are as open to possibilities as you are.

But even though we cast a wide net, we are very particular about what we offer our members.

When a group of us got together for the first time a couple of years ago to start One Spirit, we agreed that our most important mission was simple: <u>to bring you the best — and only the best — selections of their kind</u>.

Browse through the 120 selections in the enclosed brochure. Choose any 4 for only $1 each — a savings of up to $150.

You'll find <u>Talking to Heaven</u>, medium James Van Praagh's memoir of his communication with spirits from the other side.

Harness your body's natural powers with our special two-volume set from naturopathic doctor Andrew Weil: <u>Eight Weeks to Optimum Health</u> and <u>Spontaneous Healing</u>.

Find out the precise connection between intuition — "the commonest sense" — and your emotions, dreams, and memories with Mona Lisa Schulz's <u>Awakening Intuition</u>.

Fig. 1.6 Continued

You'll also discover more than 1,000 natural remedies
for the prevention, treatment, and cure of common
ailments and conditions in <u>The Illustrated Encyclopedia
of Natural Remedies</u> ... Barbara Sher's <u>It's Only
Too Late If You Don't Start Now</u>, which shows how
to map out a more conscious, centered,
and creative life after 40 ... and explore
the depth and mystery of physical intimacy in
<u>The Soul of Sex</u>.

There are books by today's foremost leaders and
thinkers, including <u>The Gifts of the Jews</u>, wherein Thomas
Cahill describes how a tribe of desert nomads changed
the way everyone thinks and feels ... and in Dr. Dean
Ornish's <u>Love and Survival</u>, the acclaimed healer who
proved that it was possible to reverse heart disease
focuses on another aspect of the heart: love.

**Tools that can change the way you think,
the way you feel, the way you live.**

One Spirit's selections also include the fantastic
true story of a scientist turned shaman in Hank
Wesselman's <u>Medicinemaker</u> ... Caitlin and John Matthews'
sourcebook, <u>The Encyclopædia of Celtic Wisdom</u> ... Neale
Donald Walsch's unique bestsellers, <u>Conversations With
God, Books One and Two</u> ... and our Sarah Ban Breathnach
<u>Simple Abundance</u> set.

And you can learn the healing secrets of herbs, vitamins,
and minerals in Jean Carper's <u>Miracle Cures</u>, or consult <u>The
Encyclopedia of Healing Therapies</u> for information on more
than 70 alternative therapies.

What's more, One Spirit features such
practical guides as <u>The Nutrition Desk
Reference</u>, <u>Don't Sweat the Small Stuff ... and
It's All Small Stuff</u> (offered along with its
companion Workbook), and Caroline Myss's <u>Why
People Don't Heal and How They Can</u> and <u>The
Anatomy of the Spirit</u>.

And books are just part of the story.
One Spirit brings together a diverse
collection of instructional and motivational
videos. So you can master an ancient art

Fig. 1.6   Continued

with <u>Yoga Journal's Yoga for Beginners</u>, hone your sense of balance with <u>David Carradine's New Tai Chi Workout</u>, or share the ancient secrets of sexual pleasure in <u>The Kama Sutra of Vatsyayana</u>.

And you can choose from today's most inspirational audiobooks and enjoyable music CDs. Among them, the otherworldly <u>Mystic Harp</u> from the legendary Chieftains' harpist Derek Bell, and <u>Tribal Winds</u>, featuring the unique styles of the Native American flute from various tribes, including the Apache, Dakota, Navajo, Ute, and Zuni.

Dramatic savings — and free books.

Your introductory selections are worth up to $165. You are under no obligation to buy anything else. Of course, we're sure you'll want to, once you see the outstanding selections we offer in the <u>One Spirit Review</u>. And you'll continue to enjoy exceptional savings on those selections — as much as 40% or more. Plus, you'll accumulate credits with every purchase that you can redeem for free books. (You pay just shipping and handling.)

Please accept our invitation for conscious, holistic, balanced living.

Select any 4 of the 120 items in the enclosed brochure for $1 each, plus shipping and handling. Indicate your choices on the enclosed postage-paid Reply Card.

I look forward to hearing from you.

Warm regards,

Linda Loewenthal
Editorial Director

P.S. There's no need to send money now. Just return your Reply Card indicating the 4 selections you want for just $1 each.

Fig. 1.6   Continued

The letter is your projected image. The recipient's *psychological* reaction is to that image; how deeply the psychological reaction colors the physical reaction to the offer is a matter of percentages . . . but the percentage is never zero.

This shows once again that the letter has a profound effect on that mystical ingredient, *rapport*. Whatever your offer, whatever your proposition, whatever miracle you represent, the offer alone can't establish rapport; if it could, mailers wouldn't need letters because other enclosures spell out the offer.

Can you see the significance of choosing a letter opening which mirrors the person you're trying to be?

Who are you?

Albert Einstein once might have begun a letter to someone with "I have a free gift for you." The *image* of Albert Einstein never would. Maybe P. T. Barnum once wrote to somebody, "It's late and I'm tired but I have to tell you this" but the *image* of P. T. Barnum wouldn't write that. The statement is in perfect sync with the image of Florence Nightingale.

(Did Lucrezia Borgia ever write, "Visualize this scenario"? Probably.)

Once you've decided who you are, the next key is to stay in character. This becomes a simple matter. Choose the right opening. Then remember who you are and don't take off your costume or your mask until the show is over!

See how simple it is? Chop off your ego, graft on your rapport, get to the point, and watch response to your sales letters rocket.

ROUTE 3, BOX 10 • ALAMO, TEXAS 78516 • PHONE 1-800-876-4733

You're one of the first to enjoy this!

Good Morning!

If you'll give me the next 3 1/2 minutes, in return I'll give you a treat that'll open up an unbelievable new world of eating pleasure for you. Fair enough?

A little background:

My family has been in the citrus fruit business just about forever. We've become slightly famous down here because our fruit is so much bigger and sweeter than the citrus you find in the store. When people have a special occasion, in they come to get some Red Cooper grapefruit.

Until a couple of years ago, we were perfectly content with our grapefruit. So was everybody else, and it sold like crazy. Ours always has been the biggest, sweetest, prettiest grapefruit in the neighborhood ... some say the whole country.

But then that big freeze came along. You read about it in the paper: We'd never had a bitter cold spell like that, down here where the climate is "grapefruit perfect." That freeze wiped out almost every darned grapefruit tree in South Texas. Our own gorgeous trees were frozen solid. That meant, literally, starting all over again.

What we did:

Even before the freeze we'd been experimenting with grapefruit. Now, we figured, since we were starting over, why not carry those experiments as far as we could go?

I'll tell you what the experiments were:

We were trying to <u>cross-breed</u> a grapefruit with a big, honey-sweet orange. If we could do it, we knew we'd have the sweetest grapefruit anybody ever grew ... a grapefruit that wouldn't need sugar because it would be so sweet on its own.

It turned out that cross-breeding wasn't the way to go. But it led us to a discovery that - if you'll let me prove it to you - will change your taste-bud pleasures forever! Our discovery was "budding" instead of grafting. We "budded" grapefruit onto an orange tree.

Fig. 1.7   This letter has been selling grapefruit for a generation. The key to its success undoubtedly is the *rapport* it quickly builds and holds with the reader. Too, the grabber first few words of text exemplify opening number 71, described in chapter 10.

Now bear in mind, when you bud you <u>wait</u>. And you <u>wait</u>. And you <u>wait</u>. The buds "take" or they don't. If they don't you start over. That's exactly what we did. We budded ... and we waited. And we budded again ... and we waited.

But you know what? We succeeded beyond our wildest dreams!

Understand, my friend: Budding doesn't mean a thing if the results aren't worth it. When I say we did it, I mean wow! We produced the sweetest grapefruit this side of heaven. I've been in this business all my life. I've tasted every variety of grapefruit anybody grows today. Nobody, <u>nobody</u> has ever produced one this sweet. We've done it! We've grown the 21st century grapefruit, and nobody else can match it.

When we got our first batch, I tried them out on my own family. They're used to the best grapefruit. But I caught them by surprise with the new ones.

First of all, the color is distinctive: It's a much richer red than even our famous Ruby Red was. Second, the sweetness is <u>light years</u> beyond any grapefruit they (or you) have ever tasted before. And third (what a bonus!) they're seedless, so whether you're eating them or making juice you'll have marvelous mellow flavor without the seeds.

My son said, "Dad, if I didn't see a great big grapefruit sitting in front of me I'd think I was eating a new type of sweet orange." That gave us the name: ORANGE-SWEET GRAPEFRUIT.

Why I'm writing you:

All right, why am I telling this to <u>you</u>?

I'll tell you why: I paid a bunch of high-powered computer guys a lot of money for the names of people they tell me will appreciate the very best gourmet treats. So if they're right about your position and lifestyle, you'll recognize and take advantage of the offer I'm about to make to you.

Understand: Our Orange-Sweet Grapefruit is just about as elite a "limited edition" fruit as anybody ever produced. Oh, sure, these are the future of grapefruit; but it'll be years and years before we send <u>any</u> of these to even the most upscale grocers. Anybody who wants them has to get them from us, <u>direct</u>.

That's what I invite you to do. And I'll make it worth your while, because you're the kind of person whose opinion can cause others to ask, "Where did you get these, and how can I get some?" You'll tell them. That's worth a lot to us for next year's crop.

So I have an offer I hope you can't refuse.

Fig. 1.7   Continued

Your Special <u>DIRECT</u> offer:

Every three weeks this winter starting in November - winter
being the time when fresh grapefruit really will bring sunshine
into your home - I'll send you a whole box of 15 great big Orange-
Sweet Grapefruit.

I don't want any money from you now. In fact, I don't want
any money until you've sampled your first shipment.

When you get them, select any four grapefruit from the box.
Chill them, then put them to your personal taste test. Surprise
your family for breakfast one morning ... or, for that matter, as
a dinner dessert, because these are so sweet they can be the most
delicious (and best for you) dessert that ever graced your table.
Or you might want to make some juice from one or two.

Only then, if you agree these are absolutely the finest and
sweetest grapefruit you've ever tasted, the whole shipment is
yours for just $20.98 plus a nominal shipping charge. If you
don't agree just write "no, thanks" on the invoice and send back
the unused fruit. I'll pay for the return shipping, and we'll
still be friends.

As a preferred Red Cooper gourmet customer, you'll get a similar shipment every three weeks early November through April. You
don't pay for any shipment until after you've sampled it. And of
course you can skip a shipment or cancel at any time.

See my note in the P.S.

I want to emphasize: This is the <u>only</u> way you or anybody can
get our Orange-Sweet Grapefruit. You owe it to yourself to at
least sample this wonderful new triumph in fine citrus fruit.

What a way to start the day! On those cold, bleak, overcast
winter mornings you'll have some real sunshine in your life,
because that's the happy effect our Orange-Sweets have!

May I have your answer quickly?

This year's crop is <u>very</u> limited. And consider, we ship only
the best of the best, just as soon as we pick them off the tree.
(They'll stay fresh for weeks and weeks.) Every piece of fruit is
hand-selected for size and sweetness.

As I told you, you're among the first to get this information. I sincerely want <u>you</u> to be our customer. And I intend to
make it worth your while to be our customer, because I want this
year's crop to be spoken for.

So please, my friend, let me hear from you right away.
Really, you're in a win/win situation, because if you like our
fabulous Orange-Sweet Grapefruit it's yours at the <u>direct</u> price;
if you don't, you haven't risked a cent.

Here's what you do:

Fig. 1.7   Continued

Just sign the Preferred Order Card I've enclosed and drop it in the mail. Nothing else to do ... except sit back and anticipate the very best grapefruit anybody ever ate, ever, anywhere on this planet.

Really, our Orange-Sweets will change forever the way you think of grapefruit. You won't again admire any supermarket grapefruit, no matter how pretty it may look in the display ... because you'll know better. You'll realize a far sweeter, far better-tasting grapefruit can be yours.

But please, please don't wait on this. I'd hate to see you miss out. And if we don't hear from you, you won't have an opportunity to sample this spectacular 21st century grapefruit for another whole year.

You have a fantastic taste treat in store. I'm delighted to be able to make the limited-edition Orange-Sweet available to you, and I'm eager to know what you think of this "King of Grapefruit."

I'll look for your Preferred Order Card on my desk. Thanks.

Sincerely,

Red Cooper

For The Cooper Family

RC/HL7

P.S. Chances are this is the only notification you'll get
     from me. To make it even more worth your while:
     Take $3.00 off the cost of your first shipment.
     It's yours for $17.98, not $20.98.

97

Fig. 1.7 Continued

2

Ten Easy Pieces

A well-written business or direct-response letter is an amalgam of sales psychology, word manipulation, and mechanical application.

I'm no longer surprised to see communication professionals fail to take advantage of mechanical procedures a reasonably bright eight-year-old can implement. They're victims of a vertical education which excludes the mechanics of force-communication . . . and also victims of a misguided professional indoctrination founded on the regrettable concept that communication is effective if it accomplishes self-glorification.

So the ten tips described in this chapter are surprisingly easy to apply . . . and, I hope, surprisingly obvious to the astute communicator. I say this with confidence because they aren't abstruse philosophical notions; they're mechanical devices, instant tools designed not to replace imagination but to showcase imagination properly.

Tip Number One:
Keep your first sentence short.

The first sentence is an early warning to the reader, and your target forms a quick impression: The letter is going to be easy to read or it's going to be hard slogging.

The short first sentence isn't an absolute, invariable law. It's just a good idea most of the time. And because it's a good idea most of the time as well as an easy idea to implement, it's on this list.

Which opener is most likely to grab and shake the reader? This . . .

I want 1½ minutes of your time.

Or this . . .

If you'll give me 1½ minutes of your time, in turn I'll give you information about an opportunity you probably never thought would be available to you in today's marketplace.

No contest. You won't have any problem activating this tool if you ask yourself as you poise your fingers to generate that crucial first sentence, "If I were speaking instead of writing, to someone who has no reason to respect my position, what would I use as an opener?"

Take a look at figure 2.1. Mightn't it have been more effective with a first sentence shorter than forty-six words?

Tip Number Two:
No paragraphs longer than seven lines.

I suggested this concept to an assemblage of professional copywriters. I guess I shouldn't have been surprised to get the question, "But what if a paragraph has to be longer than seven lines?"

The question reminded me of my own complaint when I was writing one of my earlier books. I said to my wife, "I've written considerably more than one hundred thousand words, and the book still isn't finished." Her answer cut the Gordian knot: "Yes, it is."

So my own answer to the aforementioned question: Type a period and start a new paragraph. No paragraph has to be longer than seven lines. Break up the text. One paragraph becomes two, three, or four, and reader fatigue vanishes.

Tip Number Three:
Single-space the letter; double-space
between paragraphs.

This notion is even easier to implement than the first two. It's based on ease of readership. Manuscripts and news releases traditionally are double-spaced, but that's because editors need the space between the lines to write in their blue-pencil chicken scratch.

A letter should set itself up for easy reading; a double-spaced letter not only is harder to read, but double-spacing balloons every aspect. A two-page

PRO FARMER

AG TRADER

219 Parkade, Box 6 • Cedar Falls, Iowa 50613

**Are you positioned to profit from the wild
swings in the ag markets that are ahead, as
the U.S. government exits the marketplace
after more than 60 years of price and income
support programs for farmers?**

Dear Futures and Options Trader,

   Some of the most profitable trades of the next decade are going to be in the agricultural complex, and it's not just because El Niño's retreat has sparked talk of less-than-ideal growing conditions for the heart of the Corn Belt due to La Niña. Agriculture has gone global. Uncle Sam knows he can no longer influence prices without the cooperation of the rest of the world and has effectively given up trying to do so.

   Here's one example of the changes ahead: In the future, crop acreage will no longer be determined by such things as acreage set-asides and farm programs. The acreage farmers plant each spring will now be dictated by markets.

> Only those in very close touch with farmers on a regular basis
> will get advance warning of these big acreage swings and colossal
> trading opportunities! We can put you in touch with them.

Introducing *Pro Farmer Ag Trader* newsletter.

   This four-page weekly letter is put together *just for traders* by the editors of Professional Farmers of America, the analytical team that has advised America's top farmers for more than 25 years. Each week, you'll get insight and early alerts about global farmer planting and livestock production intentions from a team of veteran analysts in constant touch with farmers, traders, users and commodity merchants all over the world.

   Most importantly, you get these insights and tips long before they are officially confirmed by the U.S. Department of Agriculture, in plenty of time to position yourself wisely in the markets. And at just $159 per year for 50 issues, a single profitable trade could easily recover your subscription price many times over!

   With *Ag Trader*, you also get a "targeted" chart service for wheat, corn, soybeans, cotton, hogs and cattle — the spotlight markets of the futures and options industry in the

(Please see over...)

Fig. 2.1   The first sentence of this letter has forty-six words. As a quick exercise, create a short grabber first sentence. Isn't your version far more readable?

Citicorp Diners Club Inc.
183 Inverness Drive West
Englewood, CO 80112

CITIBANK○

Dear Cardmember,

When you travel, are you confident that you have enough protection for yourself and your family? Diners Club® has made it easy to help get that protection with an enhanced Supplemental Air Travel Accident Insurance plan*. It's called Diners Club Flight Coverage Plus℠. Flight Coverage Plus offers you up to $1 million of Air Travel Accident Insurance in addition to the $350,000 of Automatic Travel Accident Insurance you already receive as a Cardmember. The "Plus" means that if you enroll, you also receive $150,000 of 24-Hour Travel Accident Insurance that covers you where the Air Travel Accident Insurance does not. So from the moment you leave for air travel to the moment you return, you're protected with Flight Coverage Plus. We think it's the best Air Travel Accident Insurance value in the industry.

With Diners Club Flight Coverage Plus℠, you get:

· **Protection in the Air and on the Ground.** Your coverage starts from the time you leave your door to go to the airport and continues until you return, up to 30 days later.

· **Guaranteed Acceptance.** As a Diners Club Cardmember in good standing, you're Pre- Approved for enrollment in the plan.

· **High Coverage at an Economical Cost.** You choose $1,000,000, $500,000 or $250,000 of Supplemental Air Travel Accident Insurance with no enrollment fee. Your surprisingly affordable cost is automatically billed to your account each time you charge an airline ticket with your Diners Club Card.

· **Coverage for You, Your Family, and Your Authorized Travelers.** Just charge airline tickets separately in each traveler's name to the enrolled account and protect yourself, your spouse, your dependent children, or any authorized traveler (any person whose airline ticket is charged to your Diners Club Card).

· **The "Plus": 24-Hour Travel Accident Insurance and Trip Cancellation/Interruption Insurance.** Enroll in the Diners Club Flight Coverage Plus program and automatically receive $150,000 of 24-Hour Travel Accident Insurance (covering you where Air Travel Accident Insurance does not) and up to $500 per ticket of Trip Cancellation/Interruption Insurance at no additional cost.

Everything you need to know about this important plan, including details regarding exclusions and limitations, is in the enclosed brochure. Read it carefully and find out how easily you can enroll in Diners Club Flight Coverage Plus - the $1,000,000 travel protection program that helps buy you priceless peace of mind.

Sincerely,

Lisa E. Rosenberg

Lisa E. Rosenberg
Vice President

---

* Underwritten by National Union Fire Insurance Company of Pittsburgh, PA., a member company of American International Group, Inc.

Fig. 2.2   Having no paragraphs longer than seven lines is an easy mechanical rule. But it also is a logical psychological rule. The first paragraph of this letter is unindented and runs to nine tight lines, suggesting that reading it will be a formidable task. The asterisk doesn't help. You can see how easy it would have been to break up that first paragraph into chewable bites.

letter becomes four pages, and an eight-page letter—well, don't even think about it. Worse, the page has an overall gray look because the space between paragraphs is identical to the space within paragraphs. Emphasizing specific points you want to hammer home—which is within your control as you lead the reader by the hand—is a lot harder to do.

A suggestion, if you disagree on grounds of tradition rather than reader attention: Type out your next letter both ways. Ask fifty people which is easier to read. If you're really scientific, ask those people questions based on reader comprehension.

Tip Number Four:
In a letter longer than one page, don't end a paragraph at the bottom of any page except the last; break in the middle of a sentence.

Newspapers have known this for a hundred years. Readers demand completeness. So a newspaper story on page 1 may have the legend "Continued on page 14, column 2"—and the reader is more likely to turn to page 14 if that break comes in mid-sentence, because the reader can't claim even a vestige of completeness.

If you've ended a paragraph at the bottom of the page, the reader has a reason to read on only if he or she already has a firm interest in what you're selling. Leaving the reader hanging in mid-sentence maintains the writer's command. The reader is your captive until the end of the sentence—on the next page.

This is the force-communication ploy parallel to a motion picture on television's late show. The show doesn't open with credits and titles; it opens with action. Once you've seen the first five minutes, it's too late to switch channels because you've already missed the opening of the film on the competing channel; it started with action, too.

Tip Number Five:
Don't sneak up on the reader.

An inverse way to word this tip might be, "Fire a big gun to start the battle." We're in the Age of Skepticism, and letter openings such as this one betray a 1930s selling attitude:

_____

This story begins around the turn of the century, when times were peaceful and big fortunes could be made.

Way back then, someone took a look at a contraption a lot of people still called a horseless carriage, and they said, "Gee, wouldn't it be great if we could start these vehicles without cranking them by hand? Old Silas broke his arm cranking his machine, and the danged thing never would go."

_____

I agree—it isn't dull. As this type of opening goes, it's more intriguing than most. Now read the next paragraph:

_____

Half a century later, a guy named Alan Shepard climbed into a different contraption, and a lot of smoke came out of the bottom end. Wham! Within a couple of minutes our first astronaut was not only out of sight, he'd made history.

_____

Now I'm not so pleased. It's obvious at last—we aren't talking about starters or storage batteries, and we aren't talking about outer space. We still don't know what we *are* supposed to be talking about, and we're deep into the letter.

Just for the sake of history, I'll tell you. This writer is selling vacations. It could have been any of ten thousand other possibilities, including aardvarks and Zoroastrian texts.

Firing your biggest gun first is a good idea because you can't miss. As the letter opens, you're at point-blank range, and you may never have this advantage over your target prospect again.

Tip Number Six:
Never again start a letter with "Dear Sir" or "Dear Madam."

Why not? Because these are nineteenth-century techniques. They suggest stiff-necked, old-fashioned pomposity. Warming up the readers, establishing rapport with them, is one of the great hurdles we face. A greeting such as "Dear Sir" or "Dear Madam" adds sandbags to the obstacle when we should be shoveling sand away.

In a unisex age, I occasionally see "Dear Sir or Madam." This is the kind of opening we might expect from a bill collector.

The mail-order industry has pretty much settled on some version of "Dear Friend" as a neutral substitute when we can't personalize the

50 W. 17th St., 8th flr.
New York, NY 10011
Tel. (212) 647-1415
Fax: (212) 647-1419
Hotline: (800) 828-3280

Board of Directors

Moises Agosto
Sandra Dorsey
Sheila Etheridge
Scott Hoot
Don Huppert
Jay Laudato
Vincent Martinez
Tom Viola

Executive Director

Doug Wirth

December 15

Dear Sir or Madam;

Over the past decade, we have experienced progress in the approach and treatment of HIV/AIDS. Fewer people are dying. But now there are more people living with this disease -- more men, women, children, and people of color. New treatments don't work for everyone.

It seems like some people have forgotten that we're still in the middle of an epidemic. In 1997, individual, corporate, and foundation contributions for HIV/AIDS are down across the country. Volunteerism is down. Government funding hasn't keep pace with the service demands. Aspects of the health care system seem to be crumbling. **But the AIDS crisis is not over -- yet**. Now more than ever, we need people to give, volunteer/work, and fight.

The **People With AIDS Coalition of New York** hopes that you will continue to be one of those dedicated people by sending $50, $75, $100, $250 or $500 along with the response card below.

Your gift will help fund our education, counseling, information and support programs, including our peer led hotline, support groups, treatment information services, and our publications. These services help people understand their options, make informed personal choices, and then assist them in adhering to challenging treatment regimens. **We provide information and support to tens of thousands of people living with HIV/AIDS and their care partners in New York City, across the country, and around the world.**

This is the point, at PWAC NY, we are people living with HIV/AIDS. Our mission is clear. We serve all people living with HIV/AIDS. We understand the issues like nobody else can. Our perspective and personal experiences provide a genuine sensitivity and respect for the men, women, and families that we serve.

On behalf of our Board, staff, volunteers and program participants, **thank you for your support and commitment** to helping us empower people living with HIV/AIDS.

Sincerely,

Doug Wirth

Doug Wirth
Executive Director

Tom Viola

Tom Viola
Board President

Fig. 2.3   Tip number six suggests *not* using "Dear Sir or Madam" as the greeting. Not only is it archaic; it keeps readers at arm's length. How much warmer this letter would have seemed, at its very outset, with even such a standard greeting as "Dear Concerned Citizen."

opening. Depending on the demographic complexion of a list, or on your knowledge of an individual, you can move in closer:

"Dear Fellow Member"
"Dear Executive"
"Dear Colleague"
"Dear World Traveler"
"Dear Collector"
"Dear Tennis Nut" (You can see the benefit of *equivalence* in greetings when you add a word—"Dear *Fellow* Tennis Nut.")

Figure 2.4 is addressed to "Dear Hostess." Note the multiplicity of elements above the greeting. (Overlines are discussed in the next chapter; the envelope for this mailing is figure 5.2 in chapter 5.)

A nitpicky question: Should we put a comma or a colon after the greeting?

Business letter-writing classes teach colon, not comma, but under most circumstances, I disagree . . . conditionally. The colon suggests a respect for the reader, but it also maintains an arm's-length relationship. Today we want to exploit the magical word that enhances the possibility of interpersonal relationships: *rapport*. I often make the comma-colon decision based on whether or not I'll indent each paragraph. Indenting is less formal, which makes the comma more logical.

Some strong usable substitutes for the old-fashioned opening gain their strength from suggesting the communication is limited to a special-interest group:

"Good Morning!"
"To one of a handful of sophisticated homeowners who demand pure water"
"This Private Notification Is Limited to Executives Earning More Than $50,000 a Year"
"Information for Administrators Only"
"May I call your attention, Mr. Brown, to . . ."
"I think you'll be interested in this, Mr. Brown"

Note the difference between "I think you'll be interested in this, Mr. Brown," and "This should interest you, Mr. Brown." The latter version is considerably more *assumptive*, which makes it considerably more dangerous.

"Good morning!" has become a popular opening, with or without the exclamation point. I personally dismiss the counterargument, "But what if they don't read it in the morning?" with the flippant answer, "Well, then it's

BDCLC

Everyone Loves A PARTY!

FREE GIFT with your FREE PREVIEW!

From Birthdays to Brunch and Showers to Supper — We Have
11 PERFECT PARTY PLANS FOR YOU!
— FREE FOR 21 DAYS! —

Dear Hostess,

    I know that people like you and me love to gather close friends and family together to celebrate special times or to simply enjoy each other's company.

    But we don't like getting caught up in all the details of planning a party ... what to serve and how to decorate. **THE GOOD NEWS** is that Leisure Arts has a refreshingly creative, amazingly easy-to-follow, and wonderfully detailed new party guidebook designed to please hostesses like us!

        FIND OUT EVERYTHING YOU WANT (AND NEED) TO KNOW ABOUT GIVING 11 PERFECT PARTIES!

    You're cordially invited to look over **PERFECT PARTIES – CREATIVE ENTERTAINING MADE EASY** ABSOLUTELY FREE for 21 days! There's NO RISK, NO OBLIGATION. ... There's only PARTY FUN (and your FREE THANK-YOU GIFT, which I'll tell you all about later in this letter).

    Imagine you and your favorite friends getting together

(Please turn the page →)

Fig. 2.4 The letter sells a party-planner book by quoting excerpts from the book itself. Specifics such as this aid response. (The envelope for this mailing is figure 5.2.)

on a warm evening for a relaxing, informal **Summertime Supper**. Here's how this delightful evening goes ...

> Your guests arrive praising your beautiful invitations. "You made them, Karen? How did you think of decorating them with silk flowers?" "They were so pretty, and you are so creative!"
>
> You invite everyone to join you on the patio, where they're greeted by a lush scene appointed with table and chairs draped in colorful cloth and lovely garlands of ivy. Organdy, ribbons, and bows beset the decor, along with your breathtaking centerpiece — a decorative bird cage overflowing with flowers and greenery.
>
> "Oohs" and "aahs" fill the air together with remarks like, "Who's catering this event, Karen?" ... "Look, she has little birdhouses decorating the napkin rings!" ... "See how she used flowerpots as serving pieces, how darling!" ... "Oh, we each have a chocolate egg in a little bird nest as our party favor!"
>
> And that's just the beginning. "Mmmms" abound as you serve up refreshing Sangria Spritzer, Cheesy Carrot Bites, Southwestern Steak sandwiches, Sour Cream-Lemon Cups, and other tasty dishes.
> YOUR PARTY IS A SUCCESS!
>
> Don't be surprised if guests beg you to help them plan their next gathering. Ahh ... the sweet rewards of being a great hostess (and only you and I know that you used your PERFECT PARTIES book as your guide!).

Think how proud you'll be when you witness the delight on the faces of all your guests. With **PERFECT PARTIES** at your side, it's always a great day for a party!

YOU'LL CREATE FOOD, FAVORS, AND LOTS OF FESTIVITY!

▲ "Zoo-pendous" Birthday Party. This animal-theme picnic finds the birthday boy and his friends on safari at the zoo! Essentials include "zoo buckets" you've created to carry their lunches. The menu features Gorilla Gorp Snack Mix, Paw Print Cookies, and other *grrreat* goodies!

▲ Anchors Aweigh Pool Party. Ahoy, matey ... you're really in the swim of things now as you paint nautical flags on the invitations and bake up Starfish Cookies and seashell-shaped muffins. You'll create all sorts of "see-worthy" decoration sensations, like miniature life preservers for the chair backs.

▲ Bridesmaids' Lovely Luncheon. You'll honor these special attendants with sweet touches. Sheets with delicate floral prints make decorating a breeze. And everyone will love drinking Fresh Apricot Margaritas and nibbling salad made with edible flowers!

▲ Great "Egg-Spectation" Baby Shower. When someone's "nesting," you'll help welcome the new arrival by creating a corsage of baby

Fig. 2.4 Continued

socks and a flowery egg centerpiece cradled in a twig wreath "nest." Receiving blankets serve as table scarves, and baby washcloths held by diaper pins are napkins. The menu is highlighted by a frosted sandwich loaf, Marshmallow Mints, and other yummies.

▲ **Tool-Time Shower.** Hail the groom-to-be with this great get-together. You'll easily work handsaw motifs into fun invitations. A toolbox becomes the centerpiece; and metal buckets, a dustpan, and toolbox trays (new and clean!) make handy serving dishes. Clever take-home favors are small plastic boxes topped with painted nuts and bolts. The man-pleasing menu includes "Honey-Do" Brownies.

▲ **Football Fever Party.** This event will have sports fans cheering! The fun kicks off with invitations decorated with football motifs snipped from paper napkins. At game time, big points are scored with the buffet menu, which includes Championship Snack Mix, a football-shaped Stadium Sandwich, and other winners.

▲ **Dress-Up Birthday Tea.** The birthday girl will love the whimsy of this afternoon of "let's pretend!" Playthings include oversize "lipsticks," "perfume bottles," and garland "necklaces." The little ladies will play dress-up, make picture frame favors, sip Cherry-Apple Punch, munch slices of teapot-shaped cake, and more!

WE HAVE CREATIVE PARTY PLANS FOR LOTS OF OCCASIONS!

There's also the **Quilters' Block Party** where quilting enthusiasts swap fabric pieces; the **Midnight Prom Buffet** at which teens receive colorful autograph books you've decorated; and the **Golfer's Birthday Party** with "under par" and "over par" recipes featuring light and luscious versions.

WE'VE DONE ALL THE PLANNING, SO YOU'LL HAVE ALL THE FUN!

You'll use **PERFECT PARTIES** year after happy year! Our parties are "classics," so you'll enjoy hosting any of them more than once. You may even want to adapt projects and recipes to fit your innovative party-theme ideas!

And our new book makes it easy for you to experience the best part of party-giving — the satisfaction of putting your "personal touch" on each fun project and tasty recipe!

From the inventive invitations and dazzling decorations to the "fun-tastic" favors, each project has easy-to-follow instructions to lead you, step by easy step! And our recipes are thoroughly kitchen-tested to give you the most flavorful party foods ever. Plus, you'll get vivid color photographs to show you how each finished party setting will look.

Can't wait to have a party? It's more fun than ever

Fig. 2.4 Continued

because we've taken out all the planning headaches and hassles, so you can enjoy your celebrations as much as your guests do!

GO AHEAD, TRY <u>PERFECT PARTIES</u> FOR 21 DAYS — FREE!

Your **FREE PREVIEW** will allow you plenty of time to browse through our new book, whip up a couple of treats, and see all the creative parties you'll want to give. But don't worry, <u>we'll take the book back with open arms if you don't like it</u>.

PLEASE KEEP YOUR COMPLIMENTARY GIFT!

<u>Perfect Party Punches for the Holidays</u> is your FREE GIFT just for taking a no-risk look at our new book. This 12-page recipe booklet is overflowing with delectable drinkables like Fuzzy Navel Punch, Mocha-Cardamom Cappuccino, and additional concoctions to please the palates of all your guests. <u>It's yours, compliments of Leisure Arts, no matter what you decide</u>!

And if you can't wait to be the "hostess with the mostest" and want **PERFECT PARTIES** to help, you may keep your book for the **low introductory price of ONLY $14.95** plus a small postage/handling fee. That's a **BIG 25% OFF** the $19.95 retail price. What a bargain — this comes out to around <u>$1.50 a party</u>!

Hurry, locate YOUR PARTY R.S.V.P.! Card and slip it into the postage-paid envelope we've given you. Now, simply drop it into the mailbox and be on your way to happy hostessing!

Don't wait, so **you can have a chance to win our Fast 50 PRIZE — the Creative Cook's Library**. If your R.S.V.P. Card is one of the first 50 received in our mail room, this valuable 5-book recipe collection is yours for replying early.

Don't miss the party,

Anne Childs

Anne Van Wagner Childs
Editor-in-Chief

P.S. PLEASE BE QUICK — slip your card in the mail today
    to receive your FREE preview of **PERFECT PARTIES,**
    your FREE recipe booklet to keep no matter what,
    and your chance to be among the 50 lucky people
    to WIN the Creative Cook's Library!

Fig. 2.4   Continued

morning in Japan." A more gracious answer might be, "Regardless of the time of day, this is breezy and warm without the danger of being overly aggressive."

The close isn't as crucial as the opening, but here's a tip: don't close with "Yours truly."

"Yours truly" isn't as stiffly formal as "Dear Sir" or "Gentlemen"—greetings that often begin a letter which closes with "Yours truly." But you know what it is? Antiquity without polish.

Antiquity *with* polish is a standard and often elegant selling technique. "Your servant, Sir" is an example of this writing style—which had better match in *all* components or you look dumb.

You'll find "Sincerely" (not "Sincerely yours") as the close on most letters; business-to-business often uses "Cordially" on the theory that "Sincerely" is more emotional a close than the text justifies.

Attacking "Sincerely" is like breaking a butterfly on the rack. Why do it? But if you're doggedly determined to improve the close of your letter, try adding another pinch of salesmanship:

"Yours for more vigorous health"
"For the Board of Directors"
"For your friends at [NAME OF COMPANY]"
"Bless you, my dear friend" (fund-raising only, please)

If you're writing to people who think of you as a friend, consider "Regards" an indication of affection that doesn't seem so emotional it suggests a more personal relationship than actually exists.

Tip Number Seven:
Use an overline, if it isn't stupid.

The overline is a potentially valuable element in mass mailings and warrants its own chapter in this book. (See chapter 3.)

The world of force-communication so tightly links creative rules and mechanical rules we sometimes can't separate them. For example: In a test of four identical messages—one version with a typewritten overline, one with a typeset overline, one with a handwritten overline, and one with no overline—which probably will bring heaviest response?

My fast vote is for the letter with the handwritten overline. Why? Because my experience has been that a letter with a handwritten overline is read more thoroughly by the person who gets it. In fact, it's more likely to be read at all.

But . . .

If your overline has more than about fifteen words, handwriting can slow down or even destroy readership. I used to object strongly to descendants of the old Johnson Box—that legend at the top of the letter, centered and boxed by stars or asterisks, and now in my opinion obsolete. Those descendants use display type, lots of attention-getters, and sometimes pictures. (Johnson Boxes are discussed in chapter 3.) I don't object any longer, *except* to overlong typeset overlines that can consume half a page or more and say nothing.

You can position the overline toward the right edge, or if you have a neatness complex, you can center it. But here you have another opportunity to relate mechanical rules to creative rules. I prefer having the overline on the right. Why? Because perfect balance detracts from the impact of your message.

Can you see how art direction, which can have a set of goals completely different from the goals of the communicator, can damage the communicator's message? If perfect balance detracts from the impact of your message, how does this knowledge affect your decision to type or handwrite your overline?

Let's follow a logical path here. To begin, subject to the fifteen-word exception discussed earlier, we can formulate a mini-generalization:

> ✏ A handwritten overline tends to outpull a typewritten overline.

Why? Because the typewritten overline has less contrast with the rest of the letter . . . and it more closely parallels perfect balance than a handwritten overline.

This is the stuff obsolescence is made of.

Let's suppose you agree with me. We all start following this mini-generalization. We all start writing letters with handwritten overlines. My secret system is no longer a secret. Instead, it becomes the standard procedure. Anyone who doesn't use a handwritten overline is regarded as ignorant. Then what happens?

In a couple of years we all will run afoul of a maxi-generalization:

> ✏ Sameness equals boredom; overuse equals abuse.

Whenever a mini-generalization and a maxi-generalization come into conflict, the mini-generalization loses. So sameness has produced boredom, and our mini-generalization doesn't work anymore.

And by overusing a rule we accelerate the evolutionary process. Marketing isn't a stagnant pool. The water is always running from that great, fresh spring in the heavens. We have to keep our wits about us. Mozart's symphonies and operas were sophisticated for their time, but if Mozart studied music today he'd need a far more complex type of orchestration to compete.

Now can you visualize how these little rules of force-communication we're beginning to enjoy have taken form? First we recognize that one approach works better than others. This doesn't give us the rule; it only gives us the pieces of a puzzle. We assemble the puzzle by learning more. And we learn more by additional tests. This overline outpulled that overline. This overline has something that overline doesn't have. What is it? Slowly, the rules appear for us to use.

And the rules are fluid. We can't sit back year after year and apply the same rules. Too many academicians in our colleges and universities, teaching journalism and advertising and mass communication, use the same lecture notes year after year, long after those notes have become obsolete.

So if you teach mass communication, and you tell your students that getting attention is parallel to selling merchandise, your lecture notes are twenty years out of date.

Tip Number Eight:
If you include a P.S., it should reinforce one of the key selling motivators or mention an extra benefit that doesn't require explanation.

So this P.S. adds nothing to the power of the letter:

———————————

Don't you agree this is a wonderful and unique opportunity? I urge you to respond without delay, because delay can be costly to you.

———————————

This P.S. does add power:

———————————

If you want this special private discount, be sure to mail the postage-free card or call my personal toll-free phone number within the next 10 days. I'd hate to see you miss out.

———————————

The various facets, benefits, and perils of the P.S. will be covered in chapter 4. In general, a P.S. is second only to the overline in its position as being more likely to be read than the text of the letter. Mailers point to many tests showing that what's in the P.S. can actually pull the reader into the letter . . . or push the reader away.

The postscript is standard in direct-response mass mailings; in one-to-one mailings, the key is *pertinence*. If your P.S. causes the recipient to think he or she is one of a mob of people getting a mass mailing, wow, have you goofed!

Tip Number Nine: Experiment with marginal notes.

Marginal notes are a specialty. Not every letter benefits from them, and this suggests you decide, based on the tone of the letter, whether or not they'll be beneficial.

When you do use them, the rules for marginal notes are even tighter than they are for overlines. Two of them are absolute:

1. Handwrite everything.
2. Use no more than four or five words for each marginal note.

Marginal notes draw their power from appearing to be a spontaneous outburst of enthusiasm. The writer is so excited, so enthusiastic, he or she bubbles over. Handwritten bubbling over has verisimilitude, the appearance of truth. Typed bubbling over looks contrived. We fight like tigers to avoid a contrived look, so why take the risk?

The four- or five-word maximum is a good idea mechanically as well as creatively. When you limit yourself to four or five words, you can write big enough to grab the reader's eye the way you should. There's no handwritten marginal message that can't be transmitted in four or five words.

Don't put a whole bunch of marginal notes together on the same page. Remember the maxi-generalization? *Sameness equals boredom; overuse equals abuse.*

Some boilerplate marginal notes:

"Here's your FREE bonus!"
"Read this *extra*-carefully"
"Save 50 percent"

Don't be afraid to use hand-drawn arrows, lines, brackets, or even stars for emphasis. You're creating the impression of spontaneous enthusiasm.

Marginal notes, along with handwritten overlines, should be in a second color. What color? Don't consider any color other than the one in which you print the signature, usually process blue. Why the same color as the signature? Because you're trying to project an effect: The writer is reading over the letter before signing it. He or she has pen in hand, and this pen—the one that signs the letter—is the same one that writes the marginal notes.

If the whole letter, including signature, is printed in one color, you don't have any decision to make.

For heaven's sake don't have an overline and marginal comments in beautiful writing, a showcase of fine feminine calligraphy, and then have an illegible scrawl for a signature at the end of the letter. The writing should match.

Figures 2.5 and 2.6 are examples of letters with marginal notes. But the notes are too wordy and the first, in figure 2.5, "Choose your own easy-to-remember PIN number," is oblique to the selling argument. Too, why have two signatures? Adding an external signature emphasizes the promotional nature of the letter and damages exclusivity.

An extra tip: There never is an excuse for an illegible signature on a letter. It may give ego satisfaction to an executive, but it drains intimacy from the communication. The one thing worse than an illegible signature is an illegible signature with no name typed below it.

Tip Number Ten:
Use letters to test.

The letter is the most logical testing instrument in a direct-mail package.

Testing one brochure against another is expensive, even if all the changes are in the black plate. Testing response devices such as order forms often gives muddy results because this type of test isn't always logical.

But letters! The writer becomes a hero because the four-page letter outpulled the one-page letter—or vice versa. The writer can create letters with different flavors to test the five great motivators of our era (fear, exclusivity, greed, guilt, and need for approval) against one another . . . or test one of these against the "soft" motivators (convenience and pleasure).

Best of all, letter tests are cheap. It costs next to nothing to print two versions of the letter instead of one.

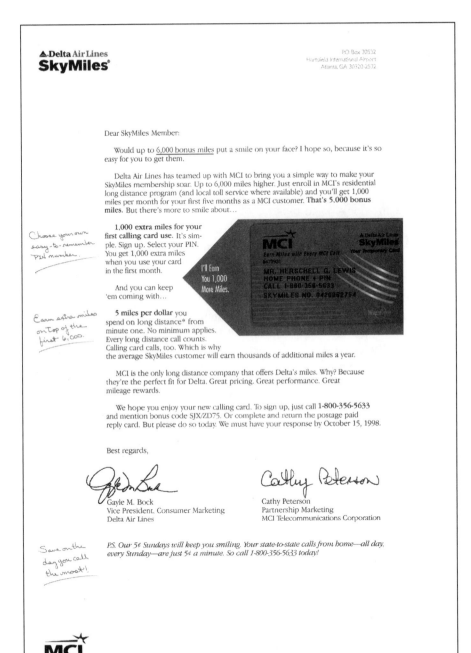

▲ Delta Air Lines
SkyMiles®

PO Box 20532
Hartsfield International Airport
Atlanta, GA 30320-2532

Dear SkyMiles Member:

Would up to 6,000 bonus miles put a smile on your face? I hope so, because it's so easy for you to get them.

Delta Air Lines has teamed up with MCI to bring you a simple way to make your SkyMiles membership soar. Up to 6,000 miles higher. Just enroll in MCI's residential long distance program (and local toll service where available) and you'll get 1,000 miles per month for your first five months as a MCI customer. **That's 5,000 bonus miles.** But there's more to smile about...

Choose your own easy-to-remember PIN number.

1,000 extra miles for your first calling card use. It's simple. Sign up. Select your PIN. You get 1,000 extra miles when you use your card in the first month.

And you can keep 'em coming with...

Earn extra miles on Top of the first 6,000.

5 miles per dollar you spend on long distance* from minute one. No minimum applies. Every long distance call counts. Calling card calls, too. Which is why the average SkyMiles customer will earn thousands of additional miles a year.

MCI is the only long distance company that offers Delta's miles. Why? Because they're the perfect fit for Delta. Great pricing. Great performance. Great mileage rewards.

We hope you enjoy your new calling card. To sign up, just call **1-800-356-5633** and mention bonus code SJX/ZD75. Or complete and return the postage paid reply card. But please do so today. We must have your response by October 15, 1998.

Best regards,

Gayle M. Bock
Gayle M. Bock
Vice President, Consumer Marketing
Delta Air Lines

Cathy Peterson
Cathy Peterson
Partnership Marketing
MCI Telecommunications Corporation

Save on the day you call the most!

P.S. Our 5¢ Sundays will keep you smiling. Your state-to-state calls from home—all day, every Sunday—are just 5¢ a minute. So call 1-800-356-5633 today!

MCI

Fig. 2.5   Relating to tip number nine, this letter uses marginal notes; but the wording of these notes in no way is as exciting as "6,000 FREE miles for you!" or "Get this: 5¢ a minute!"

ENJOY UP TO 6,000 ONEPASS® MILES.
5,000 MILES FOR JOINING MCI AND 1,000 WHEN
YOU USE YOUR CALLING CARD.*

Ms. Margo E. Lewis
340 N. Fig Tree Ln
Plantation FL 33317-2561

Dear Ms. Margo E. Lewis:

You're just one call away from OnePass bonus miles and *that much closer to earning a reward ticket on Continental Airlines.*

Simply choose MCI for your residential long distance and local toll service (where available), and up to 6,000 bonus miles will be credited to your OnePass account. Just call 1-800-319-9194 to enroll right away.

Earn 5 Miles for every dollar you spend

As an MCI customer, your voice will take you far. Every time you make a long distance call *you'll earn 5 miles for every dollar* you spend. Plus, you'll receive 1,000 miles for using the MCI Card® by the end of your first full billing cycle.

SAVE WITH 5¢ SUNDAYS

You won't just be adding miles, you'll be adding long distance savings, with MCI's low rates. As an MCI customer, you can enjoy our 5-cent rate on state-to-state calls from home all day every Sunday**.

ENJOY MCI SERVICE AT HOME OR ON THE ROAD.

As an MCI customer, you'll also receive the MCI Card® with WorldPhone® service that you can use to call from the U.S. to more than 280 places worldwide. So you'll never be out of touch with the people most important to you.

Turn one call into 6,000 bonus miles

There are up to 6,000 OnePass bonus miles waiting for you. Just call 1-800-319-9194. Or sign and return your certificate in the enclosed envelope. Don't delay, this offer expires October 15, 1998

Sincerely,

Shari Kapelina
Program Manager, Partner Marketing
MCI Telecommunications Corporation.

Scott Dunphy
Director, Partner and Membership Marketing
Continental Airlines

P.S. Call 1-800-319-9194 today and earn up to 6,000 OnePass bonus miles.

Fig. 2.6 This offer, for a competing airline, is identical to the one shown in figure 2.5. Marginal notes are printed, not handwritten, and a different individual's signature represents the telecommunications company. As with figure 2.5, two signatures seem unnecessary and damage rapport.

While you're at it, consider testing a tinted paper stock against white. The text has to be identical, or you destroy the purity of test results. Color psychology is itself one of the creative aspects of communication.

Following these ten little tips can result in a quick spurt in the effectiveness of your letter-writing. Print the ten tips on a small sheet of paper and keep it visible when you're writing. If one of them jogs loose an effective thought, you're already ahead.

3

What's on Top? And What's in the Middle?

Until the mid-1970s, a letter was a letter. Gimmickry and tampering with the standardized format—date, greeting, text—weren't considered because nobody had yet thought of new and effective ways to grab and shake the reader's attention.

The overline came into its own when experiments revealed two results: First, a properly constructed overline is the most read part of the letter. This is both natural and expected because the overline is the first element the reader sees; the reader's reaction to the overline determines whether that individual will continue reading.

Second—and considerably more significant—many head-to-head tests verify that a letter with an overline will outpull an identical letter with no overline.

The First Law of Overlines

As you can see from some of the samples reproduced in this book, the mechanical choice of overline techniques is unlimited. Want to have one giant word set in 120-point type? Why not? Want a handwritten message? Why not? Want a heading and subhead, as though the letter is an ad? Why not? The space is available . . . and the mechanical constraint is subject only to the creative constraint—the First Law of Overlines:

> ✏ The overline should generate or enhance the reader's desire to keep reading. This means the overline should not synopsize the offer.

Too many of the ineffective overlines we see summarize the offer *before* the reader is conditioned to accept the premise. So an overline with the words:

_____

Save 20% on your automobile insurance!

_____

isn't as effective as:

_____

Put an extra $100 a year in your pocket!

_____

An overline shouldn't be a document in itself. If the writer needs five handwritten lines, warning flags should go flying up. That's too long for handwriting, a candidate for typesetting.

Figure 3.1 is an overline which specifies the purpose of the letter. Unquestionably it spurred readership.

Figure 3.2 is an example of an overline which seems to deliberately avoid specifics. Aimed at those who know the publication but aren't subscribers, it damages itself by offering puffery without specifics.

When Should You? When Shouldn't You?

With one exception, overlines have little place in one-to-one correspondence. That's because they're implicitly "pitchy." They're suggesting an offer, which puts the writer in a selling posture.

What's the one exception? When the writer wants the reader to feel he or she is reading over the letter before mailing it and has a spontaneous burst of enthusiasm. So this type of overline should be handwritten and not look "produced."

The most effective and most common overlines are those on mass mailings, because the recipient either has no prior relationship with the sender or, as a prior customer, has the standard buyer-to-vendor relationship.

Figure 3.3 shows an interesting relationship between the overline and the letterhead. Had "Health & Nutrition Letter" been set in the same size as "Tufts University," readership would have been much lower. By screaming "Health & Nutrition Letter" (in bright purple) and following with questions, the opening spurs reader interest . . . although the questions are weaker than they might be.

CNA Plaza, Chicago, Illinois 60685

**This is a new benefit
exclusively for employees.
Please read this now.**

Dear Employee,

If I may have your attention for about three minutes ...

    CNA is pleased to be able to offer you a voluntary employee benefit that is not available to the general public - auto coverage at special group rates in most states.

    I invite you to participate in this exclusive program, and I believe it will be worth your while from two viewpoints:

  1. Money.
  2. Peace of mind.

    Both money and peace of mind relate to a subject you probably <u>don't</u> want to think about right now: automobile insurance.

Money - a good way to keep score.

    One statement I've heard all my professional life is, "What difference does it make who carries your insurance? They're all about the same."

    Just one thing wrong with that statement.

over, please ...

Fig. 3.1   An exception to the handwritten overline is one whose effectiveness is damaged if the appearance is not totally businesslike. This one, a dozen words in oversize typewriter effect, demands readership.

Consumer Reports

Remember Consumer Reports?

The magazine you used to think of checking before you bought a car?

Well, please rethink Consumer Reports. Because now there are even more important reasons to read it.

Yes, we can still save you hundreds of dollars on the products you buy.

But now, more than ever, we can also save you thousands of dollars on the services you buy. And help you make the high-stakes financial, health and safety decisions that could affect the quality of your life for years.

You need Consumer Reports more than ever. Here's how you can get it on very special terms.

Dear Friend:

    I'd like to make you an offer I think and hope you'll find irresistible. I'd like to send you:

1. A sample issue of Consumer Reports ($2.95 at the newsstand).

2. A free copy of the 1998 Consumer Reports Buying Guide (regularly $8.95) with hundreds of brand-name product ratings.

3. A free copy of our $11.95 book, How To Clean Practically Anything. Updated, fourth edition.

                             (over please)

Fig. 3.2　What is your opinion of the lengthy Johnson Box at the top of page 1 of a four-page letter? Is it that it lacks a single specific to spur ongoing readership? In the body of the letter are subheads such as "How to save $52,000 on a mortgage." Wouldn't such a reference have been many times more powerful?

TUFTS UNIVERSITY
Health & Nutrition Letter

What should you believe when they tell you margarine is "good for you" one week...and "bad for you" the next?

What should you believe when you read that drinking coffee hurts your heart?

What should you believe when they say drinking red wine helps you live longer?

Well, you can keep on being confused by contradictions in the media — or you can send for our next issue ABSOLUTELY FREE!

Dear Friend:

Once upon a time life was simple...

You sat down with the whole family for a hearty meat-and-potatoes dinner...and words like "cholesterol" and "fiber" and "antioxidants" were nowhere to be heard!

- NOBODY warned that the meat loaf might be loaded with harmful bacteria.
- NOBODY thought twice when you asked them to "please pass the salt."
- NOBODY had ever heard the term "saturated fat." Life was simple.

And then things got complicated. Maybe too complicated.

Eating became a health risk. Scores of "experts" came out of the woodwork declaring that you SHOULDN'T eat this but you SHOULD eat that...and then still more experts popped up to say that the other experts had it all wrong!

Pretty soon, eating became as complex as trying to figure out your tax returns and just about as much fun, which is why...

          I'VE GOT TERRIFIC NEWS FOR YOU...

                                        (over, please)

Fig. 3.3 The huge "Health & Nutrition Letter" heading strikes home. But the questions are curiously mild. "What should you believe when you read that drinking coffee hurts your heart?" is oblique to reader interest. Better might have been, "For years you've been told coffee hurts your heart. Oops!"

Rules and Techniques of Overline Writing

A handwritten overline is an unequaled attention-getting device for any letter. But if we're on the verge of formulating rules for overlines, we can't just accept this as fact. We must ask why the overline has such potential.

The answer is that, except for huge bold handwriting as a greeting or just after the greeting, the handwritten overline is the most read element of the letter. The reader's eye goes there first. That's what gives it strength . . . and that's what makes it so dangerous. As an attention-getting device, in the Age of Skepticism, it has a double responsibility:

1. It has to grab and shake the reader's attention.
2. It has to make the reader eager to continue reading.

Let's look at the first responsibility. Grab and shake the reader's attention . . . but don't give away your message in the overline. I read this overline on the letter in a fat, heavily produced mailing:

If you've driven accident-free for the past three years, you can save 10 percent to 20 percent on your automobile insurance.

I'd have said, "let me show you how to save" rather than "you can save." But my objection to this overline isn't based on one little refinement, it's based on this: instead of improving reading, comprehension, and pre-acceptance, these words blunted my interest and lost me as a reader. Too much too soon.

The purpose of the overline parallels the purpose of envelope copy. Envelope copy is like a kamikaze dive, with one purpose only: to convince the reader to open the envelope. That's it. If the writer tries to go beyond this purpose, chances are envelope copy will be weaker, not stronger. (See chapter 5.)

Similarly, the overline has one purpose only: to get the reader into the letter, with more enthusiasm or anticipation than the writer can generate without the overline.

In my opinion, even simple and primitive calls such as "This is a private offer" or "Do you qualify?" are stronger overlines than the "accident-free" wording.

Years ago, college courses in advertising dismissed outdoor advertising with a single direction: "No message longer than fifteen words." As a general rule (and as you'll see, Alexandre Dumas was quite correct when he said, "All generalizations are false, including this one") we might revive

CATFANCY®

TRUE OR FALSE

1. Cats cannot be leash trained.
2. Kittens from the same litter can have different fathers.
3. Any medicine that is safe for humans is also safe for cats.
4. Cats can help people heal.

Dear Friend:

So much has been said and written about cats over the years that it's hard to separate fact from fiction. Just where do you go for the truth?

For over 26 years many thousands of cat lovers like you have relied upon CAT FANCY magazine to explode the myths, define the facts and explain it all in terms that are easy to understand.

And now, for a limited time, you can get this truth-packed publication at a very special introductory rate:

1 Full year (12 issues) for Only $11.99
That's 50% Off the regular price!

Yes, it's true. CAT FANCY, the world's most popular magazine about cats and kittens will be coming to your home each month at HALF PRICE. We guarantee this is the best rate available. And along with a great bargain, you'll be getting the most up-to-date information on cat care, health, nutrition and safety.

Do you sometimes wonder why your cat acts the way it does? CAT FANCY's behavior experts will answer your questions and help you better understand your cat. For example, did you know...

Cats will drink more water if you place the bowl well away from the food dish.

It's normal for an adult cat to sleep an average of 18 hours a day.

You can often tell what mood your cat is in from the position of its ears and tail.

P.O. BOX 52864, BOULDER, CO 80322-2864

Fig. 3.4   Who can resist a quiz like this, especially in a mailing targeted to a specific interest group? This message *forces* readership. (The answers, at the bottom of page 2: 1-F; 2-T; 3-F; 4-T.)

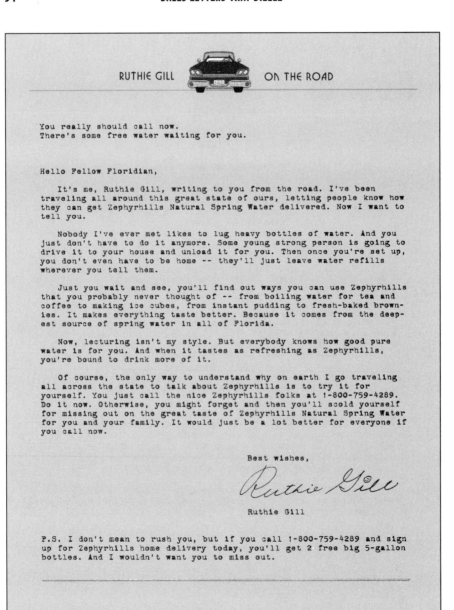

RUTHIE GILL   ON THE ROAD

You really should call now.
There's some free water waiting for you.

Hello Fellow Floridian,

    It's me, Ruthie Gill, writing to you from the road. I've been
traveling all around this great state of ours, letting people know how
they can get Zephyrhills Natural Spring Water delivered. Now I want to
tell you.

    Nobody I've ever met likes to lug heavy bottles of water. And you
just don't have to do it anymore. Some young strong person is going to
drive it to your house and unload it for you. Then once you're set up,
you don't even have to be home -- they'll just leave water refills
wherever you tell them.

    Just you wait and see, you'll find out ways you can use Zephyrhills
that you probably never thought of -- from boiling water for tea and
coffee to making ice cubes, from instant pudding to fresh-baked brownies. It makes everything taste better. Because it comes from the deepest source of spring water in all of Florida.

    Now, lecturing isn't my style. But everybody knows how good pure
water is for you. And when it tastes as refreshing as Zephyrhills,
you're bound to drink more of it.

    Of course, the only way to understand why on earth I go traveling
all across the state to talk about Zephyrhills is to try it for
yourself. You just call the nice Zephyrhills folks at 1-800-759-4289.
Do it now. Otherwise, you might forget and then you'll scold yourself
for missing out on the great taste of Zephyrhills Natural Spring Water
for you and your family. It would just be a lot better for everyone if
you call now.

                                Best wishes,

                                Ruthie Gill

                                Ruthie Gill

P.S. I don't mean to rush you, but if you call 1-800-759-4289 and sign
up for Zephyrhills home delivery today, you'll get 2 free big 5-gallon
bottles. And I wouldn't want you to miss out.

Fig. 3.5   This is an attractive letter … except for the overline, whose wording is peculiar. "Free water," unexplained, doesn't seem to be much of an incentive, and in fact, detracts from the bright greeting and first sentence.

United States Historical Society

ANTIQUE ARMS COMMITTEE

R. L. WILSON	LES LINE	MICHAEL KORDA	MEL TORMÉ	KEN WARNER	JEFFERY BELCHER
Chairman	*Editor*	*Editor-in-Chief*	*Entertainer*	*Editor*	*Chief Gunsmith*
Author/Historian	*Audubon Magazine*	*Simon & Schuster. Inc.*	*Antique Firearms Collector*	*Gun Digest*	*Society of Arms & Armour*

　　　　　　　　　　You are invited to own a pistol
　　　　　　　　　　of remarkable beauty and
　　　　　　　　　　historical importance - the
　　　　　　　　　　gold decorated Buffalo Bill
　　　　　　　　　　Centennial Pistol.

Dear Friend:

　　　A hundred years ago, a Pony Express rider galloped madly
toward his destination. A band of howling Indians cut him off.
Amid a volley of shots and arrows, he escaped to safety.

　　　No sooner had he disappeared from view than the Deadwood
Stage thundered past, its driver firing round after round from
his trusty Colt at the marauding Indians, led by the stony-faced
Chief Iron Tail.

　　　Any onlooker, watching the wide open action, responded in
the only logical way: he applauded.

　　　The event was Buffalo Bill's Wild West Show. The date
was almost exactly a century ago. The Pony Express,
the Deadwood Stage, Chief Iron Tail and incredible
crack-shot Annie Oakley packed the house for
performance after performance, all over the world.

　　　But the star of stars was Colonel William Cody
himself -- Buffalo Bill, who already was a legend as
a buffalo hunter, a U.S. Cavalry hero and a government
scout. From 1883 until his death in 1917, the legend
grew as the flamboyant western panjandrum wheeled his
horse and twirled his ivory-handled Colt .44's.

　　　Photographs of Buffalo Bill show him with his constant
companion, his 1860 Army Colt revolver. This pistol probably is
the most famous hand-weapon ever built, and now I invite you to
be one of only 2,500 individuals in the world who own an exact,
working reproduction of the celebrated firearm, the official
Buffalo Bill Centennial pistol.

First and Main Streets • Richmond. Virginia 23219 • (804) 648-4736 • Telex (804) 379-2638 • FAX (804) 648-0002

Fig. 3.6　How much more dramatic the opening of this letter would have been *without* the five-line "invitation to own a pistol." Yes, that's what's for sale, but introducing the for-sale element dilutes the drama of the opening. Where might those five lines have had a logical home? How about the envelope?

this suggestion today as a safety net for most, but by no means all, over-lines. One exception: The "dialogue" overline, in which line 1 poses a problem and line 2, in a different voice (possibly in a different handwriting or typeface), solves the problem.

Now let's look at the second responsibility. The overline should make the reader eager to continue reading . . . which eliminates overlines that tell too much and steal the selling argument from the letter itself.

So an overline such as "Save twenty percent on automobile insurance"— even though it's short—is *less* effective than "Just mail the card and you'll save $100 to $200." The first overline makes it unnecessary for the recipient to read the letter, while the second impels the recipient to read the letter.

Even though both are handwritten and both promise benefit, the first tells too much, and it violates the second responsibility of a valid overline.

Printed Legends and Pictures

The technique of having *something* before the greeting has become so widespread many professional letter writers wouldn't consider sending out a mass mailing without it.

Note the qualifier: *mass* mailings. In one-to-one correspondence, hand-writing maintains the personalized aspect; a printed legend or a picture doesn't.

Now that pre-greeting attention-getters have become commonplace, we see four- and five-paragraph pre-greeting messages. Is it too much? The decision lies in the hands of those who get the letter. Certainly length is not a deterrent if the message is lyrical and provocative.

A fairly new technique is the "Rebus" letter, in which pictures break up the text. In such a letter, a photograph or illustration replaces or exempli-fies a description.

Johnson Boxes

The origin of the term *Johnson Box* is murky, although many knowledge-able historians of the writing craft attribute it to Frank Johnson, who used it in subscription promotions in the 1970s.

A Johnson Box is a typed legend above the greeting. It's usually centered and boxed with a border of asterisks or stars. And invariably it tells the reader what the letter is about. The writer wants to interest the reader in insurance, or a subscription, or collectibles.

shutterbug®

I'll keep this open for you for 30 days. Please read.

Dear Fellow Photographer,

I was reading an article about night photography in a recent issue of SHUTTERBUG.

I've been publisher of this magazine (and of course a photographer) for years, but I admit — I never even thought about using a red or blue filter for night shots. The whole idea is exciting, and it's one I'd <u>never</u> have seen if I hadn't been reading SHUTTERBUG.

Blue Filter "Cold" effect

Another article was about shooting portraits <u>outside</u>, using natural settings. We've all done that, but this article told me when to shoot from a lower angle to solve a reflection problem I often encounter.

This same article told me (and all SHUTTERBUG readers) how to make a black and white outdoor portrait shot. It specified which paper to use to hold soft skin tones and still get high contrast.

Ilford MGII Paper, filtered at 2.5

Like all the articles in SHUTTERBUG, the descriptions were so clear a beginner could follow them easily. And the subject was so useful a professional could benefit from them. (We have letters to prove it.)

<u>Will You Look at a Free Issue?</u>

I invite you to become a subscriber to SHUTTERBUG, at a very special price ... far, far below the cover price.

Please, before you make a quick decision to toss this mailing into the wastebasket, understand what I'm offering you. Yes, I want you to become a subscriber. No, I don't want you to decide — yes or no — until you've seen a sample issue.

I'll tell you why: I can sit here all day, writing about SHUTTERBUG, and not be able to transmit a fraction of what you can expect to find in the pages of this magazine.

Fig. 3.7   A subscription test of various approaches and formats made this the winner in terms of bringing the highest percentage of response: a letter combining a handwritten overline, marginal notes, and a photograph.

Pioneering in its day, in the twenty-first century we quickly recognize the pro and the con of this technique. Pro: Someone who might not read the letter sees the Johnson Box, thinks, "Oh, I might be interested in that," and then does read the letter. Con: Someone the letter might convince to buy insurance sees the pitch before a logical sales argument has a chance to make a point, thinks, "Oh, I'm not interested in that," and tosses the letter unread into the wastebasket.

I admit, I'm not a fan of Johnson Boxes. It's because almost every one seems to remove suspense rather than heighten it. Almost every one uses a closing line before the sales argument even begins.

A typical Johnson Box says, "Here's a bet you can't lose . . . on a motivational poster program that's a proven winner!"

See what's wrong here? The writer has given away the point of the letter before making the point. The reader quickly says, "I don't want a motivational poster program." And the reader is right because we've leaped into the close without offering any benefit. Visualize the letter without the Johnson Box and see how it leaps to life. When I say "Get to the point," I don't mean "Start with the close."

If you're going to have a legend above the greeting, write that legend with one goal in mind—to force the reader to continue reading.

What Else Is "In"?

We've begun to see two powerful devices used together—handwriting and a rubber-stamp effect. Rubber stamps and stick-on notes are *in*.

A rubber stamp *implicitly* says, "Personal and important." A stick-on note *implicitly* says, "I thought of this after the letter was written and want to be sure you see it."

But some writers who know stick-on notes are in don't know how to use them. A mailing that came to me had a note affixed to the front sheet. The message began:

Since the invitation enclosed includes several months of *Smithsonian*, I want you to know that we make every issue . . .

Nope. That's not what stick-on notes are for.

Stick-on notes are useful in subscription renewal mailings, fund-raising, collection letters, and any notification of an expiration date, as the cry of "Wolf!"

```
* * * * * * * * * * * * * * * * * * * *
*                                     *
*    HERE'S A BET YOU CAN'T LOSE ...  *
*                                     *
*    ON A MOTIVATIONAL POSTER PROGRAM *
*    THAT'S A PROVEN WINNER!          *
*                                     *
* * * * * * * * * * * * * * * * * * * *
```

Dear Executive:

    I have a small bet that I'd like to make with you -- a bet that you simply can't lose!

    It has to do with a subject that I know is of great importance to you: motivating your employees, day in and day out, to do the best possible job for you and your company.

                Here's the bet: right now, while it's close at hand, display the enclosed HERMAN ® Poster somewhere in your office. Don't say anything about it to your employees -- just watch their reactions when they see it, and listen to their comments.

                I'll wager, in fact I'll guarantee, that eight out of ten will smile, three out of five will chuckle, and at least one or two will <u>say</u> something favorable about the poster.

    If you don't get this kind of reaction, then the laugh's on me -- and the bet won't cost you a penny. But I'm confident that even this one HERMAN Poster will have a positive impact on your employees' attitudes -- and that you'll want to keep these outstanding posters coming in the weeks and months ahead, beginning with <u>four FREE weekly issues</u>!

    To do so, you need only drop the enclosed "HERMAN Poster Certificate" in the mail. (It's postage-paid for your convenience.) That's all there is to it.

    But once you've begun using your new posters ... and seen how much your employees enjoy and respond to them ... I'm sure you'll appreciate why HERMAN is <u>the most popular motivational poster program in America today</u>.

    So, take me up on my bet, won't you? And take advantage of our Special Introductory Offer at the same time. We'll start you with as many copies of

                          (over, please)

CLEMENT COMMUNICATIONS, INC.
Leaders in Management-Employee Communications

Concord Industrial Park · Concordville, Pennsylvania 19331 · 1-800-345-8101

Fig. 3.8   This typical Johnson Box adds nothing and certainly must kill off some who might have read the letter. Without an explanation of benefits, who wants a motivational poster program?

R E P O R T

EXECUTIVE SUMMARY

- Many travelers and arrangers use the hotel information found in the OAG Business Travel Planner as an invaluable "single source" for hotel selection and business travel planning. Others use it to supplement the information they may be obtaining via computer or other sources.

- Regardless, nearly all subscribers confirm it is a <u>necessity</u> to use and keep handy for its comprehensive hotel and city facts and details.

- Nearly <u>all</u> subscribers agree it <u>pays for itself</u> by improving the <u>efficiency</u> of business travel and travel planning.

- Nearly <u>all</u> subscribers renew their subscriptions because they discover it to be an <u>unsurpassed value</u>.

- You've been <u>exclusively</u> selected to receive the OAG Business Travel Planner at a <u>67% savings</u>. That's <u>$201 OFF</u> the combined single issue price of $300.

- You've been <u>exclusively</u> selected to receive a special <u>FREE GIFT</u> just for replying before December 31 with your paid order!

Dear Business Traveler or Arranger:

What's your idea of convenient business travel? What does <u>efficient</u> travel arranging and travel planning mean to you?

In canvassing hundreds of professionals like you, we discovered professionals wanted all their hotel information — locations, phone numbers, directions — <u>all in one place</u>. They wanted a reference tool that has information conveniently listed, alphabetically by city.

The OAG Business Travel Planner is the answer. And now — for a limited time as a qualified business traveler or arranger — OAG is offering astonishing savings on the Travel Planner ... <u>four quarterly issues for just $99</u>!

That's <u>$201 OFF THE COMBINED SINGLE COPY PRICE</u> ... or a <u>67% savings</u> on a publication that has become the handiest source of valuable information about business travel destinations.

Let's say you have the address of your meeting. But where is it located and what hotel is nearby? Does the hotel have suites? Does it have fax service? Does it have meeting facilities? What credit cards does it accept? Does it have an airport shuttle?

In addition to those questions, the OAG Business Travel Planner answers others: Where is the airport? What roads to take? What special events are happening while you're in town? Where exactly is Gate B9 located at the airport?

The OAG Business Travel Planner contains complete information on <u>more than 29,000 hotels in over 14,700 destinations</u> throughout North America. Called the #1 Directory for Corporate Travel, it now features more than <u>1,000 Latin American accommodations</u> — a

(Over, please)

Fig. 3.9   The phrase "Executive Summary" isn't in itself a damaging element. But this old-fashioned Johnson Box not only doesn't create excitement, it suppresses it by starting off in low gear and staying there. Many will not read beyond the twenty-seven-word first sentence in this box, which to the veteran traveler, at whom this communication is aimed, is neither informative nor helpful.

```
* * * * * * * * * * * * * * * * * * * * * * * * *
*                                                *
*    Here's great news for AAA members between   *
*    45 and 75!  You can now buy between $2,000   *
*    and $10,000 in life insurance -- at a very   *
*    affordable cost.  And as a AAA member --     *
*    you can't be turned down for this policy ... *
*    even if you're in poor health.  You are      *
*    guaranteed this insurance.                   *
*                                                *
* * * * * * * * * * * * * * * * * * * * * * * * *
```

Dear Member:

    What I said above really _is_ good news! It's so good that I urge you to send in your application and payment today -- to be certain you beat the reply date shown on your application.

    I'm talking about our AAA Guaranteed Life insurance policy. It has so many great features I'll have trouble describing them all in this letter. So I better start right now. Here's a brief listing of advantages this policy brings you:

      ✓ You buy it by mail -- with no medical exam and no questions to answer about your health.

      ✓ It insures you for your entire life. (At age 100, you receive the full policy amount.) You can't be canceled because of age or poor health.

      ✓ You never get a rate increase either because of age or health. And the amount of your insurance is never reduced because of age or health.

      ✓ You can't be turned down for _any_ reason -- as long as you're a AAA member and between 45 and 75. Even if you have cancer or heart trouble -- even if you have a dangerous occupation or hobby. We guarantee to accept your application.

      ✓ Pays benefits for death due to illness or injury. In order to guarantee your acceptance, death benefits payable for natural causes are reduced during the first two years you own the plan -- paying 125% of the annual premium in the

Over, please

AAA Life Insurance Company • Administration and Service Center • Dodge at 33rd • Omaha, Nebraska 68175

Fig. 3.10 Does the Johnson Box at the top of page 1 of this four-page letter help or damage the possibility of response? One can make an argument both ways. As a general rule, a provocative message is more likely than a synop--sis to bring the reader into the main message because rapport hasn't been established and sales points haven't been developed.

Even if you never send for things — return this card to receive three free gifts to make you happier, healthier and wealthier

I know you're busy.

I know you have too much to read.

And yet, that's exactly why I want to send you THREE FREE ISSUES of BOTTOM LINE/PERSONAL -- the magazine for busy people.

FREE GIFTS NO CONTEST NO PURCHASE NECESSARY

Dear Reader:

In the olden days (actually, not long ago) life was simpler and slower.

When Mom and Dad were born, people took trains, not planes. They didn't trust cars or roads for long trips. There were no TV's, no computers, no fax machines, no cellular phones. Nobody ever heard of cholesterol, crack, junk bonds, or nuclear energy. Tax rules were understandable.

Then things started changing too fast.

The world speeded up. Scientific discoveries multiplied. Finance and money management became complicated. Rules of sexual relations were revised. Staying fit became everyone's No. 1 priority. We jogged, walked, and even stopped eating many of the foods that we loved. We learned how to use computers and program VCRs.

Soon we were drowning in a flood of information. It became almost impossible to find enough time to be well-informed.

Never mind. I have good news for you...

As more than 400,000 families already know, BOTTOM LINE/PERSONAL seeks out the new knowledge you need -- and zips it to you regularly twice-a-month in 16 pages of brief, intelligent, and easy-to-read super-useful form.

There is no fiction, no advertising, no pretty pictures -- just facts, ideas and advice to help you live better and live smarter -- digested to save you time.

*   *   *   *   *   *   *

But I am NOT asking you to buy anything. I'm NOT asking you to spend a penny.

All I ask is that you accept some sample issues (three, to be exact) and see BOTTOM LINE/PERSONAL for yourself. Then, if you like it, buy it -- or if you don't like it, don't buy it. You're the boss. Sure, this is a *over*

Fig. 3.11 The word describing heavy handwriting coupled with a rubber stamp: *excitement.* Excitement carries through the pre-greeting message; then after "Dear Reader" the mood slackens momentarily. A suggestion: Eliminate the "In the olden days ..." line and pace continues at a gallop.

Dear Reader,

You are there!

You're there when Admiral Farragut shouts, "Damn the torpedoes!"

You're there when the residents of Gettysburg cower in the corners of their homes, fearfully waiting to discover whether they'll be citizens of the Union or the Confederacy.

You're there to see many observers misrepresent the outcome of the battle between the USS Monitor and the Merrimack.

Ah, you're there at the very shoulder of a tough Union sergeant about to repel Robert E. Lee's last offensive north of the James River at Darbytown, Virginia. You're so close you can see the insignia on the bridle of his horse.

And you're there to see a Union raider you never heard of before, a former Illinois music teacher named Benjamin Grierson, literally dismantle 50 crucial miles of railroad and telegraph lines in Mississippi.

Where are you? In the exciting, exhilarating, colorful pages of a classic magazine unlike any other: AMERICA'S CIVIL WAR.

Should YOU Have This Extraordinary Magazine?
Read On for a Special Private Offer

It's no coincidence that I'm writing, specifically, to you. You have reason for pride, because the source from which your name came to us indicates you're both educated and thoughtful.

We cheerfully admit, AMERICA'S CIVIL WAR isn't for everyone. But it <u>is</u> for you, and I intend to prove that point <u>at no risk to you whatever</u>.

Please consider this proposition:

Six times a year AMERICA'S CIVIL WAR brings you page after page of absolutely fascinating (and absolutely factual) knowledge of the

(over, please)

Fig. 3.12 "You are there!" is provocative without betraying what's in the letter; the rubber stamp adds immediacy and an appeal to greed. Quite properly, the letter begins with the theme of the handwritten line, *then* validates the "free issue" offer.

DAY-TIMERS, Inc.

Mr. Herschell Lewis:

Seeing is believing!

So please use the enclosed free sample for a full month and ask yourself if it didn't help you work smarter...get more done...and give you more time to yourself.

I think you'll answer "Yes" to all!

Steve Rowley, President
Day-Timers, Inc.

Planner/Diary...and cordially invite you to...

...DISCOVER FIRSTHAND THE BENEFITS OF OUR SYSTEM WITH *NO* RISK, COMMITMENT, OR OBLIGATION ON YOUR PART.

You've probably known about Day-Timer planners for years...seen them wherever you've traveled...and wondered just how anything that fits into a coat pocket or purse could be so indispensable to more than 4,000,000 men and women around the world, all distinguished by their success.

I know your sample will show you why at once! Suddenly, everything about your job and life is going to be a little easier. You should sense the difference almost immediately:

- *Your days will literally organize themselves*
- *Your schedule will be less wearing*
- *Your "memory" will improve dramatically*
- *Your "To Do" list will be prioritized and help you plan better...short- and long-term*
- *Your output will improve noticeably*
- *Your time off the job will be better, too*

And, at the same time, you'll find that you're no longer forgetting meetings, overlooking details, or having the usual problems keeping track of bills, receipts, and other expenses.

Beyond that—and, perhaps, most importantly—you won't have to change the way you do things to enjoy Day-Timer benefits! That's what makes it great. You're already very good at what you do. Otherwise, you wouldn't have received this note.

So we'll gladly let you manage your work. We'll help manage your time. *And nothing more.* Quickly. Naturally. Effortlessly. Without the paralysis of analysis or creating yet another new job for you!

Fig. 3.13   This stick-on note, which conceals a lasered personalization, includes the recipient's name—a near-triumph of technology ("near" because the lasered personalization on the letter doesn't quite match the typeface of the letter itself). Does such a device increase the possibility the recipient will read the letter? Unquestionably. Will improved results be in excess of the additional cost? Only an actual test can answer that question.

United States Committee for

unicef 🌐

United Nations Children's Fund
333 East 38th St., New York, NY 10016

Please be sure to read the important situation report I've enclosed
A/S

A Future for Every Child

Dear Friend:

In the ten seconds it took you to open and begin to read this letter, four children died from the effects of malnutrition or disease somewhere in the world.

No statistic can express what it's like to see even one child die that way ... to see a mother sitting hour after hour, leaning her child's body against her own ... to watch the small, feeble head movements that expend all the energy a youngster has left ... to see the panic in a dying tot's innocent eyes ... and then to know in a moment that life is gone.

But I'm not writing this letter simply to describe an all-too-common tragedy.

> I'm writing because, after decades of hard work, UNICEF -- the United Nations Children's Fund -- has identified four simple, low-cost techniques that, if applied, have the potential to cut the yearly child mortality rate in this decade by one third.

These methods work immediately -- even before large-scale solutions like increasing food supply or cleaning up contaminated water can be implemented. They can be put into effect before a single additional bushel of wheat is grown, or before a single new well is dug.

They may depend on what you decide to do by the time you finish reading this letter. You see, putting these simple techniques to work requires the support of UNICEF's programs by people around the world. In our country, it means helping the U.S. Committee for UNICEF contribute to that vital work.

> With your help, millions of children can be given the chance of a lifetime -- the chance to live -- to grow up healthy and strong. Without your help, more children may continue to die painfully, slowly, and needlessly -- children like the four who have died in the past ten seconds.

The first method is called oral rehydration. Most children who die

over, please ...

Fig. 3.14 Any device which increases the one-to-one intention of a fund-raising letter is a worthwhile addition. That's what the note affixed to this letter accomplishes. It transmits no message but says to the reader, "This is from me to you."

Important Cancer News from
Memorial Sloan-Kettering Cancer Center

SUBJECT: Recent Advances

Prostate Cancer. MSK has opened an important

> Mr. Lewis,
>
>   The cancer research we are doing right now may someday benefit you or someone close to you.
>
>   Please read this important letter and see how. Thank you!
>
>   Bob Wilkens

therapy, to prevent or cure the cancer.

Ovarian Cancer. Based on a pilot study conducted at MSK, the Gynecologic Oncology Group (a national research organization) has opened a prospective trial of dose-intense chemotherapy for patients with newly diagnosed ovarian cancer. This dose-intense regimen uses high doses of taxol and carboplatin administered at three-week intervals with autologous stem cell support. MSK is one of four institutions in the United States conducting this trial.

Melanoma Vaccine. MSK researchers are working on an exciting new weapon against cancer: a group of agents that stimulate immune responses as a means of fighting disease. Large - scale clinical trials have begun for patients with melanoma, the most serious form of skin cancer.

Larynx Preservation. The ability to speak — once the price paid for effective treatment in advanced cancer of the larynx — can now be preserved in many patients as the result of a new

(open, please)

Fig. 3.15a   The personalized stick-on note transforms a bland fund-raising appeal into a timely one-to-one entreaty, personalization adding a dollop of guilt to the mix. (Figure 3.15b shows the brochure and stick-on note separately.)

Mr. Lewis,

The cancer research we are doing right now may someday benefit you or someone close to you.

Please read this important letter and see how. Thank you!

Bob Wilkens

Important Cancer News from
Memorial Sloan-Kettering Cancer Center

SUBJECT: Recent Advances

Prostate Cancer. MSK has opened an important new Prostate Diagnostic Center, and MSK researchers have expanded their efforts to identify early genetic markers of prostate cancer, to evaluate other markers for early detection such as PSA (prostate-specific antigen), and to develop cancer vaccines that stimulate the patient's immune system to attack the cancer.

Breast Cancer. To help determine the best treatment for women with breast cancer, MSK investigators are evaluating the prognostic value of hormone receptors, cancer-related genes called oncogenes, and enzymes that help breast cancer to spread. In our research laboratories, MSK scientists are seeking to understand the role genes play in breast cancer, to identify genetic markers that correlate with increased risk, and to find ways of intervening, possibly through gene therapy, to prevent or cure the cancer.

Ovarian Cancer. Based on a pilot study conducted at MSK, the Gynecologic Oncology Group (a national research organization) has opened a prospective trial of dose-intense chemotherapy for patients with newly diagnosed ovarian cancer. This do   ntense regimen uses high doses of taxol anc   boplatin administered at three-week intervals with autologous stem cell support. MSK is one of four institutions in the United States conducting this trial.

Melanoma Vaccine. MSK researchers are working on an exciting new weapon against cancer: a group of agents that stimulate immune responses as a means of fighting disease. Large - scale clinical trials have begun for patients with melanoma, the most serious form of skin cancer.

Larynx Preservation. The ability to speak — once the price paid for effective treatment in advanced cancer of the larynx — can now be preserved in many patients as the result of a new

(open, please)

Fig. 3.15b

What About Highlighting?

We occasionally see a letter which highlights, in yellow or green, specific words, phrases, and sentences.

I've dabbled with this technique and retired from it. Highlighting does emphasize the words it attacks; but unlike rubber stamps and stick-on notes, highlighting *damages* the impact of the rest of the letter. The reader tends to see only the highlighted portions and ignores completely, as unworthy of attention, any unhighlighted words. (Figure 3.16 is an example of highlighting.)

So what happens? The writer either highlights too much of the letter, so the ploy becomes transparent; or the writer settles for less than maximum effectiveness. The impact disappears.

You know the equation for overemphasizing: $E^2 = 0$. When you emphasize everything, you emphasize nothing. And you know the penalty for limp substitution of form over substance.

Handwriting Within the Letter

If handwriting works for an overline, how about handwriting *inside* the letter?

This development was experimental in the very late 1970s, fell into disuse in the 1980s, became an established winner in the mid-1990s, and is flourishing madly as this book goes to press. If you're reading this after, say, 2005, look closely for overuse. You know the rule: *Sameness equals boredom; overuse equals abuse.* Novelty has a short, happy life. Stay with it while it's happy.

> ✏ The simple rule: Don't overdo handwriting within the letter.

An example of handwriting well inside the body of the letter:

_____

I want to send you this Premier Issue—free.

_____

If you're worried about reader fatigue—and you shouldn't be if you break up your letter into chewable bites—an occasional handwritten chunk lets the reader breathe.

In one test to which I was privy, handwriting within the letter well outpulled the identical letter without handwriting.

PR NEWS

The International Weekly
For Public Relations,
Public Affairs
And Communications
Executives

1201 Seven Locks Road, P.O. Box 61130, Suite 300, Potomac, Maryland 20859-1130 USA

Welcome to the PR NEWS Information Service!

Dear PR Colleague,

You've been chosen to receive a FREE trial to the PR NEWS
Information Service. Over the next 6 weeks this Service
brings you proven tips, tactics and "stealable" ideas to
improve your PR and advance your career.

You'll receive weekly Case Studies... you'll learn how to
pitch to different news mediums with our Media Insight
Chart... you'll discover why top professionals turn to PR
NEWS first for guidance on justifying PR costs, measuring
program effectiveness, and dealing with crisis
communications.

As a paid subscriber to the PR NEWS Information Service,
you'll also receive these 4 exclusive resource guides (a
total value of $268.85 — free with your paid subscription):

1 **PR NEWS Annual Salary Survey and Exclusive Guide to
Executive Recruiters**
Provides verified data on corporate and agency
salaries by practice, title and geographic region.
Plus, the industry's most complete listing of the
names and addresses of recruiters with major practices
in PR. *Published each Spring. (Value — $49.95)*

2 **PR NEWS Guide to Media Relations Services**
Comprehensive source for products and services
executives rely on for conducting and succeeding in
media relations. *Published each Summer. (Value —
$99.00)*

3 **PR NEWS Media Insight Guide**
Full contact details for major newspapers, magazines,
TV shows and radio programs, complete with editors'
names, phone and fax numbers as well as their pet
peeves, days to contact them and days to avoid.
Published each Fall. (Value — $59.95)

4 **PR NEWS Annual Calendar of PR and Marketing Events**
Features more than 350 PR, public affairs, investor

(over, please)

Fig. 3.16   In the original, green highlighting emphasized "FREE trial," "weekly Case Studies," "Media Insight Chart," and "these 4 exclusive resource." On the reverse side was additional highlighting. Why?

LEISURE ARTS   LFL96B-3

leaflets
FOR LESS

C   L   U   B

Here's a quiz you'll like:
    Which four Leisure Arts Leaflets do you want ...
                                        FREE!

Hello, Fellow Needlecrafter!

    I'm thrilled to invite you to join a wonderful Club.

    This Club doesn't have any meetings. It doesn't have any dues.
It has just one purpose: Enjoyment. Who's the president? I don't
know ... I guess *you* are, because you certainly are the boss!

    As a member (or president) of the Club, you get a bimonthly
magazine. And what's the magazine about? More enjoyment. More
fun. More money saved on your favorite, most satisfying hobby.

I guess I'd better explain. You'll be _thrilled_!

    Leisure Arts is famous throughout the world for our
Leaflets: Cross Stitch Leaflets. Knit and Crochet Leaflets.
Plastic Canvas Leaflets. Crafts Leaflets. Leaflets, Leaflets,
Leaflets. Hundreds of them. New ones every month.

    A Leisure Arts Leaflet is a terrific bargain, because it's
100% complete. I'm looking at our <u>Wind Chimes</u> Leaflet. Here are
three exquisite designs for your house or garden. They're shown
in charming color. Every one is tested and re-tested for *oh-so-
easy-to-follow* step-by-step instructions.

    But you already know that. So here's what's new.

    The Leaflet I've described sells for $4.50. That's a real
bargain. But you know how much you'll pay for this Leaflet if
you want it right now?

Fig. 3.17   Although subheads are set in Brush typeface, the effect is one of handwriting throughout the letter. Many stimuli here: A question suggesting a choice of free items is sure to promote readership. "Why? Because ..." is an automatic way of getting to the point, as described in chapter 1. This letter is from the mailing whose envelope is shown in figure 5.9, asking a "Why" question.

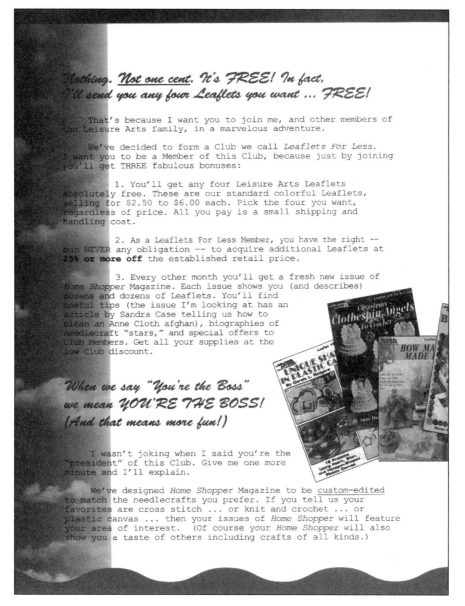

*Nothing. Not one cent. It's FREE! In fact,
I'll send you any four Leaflets you want ... FREE!*

That's because I want you to join me, and other members of the Leisure Arts family, in a marvelous adventure.

We've decided to form a Club we call *Leaflets For Less*. I want you to be a Member of this Club, because just by joining you'll get THREE fabulous bonuses:

1. You'll get any four Leisure Arts Leaflets absolutely free. These are our standard colorful Leaflets, selling for $2.50 to $6.00 each. Pick the four you want, regardless of price. All you pay is a small shipping and handling cost.

2. As a Leaflets For Less Member, you have the right -- but NEVER any obligation -- to acquire additional Leaflets at **25% or more off** the established retail price.

3. Every other month you'll get a fresh new issue of *Home Shopper* Magazine. Each issue shows you (and describes) dozens and dozens of Leaflets. You'll find useful tips (the issue I'm looking at has an article by Sandra Case telling us how to clean an Anne Cloth afghan), biographies of needlecraft "stars," and special offers to Club Members. Get all your supplies at the low Club discount.

*When we say "You're the Boss"
we mean YOU'RE THE BOSS!
(And that means more fun!)*

I wasn't joking when I said you're the "president" of this Club. Give me one more minute and I'll explain.

We've designed *Home Shopper* Magazine to be <u>custom-edited</u> to match the needlecrafts you prefer. If you tell us your favorites are cross stitch ... or knit and crochet ... or plastic canvas ... then your issues of *Home Shopper* will feature your area of interest. (Of course your *Home Shopper* will also show you a taste of others including crafts of all kinds.)

Fig. 3.17   Continued

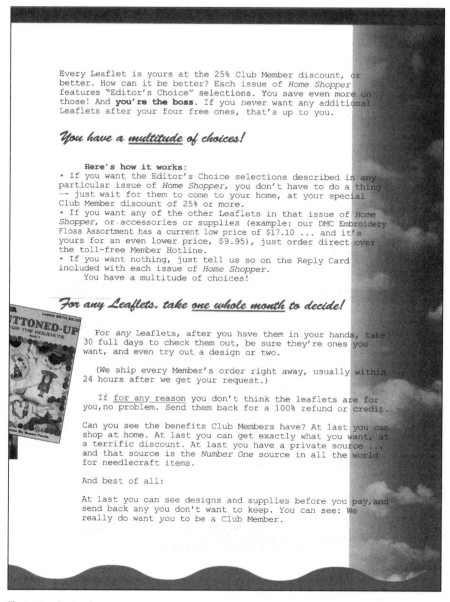

Every Leaflet is yours at the 25% Club Member discount, or better. How can it be better? Each issue of *Home Shopper* features "Editor's Choice" selections. You save even more on those! And **you're the boss**. If you *never* want any additional Leaflets after your four free ones, that's up to you.

You have a multitude of choices!

Here's how it works:
· If you want the Editor's Choice selections described in any particular issue of *Home Shopper*, you don't have to do a thing -- just wait for them to come to your home, at your special Club Member discount of 25% or more.
· If you want any of the other Leaflets in that issue of *Home Shopper*, or accessories or supplies (example: our DMC Embroidery Floss Assortment has a current low price of $17.10 ... and it's yours for an even lower price, $9.95), just order direct over the toll-free Member Hotline.
· If you want nothing, just tell us so on the Reply Card included with each issue of *Home Shopper*.
　　You have a multitude of choices!

For any Leaflets, take one whole month to decide!

For *any* Leaflets, after you have them in your hands, take 30 full days to check them out, be sure they're ones you want, and even try out a design or two.

(We ship every Member's order right away, usually within 24 hours after we get your request.)

If for any reason you don't think the leaflets are for you, no problem. Send them back for a 100% refund or credit.

Can you see the benefits Club Members have? At last you can shop at home. At last you can get exactly what you want, at a terrific discount. At last you have a private source ... and that source is the *Number One* source in all the world for needlecraft items.

And best of all:

At last you can see designs and supplies before you pay, and send back any you don't want to keep. You can see: We really do want *you* to be a Club Member.

Fig. 3.17　Continued

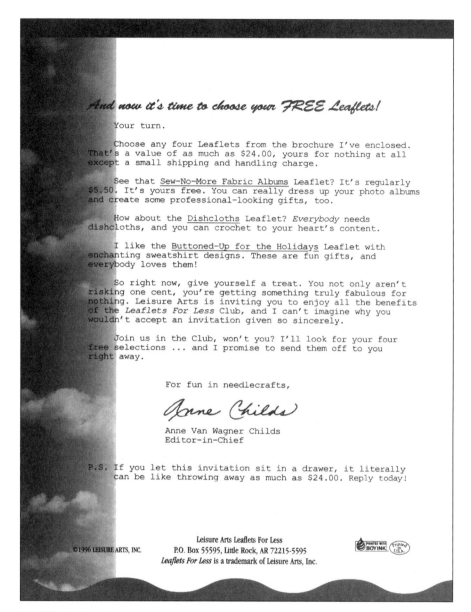

And now it's time to choose your FREE Leaflets!

Your turn.

Choose any four Leaflets from the brochure I've enclosed. That's a value of as much as $24.00, yours for nothing at all except a small shipping and handling charge.

See that <u>Sew-No-More Fabric Albums</u> Leaflet? It's regularly $5.50. It's yours free. You can really dress up your photo albums and create some professional-looking gifts, too.

How about the <u>Dishcloths</u> Leaflet? *Everybody* needs dishcloths, and you can crochet to your heart's content.

I like the <u>Buttoned-Up for the Holidays</u> Leaflet with enchanting sweatshirt designs. These are fun gifts, and everybody loves them!

So right now, give yourself a treat. You not only aren't risking one cent, you're getting something truly fabulous for nothing. Leisure Arts is inviting you to enjoy all the benefits of the *Leaflets For Less* Club, and I can't imagine why you wouldn't accept an invitation given so sincerely.

Join us in the Club, won't you? I'll look for your four free selections ... and I promise to send them off to you right away.

For fun in needlecrafts,

Anne Childs

Anne Van Wagner Childs
Editor-in-Chief

P.S. If you let this invitation sit in a drawer, it literally can be like throwing away as much as $24.00. Reply today!

Leisure Arts Leaflets For Less
P.O. Box 55595, Little Rock, AR 72215-5595
Leaflets For Less is a trademark of Leisure Arts, Inc.

© 1996 LEISURE ARTS, INC.

Fig. 3.17 Continued

What about a *totally* handwritten letter?

Well . . . that's how correspondence began. And after all, if we don't seize the reader's attention we've lost the battle because our ammunition got wet.

But careful! First of all, computerized handwriting can go only so far. If your letter is more than a few paragraphs, you'll do a better job of avoiding reader fatigue by using *some* handwriting, together with other devices.

Ah, but how about a handwritten envelope?

Good idea. We'll come to that in chapter 5.

Conclusion

Are gimmicks good?

What a question! Per se, gimmicks—and in this pile I include all the mechanical devices we've looked at, plus stickers and scratch-offs and pads of name and address labels and, for that matter, sweepstakes—are artifices.

But don't let that throw you. What matters is response—and all of us should applaud, embrace, and vigorously use professionally applied gimmicks that increase response.

4

What's at the End?

Some years ago, I was privy to a test originated by one of the most alert and sophisticated fund-raisers, St. Jude Children's Research Hospital of Memphis, Tennessee. We tested the identical letter with and without a postscript. The one with the P.S. pulled an astonishing 19 percent better. (At the time, the late Danny Thomas was the spokesperson for St. Jude.)

This was the wording of the P.S.:

I hope that your own family never suffers the tragedy of losing a child to an incurable disease. At St. Jude, we're fighting to conquer these killers, and one day someone in your own family may live because we succeeded.

So powerful was this P.S. that years later different letters, with a different signature, retained this same wording.

The Rule for P.S. Writing

Think for a moment: *Why have a P.S.?*

The question generates its own answer. We put a postscript on a letter so the letter will end with a bang, not a whimper. So a P.S. which does nothing to add to the reader's desire to respond is a waste.

The overline is the most read part of a letter, and the P.S. is next. Automatically the format itself gives us thunderbolts to throw. Let's not take the electricity out of them.

The Postscript Rule is tip number eight described in chapter 2:

> ✏ If you include a P.S., it should reinforce one of the key selling motivators or mention an extra benefit that doesn't require explanation.

Public-Domain Postscripts

If you're unsure what to put into a P.S., here are some "public-domain" postscripts you're free to use without fear of damage:

1. "To get your [WHATEVER], be sure to call our toll-free number before the expiration date."
2. "Don't risk losing out on this exclusive private offer. Use the postage-free envelope I've enclosed. I'll look for it on my desk."
3. "An *extra* bonus! If we hear from you by May 31, we'll include an extra gift."
4. "Please don't put this in a drawer thinking you'll get to it later. You'll run the risk of missing an opportunity that may never be repeated."
5. "I wouldn't be writing you if I didn't know you're the kind of person who cares . . . and who will do something about it."
6. "God bless you for caring."
7. "I'm waiting to hear from you. If you prefer, call my toll-free number or send an online message to my private e-mail address."
8. "Much as I'd like to, I can't send you another reminder of this offer. Electronic curbs mean this is the *only* notification I can send you, so please respond as quickly as possible. Thanks."

"Thanks" is a safe and reader-friendly way to end a P.S.

Experiments, Good and Bad

Depending on other enclosures (and your budget) a handwritten P.S. on a separate sheet of paper can be remarkably effective because it adds separate emphasis and still carries the P.S. label.

If you try this, keep the piece of paper small—I'd say four by six inches (ten by fifteen centimeters) maximum. Blue ink on cheap paper, please. Otherwise overproduction causes you to lose the P.S. effect.

Obviously, if you do this, you won't have a conventional P.S. on the letter proper.

Another experiment is a P.S. so long it dwarfs the letter. I've seen this a couple of times, but I've never seen a mailer repeat it, which confirms my own negative view of such a procedure.

A gigantic P.S. doesn't just violate the Postscript Rule . . . it destroys it. The P.S. isn't really a P.S., and reader interest leaks out the bottom instead of being sharpened and honed. If you can't read the P.S. without taking a breath, you've written too much.

One P.S. per Customer, Please

Here's another mini-rule, and it couldn't be simpler:

✏️ If you enclose two letters in your mailing, don't put a P.S. on more than one of them.

When might you have two letters? In subscription mailings, for example. The second letter, which some direct marketers call the "lift" letter, is also called the "publisher's" letter.

Even more destructive, assuming the first letter has a P.S., you're exposing the device *as a device* if you put a P.S. on the second letter.

A typical mass mailing has a letter, a brochure, and—as an option—a validating enclosure. Often the second letter is the validating enclosure. Why not? It's easy to write and it's inexpensive to produce. If you're using a second letter in your mailing, please observe two logical rules:

Lift Note Rule 1:

✏️ No matter how long that first letter is, keep the second letter down to one page.

Lift Note Rule 2:

✏️ Under no circumstances should the typeface for the text of a lift note parallel the typeface used for the basic letter.

(Figure 4.2 is the lift note that accompanied figure 4.3, the "Personal Power" upgrade letter.)

Two Postscripts? No Postscripts?

We've all seen letters with a P.S. and then a P.P.S. Cute, huh?

Ugh.

The concept of a P.P.S. betrays insecurity. "Oh, God, I really haven't done a strong enough selling job."

TUFTS UNIVERSITY

SCHOOL OF NUTRITION SCIENCE AND POLICY

Dear Friend,

It seems as if there are thousands of voices out there dispensing "health" and "dietary" advice --

> ...and the distressing news is that so much of that advice lacks medical and scientific authority. You often get misleading or unsound nutritional advice.

Which leads me to the two major reasons you can put your trust in every fact you read in the TUFTS UNIVERSITY HEALTH & NUTRITION LETTER...

1. Every fact comes to you fully researched by the editorial staff and the Tufts University School of Nutrition Science and Policy, an acknowledged leader in the field. Tufts, I'm proud to say, attracts America's top specialists in nutrition and health. Many of today's landmark nutrition advances were achieved by the men and women of Tufts.

2. Every fact comes to you without compromise. The TUFTS LETTER carries no advertising. This gives the editors the freedom to reveal the truth (and name names) unbeholden to advertisers. What's more, the TUFTS LETTER is quick and easy to read. It's written in plain everyday English, not medical jargon.

We stand on the brink of even greater discoveries in nutrition and health. I truly believe these advances will give you extraordinary personal power to make choices that enable you to feel better, look better and live longer.

That's why I sincerely hope you'll accept the invitation of my colleague, Dr. Stanley Gershoff, editor-in-chief of the TUFTS LETTER, to send for a sample issue to read and keep as his guest. This is a superb opportunity to experience how this extraordinary publication can make a real difference in your life.

Cordially,

Irwin H. Rosenberg, M.D.
Director, Jean Mayer USDA Human Nutrition Research
Center on Aging at Tufts University

Fig. 4.1   The rule: If you enclose two letters, don't put a P.S. on both of them. This lift note supplemented the Tufts University Health & Nutrition Letter mailing (figure 3.3), which ends in a P.S. on the fourth page. Aside from its weakness in not stimulating a buying impulse, the lengthy set of credentials below the signature seems pompous. The typical recipient neither knows nor cares who "Jean Mayer" might be; "Director, Center on Aging at Tufts University" would have been stronger. And as director of a center on aging, the writer's comments related to aging would have had an impact among the newsletter's best prospects.

A QUICK NOTE FROM *An*

A personal note from Anthony Robbins... Please read first.

Hello, Maria Izquierdo,

What a pleasure it is for me to
to you!

I am truly delighted to see that
to acquire "Personal Power II: T
an advantageous price. I am even
this new program to you in compac
you can pinpoint, instantly, any individual component you
want for reinforcement or emphasis.

When you experience CD number 12 - "The Six Human Needs" -
I really do think a new world of opportunity will open up to
you. To prepare this new element, I studied literally hundreds
of thousands of individuals, discovering what really drives
them and inspires them.

Maria, I'm eager to have your reaction to "The Six Human
Needs" because I'm convinced this can make a major difference
in your own lifestyle, your career, and your ongoing sense of
well-being.

When you replace your existing "Personal Power" with this
new version, may I make a suggestion that truly can have a
profound effect? Give your older "Personal Power" to a friend.
Let that friend have the benefit of building and maintaining
a driving force within himself or herself, as you have done.

Please make your decision within the next ten days. I have
been asked to emphasize that this is a special private offer,
one whose advantages you certainly recognize.

Enjoy "Personal Power II: The Driving Force!" And enjoy life!

With warm regards,

Anthony Robbins

Fig. 4.2 Accompanying the six-page basic letter shown as figure 4.3 is this lift note signed by the name principal. The addition of a stick-on note, such as the one used here, invariably increases readership. When using lift notes, two rules apply: (1) no P.S. on the lift note; (2) different typefaces for each letter.

How is your life today? However <u>marvelous</u> it is, let's just see if we can make it even better.

And I'm talking about every aspect of the quality of your life! Anthony Robbins wants to share the next step beyond with you so everything will be even better than it already is for you: income, romance, satisfaction, even sports.

Good Morning!

Do I have your attention? I certainly hope so.

I want you to get this news from us *first*, before others have any opportunity to take advantage of it.

As Anthony Robbins' publisher, I feel confident in reminding you that you have the privilege of enjoying many pleasures of life. You can tap into the mighty force of Personal Power, for which Mr. Robbins is so justifiably famous.

I'm writing you today (and please stay with me while I explain everything) because we have something new and wonderful for you.

(over please)

Fig. 4.3   This letter combines a big-type overline, a handwritten overline, and a rubber stamp. Note the greeting—"Good Morning!"—and the short first sentence. The lift note accompanying this letter is figure 4.2; the envelope is figure 5.7.

You, more than most people, know that as life goes on, your vistas constantly are changing and enlarging. We who are aware of the effectiveness and intensity of Personal Power expand our vistas every day. For us, expanding and growing has become as natural as breathing.

So I tell you it's both natural and beneficial that
Personal Power II: The Driving Force **now is available to you, in the newest, most "state-of-the-art" format!**

Personal Power II: The Driving Force! is the successor to the version of Personal Power you own. We want you to have this newest burst of power, the ultimate focus of all your energies. I'm about to not only tell you why, but also make certain that my proposal makes sense for you.

First of all, Personal Power II: The Driving Force! is available to you not only on cassettes but also in a series of compact discs. As near-perfect as the cassettes are, the compact discs deliver a quality of sound so incredibly real you'll feel you're right there in the room with Tony.

> But even more valuable: the CDs give you <u>instant access</u> so you quickly can get to any specific section as a refresher, a reminder, or a quick boost. This is "audio indexing" carried to a very high, very useful level!

You can reach and benefit from any "refresher" almost instantly. Any point, any inspirational thought, any one of the many thousands of tidbits of help that in combination represent the might and strength of Personal Power ... any and all are at your fingertips in seconds.

Personal Power II: The Driving Force! is yours on 25 CDs.

From this expanded number alone, you can see that this is an upgrade. And right now, it's available, at a special direct "insider" price, only to an elite group ... of which, happily, you are one: Owners of Personal Power.

Volume 12, with THREE CDs,
is new. It's exciting. You should have it.

Let me reassure you that this 21st Century "update" of *Personal Power* includes new concepts that will give you an even greater understanding and competitive edge.

Volume 12 includes, on an extra CD, "The Six Human Needs" that are part of Tony's personal strategy for creating a balanced life.

(next page)

- 2 -

Fig. 4.3   Continued

Anthony Robbins has been working on the right way to bring this to you for two years, and the completed work — diagnosing and analyzing what motivates hundreds of thousands of people, then distilling that diagnosis and analysis into useful information you can start using tomorrow — in my opinion is <u>worth far more than the total cost of **Personal Power II: The Driving Force!** even without your special preferred pricing.</u>

Also in Volume 12 is "Meetings with Masters" — a wealth, a treasury of golden nuggets taken from four different interviews with some of the Master Mentors of our time — Stephen Covey, Deepak Chopra, Barbara deAngelis, and John Gray. Their insights are the core of the final session, and the word "golden" is the right word all right, because the useful wisdom that pours into you on this one is pure gold.

Along with this advanced format you'll get a big new SUCCESS JOURNAL. It's custom-designed for **Personal Power II** and has more than 150 pages. Use it, profit from it, put your personal chronicle of progress in it. It's a major key to Anthony Robbins' new 30-day audio coaching system.

Wait, please: I'm just getting started.

Notice, I started the description with "First of all." Believe me, you get more.

The core of "more" is a brand-new video, "Life Management Systems." This is part seminar content and part Anthony Robbins, talking to you.

"Life Management Systems" is a good 75 minutes long. I suggest you sip it, the way you would fine wine, not gulp it, the way you would a glass of milk.

"Life Management Systems" is a uniquely powerful tool. Neither I nor anyone can describe it properly. You have to see it for yourself to see how these systems increase the quality of your life by changing the quality of any experience. Just to give you an idea of what this video can mean:

By eliminating urges that don't support you and intensifying those that do, you will MASSIVELY increase the quality of your life. Period.

You know better than most: Who but Anthony Robbins could bring this bonus to your lifestyle?

And "Life Management Systems" is yours free with **Personal Power II: The Driving Force!** You don't pay one penny extra for it.

The famous Stephen R. Covey, author of "The 7 Habits of Highly

(over please)

- 3 -

Fig. 4.3   Continued

Effective People" and a participant in the twelfth volume, calls Mr. Robbins "one of the great influencers of this generation." In a recent conversation, Mr. Robbins told me that while he is flattered, what he wants to have happen isn't to influence everybody; he wants to influence you.

You and Anthony Robbins are family, in a sense. He wants his family to have and enjoy the best of everything. And that means a lifestyle upgrade! It's yours, right now.

You get yet another bonus.

If this letter has a rubber stamp toward the top of the first page, we're throwing in another bonus. (You can see: We really do want you to have every benefit that's yours with **Personal Power II: The Driving Force.**)

That bonus is a certificate worth a cool one hundred dollars toward the cost of admission to any multi-day Anthony Robbins in-person program, anywhere. It's numbered, it's personal, it's real, and it's yours to use any way you like, for any live event.

I think it's safe to assume that you're asking, "how do I get **Personal Power II** and what does it cost?"

Good question. And we have a good answer!

The CD version, on 25 discs, has a publication price of three payments of $69.95. Forget that. Because you are who you are — and I'm very serious about that — your direct personal price is three payments of $54.95. That's $45.00 off the regular price.

This includes The Six Human Needs, a revelation even for those who, like you, have experienced the strength of Personal Power. Imagine being able to implement an effortless change! Well, you won't have to imagine. The secret is right there for you to hear and use.

A 24-cassette version also is available. It has a publication price of three payments of $59.95. If you prefer this lower-price version, your direct personal price is three payments of $52.95. That's $21.00 off the regular price.

Note, please: These private preferred prices apply for the next 10 days. I certainly hope you can decide by then.

**The Anthony Robbins destiny-shaping materials
have NEVER been offered to ANYONE at a special preferred price.
They may never again.**

(next page)

- 4 -

Fig. 4.3   Continued

I want be sure you understand how much you're going to get.

We'll send you the brand-new ***Personal Power II: The Driving Force,*** in your choice of 25 CDs or 24 cassettes.

We'll send you a big new Success Journal.

We'll send you the powerful video, "Life Management Systems."

We'll send you a $100 Certificate good for any Anthony Robbins multi-day seminar, anywhere.

And they're all yours, for a limited time, at a special preferred price.

> You may be asking: "When I get ***Personal Power II: The Driving Force,*** what should I do with the earlier version of Personal Power?"
>
> I've discussed this with Mr. Robbins, and I suggest you read his note to you, in this mailing.
>
> Want to do a special friend a special favor? Want to get a special friend started on a road to success he or she never dreamed existed? Give that friend your old Personal Power.

I have an even more significant suggestion: If you want to give someone special a super-special business or personal gift, or just as a spectacular show of friendship, give that lucky person the new ***Personal Power II: The Driving Force.*** Your private preferred price entitles you to two, so you can get one for yourself and one for a friend.

I really do hope you'll take me up on this offer, not only because ***Personal Power II: The Driving Force*** has so much new information but also because by having it on CDs you'll be able to refer to (and profit from) any refresher-section quickly and easily.

You know already that Anthony Robbins wants you to be on a plateau so far above any height you've reached before that you'll literally be astounded. He wants you to live the good life ... even brighter, more vigorous, more dynamic than ever before.

He wants you to enjoy the best he can give you. And the best he has ever delivered is right here for you in ***Personal Power II.***

(over please)

- 5 -

Fig. 4.3   Continued

Earlier, I made you a guarantee. I speak for both Anthony Robbins and myself when I tell you:

After **Personal Power II** is in your hands, if, at the end of 30 days, you aren't 100% satisfied — no, make that 150% thrilled, bursting with new energy and success — send back the CDs or the cassettes and we'll refund every cent you've paid so far, for everything except actual postage. Keep your Success Journal, your $100 Certificate, and even the "Life Management Systems" video for your trouble.

I'll look for your Private Preferred Reservation on my desk. It's as easy and straightforward as calling, toll-free: **1-800-543-1903.** But one caution: Don't wait. This really is a one-time-only private offer. It's yours for the next 10 days, and that's it.

Anthony Robbins says there's no limit to what you can achieve. Do you agree? I certainly hope you do.

For Personal Power II,

Shari Altman

Shari Altman
Publisher, Guthy-Renker

P.S. Every day is golden. The call is toll-free. Make it now:
1-800-543-1903. Great!

Fig. 4.3 Continued

Probably true. But the key reason to have no more than one P.S. is our old friend, the equation: $E^2 = 0$. When you emphasize everything, you emphasize nothing. Two postscripts are weaker than one because emphasis is split.

What about having *no* P.S.?

I've read statements by professional copywriters that every letter should have a P.S. What these writers mean is that every letter they write has a P.S.

The rule isn't invariable. I can envision many business-to-business circumstances in which a postscript gives the letter a prefabricated bulk-mailing look. If, after writing a P.S., you reread your letter and feel it seems to lose personalization at the end, eliminate the P.S. and incorporate its message into the letter proper. Many a letter has benefited by shifting the P.S. upward to become the final paragraph.

This gives us another imperative: If you move the P.S. up into the letter and agree the letter is stronger, it's a signal your P.S. wasn't so hot to begin with. Try again.

A polished P.S. is more than a work of art; it's a terrific sales closer. If you've been dismissing the P.S. as a necessary but not very significant chore, give this element more respect and it, in turn, will give you more response.

5

Envelopes: Crucial and Too Often Overlooked

"Who looks at the envelope?"

Man, oh, man, if ever we looked for proof that arrogance and naïveté go hand in hand, we've found it here.

This unsurprisingly arrogant and astonishingly naïve question—actually, an editorial opinion masked as a question—came from someone who gets paid to write professional copy. Hard to believe.

The answer, of course, is: *everybody*.

I think it's strange that the most obvious, most visible, and potentially most effective attention-getter a piece of mail has is also—too often—the most overlooked element.

The circumstance is exactly the same as that old riddle about a tree falling in the forest and nobody hearing it. Has it really made a sound?

If we mail the most brilliantly written, most beautifully produced letter ever and nobody opens the envelope, have we really exposed prospects to this package?

Part of the question—and part of the answer—is whether we should put any legend at all on the envelope.

The First Rule of Envelope Copy

Let's introduce the First Rule of Envelope Copy:

> ✉ Put a promotional legend on a one-to-one piece of correspondence only when you're reasonably certain the recipient is unlikely to open the envelope unless you add a dramatic "Open me!" imperative.

I'll tell you two reasons why this rule isn't a truism:

First, you have to have a modicum of professional astuteness to know when your letter probably won't reach its target unless you add an incentive.

Second, a legend on a one-to-one envelope from an unknown source may get that envelope opened, but the attitude of the recipient is likely to be condescending or skeptical.

So if you're writing to someone who knows you, decide if your name in the upper left corner gives ample incentive to keep you out of the wastebasket.

How About Direct Mail?

Many battle-scarred direct-response veterans will tell you envelope copy is a must—it always helps.

Uh-uh.

Envelope copy is *always* worthy of testing. Sometimes it gives response a huge boost; sometimes it suppresses response; sometimes changing a word or two, or changing a printed message to handwritten, or adding a rubber-stamp effect, or switching to a more dynamic color can have a dramatic impact on results.

Many mailers, especially in the financial world, feel envelope copy isn't dignified. It costs them image. Sometimes they're right, but companies can drown in their own image. What matters is whether your mailing gets the phone or the cash register ringing.

(That's one benefit of a handwritten envelope: It can crack the otherwise impenetrable secretarial barrier, where the most clever or most highly produced printed message still winds up in the circular file.)

On the other end we have full-color custom-converted envelopes that cost as much as the rest of the mailing. Are they worth the extra money?

Figure 5.1 is a custom-converted envelope, full color. This mailer constantly experiments and tests, and for this type of offer a colorful envelope seems to have been most successful. Note the handwriting, which seems to personalize what is obviously a mass mailing.

Some mailers in the world of publishing insist they have to compete with the giants by covering every millimeter of the envelope with color separations and tint-blocks and screaming type. This attitude is the result of an analysis by art directors, not by marketers, because the only way to determine whether custom-converted envelopes work for you is to *test* them against less lavish envelopes with the same copy.

My own philosophy is to spend your money to reach more people, not to win art directors' awards.

Fig. 5.1　This envelope, in full color on both front and back, typifies the approach regularly adopted by a highly sophisticated mailer who, constantly testing, has concluded that the excitement a colorful oversize envelope generates justifies the comparative expense. Note the handwriting, which personalizes the image.

Fig. 5.2　"Free Gift Inside!" will cause many who otherwise might not open this envelope to see the free gift. In this instance, the gift isn't enclosed; it's a publication that will accompany a book sent on approval.

Envelope Sizes

The uninitiated, hearing terms such as *Number 10* and *Baronial* and *Jumbo*, think of exotic envelope sizes. They aren't. These three are the most common sizes.

A number 10 is the standard business envelope. Actual dimensions are 4⅛ by 9½ inches. Smaller standard "commercial" sizes run from number 9 (3⅞ by 8⅞ inches) down to number 6¼ (3½ by 6 inches). Bigger commercial sizes run from number 11 (4½ by 10⅜ inches) up to number 14 (5 by 11½ inches).

The 6-by-9-inch is a standard "booklet" envelope. Sizes run upward, the most common being 7 by 10 inches, 10 by 13 inches, and of course, 9 by 12 inches. Other envelope types are "announcement" envelopes, ranging from the A-2 size (4⅜ by 5¾) through A-10 (6 by 9½ inches); "catalog" envelopes, ranging from 5½ by 7½ inches through 12 by 15½ inches; and specialty envelopes such as remittance, teller, policy, and coin envelopes.

The difference between many of these types is the position, shape, and size of the flaps. Within each category, the two standard colors are white and manila (kraft).

The choice is wide; yet many mailers opt for custom-converted envelopes. Actually, in a mailing of fifty thousand pieces or more, the price difference between a custom-size and a standard envelope is nominal.

Does this mean a mailer should arbitrarily choose a size? Hardly. It means testing standard sizes should yield information which can lead to a response-increasing decision.

If you want your envelope to jump out of the stack of daily mail, whether you're mailing one piece or one million, try a number 11. You can print the other elements—except the response device if it's supposed to show through a "window." You'd be absolutely amateurish to produce the device smaller than a snug fit . . . a mistake that might cause the address to slide out of view.

The Second Rule of Envelope Copy

The physical purpose of an envelope is to keep the components from spilling out onto the street. But the psychological purpose?

That's the Second Rule of Envelope Copy, which for commercial purposes might be called the *Cardinal* Rule of Envelope Copy:

> ✏ The only purpose of an outer envelope is to get the recipient to open it.

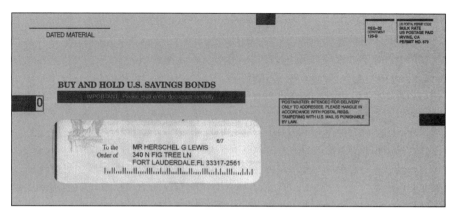

Fig. 5.3   Official-looking envelopes, especially those that seem to have a check enclosed, fool the eye … and get opened. Is it duplicity? Those who use this device point to the Cardinal Rule of Envelope Copy—that the purpose of the carrier envelope is to get itself opened. Note the legends on this manila envelope, all three of which on analysis have no significance but *seem to* suggest an official source: "Buy and hold U.S. Savings Bonds"; the reversed line "IMPORTANT: Please read entire document carefully"; and "Postmaster: Intended for delivery only to addressee…."

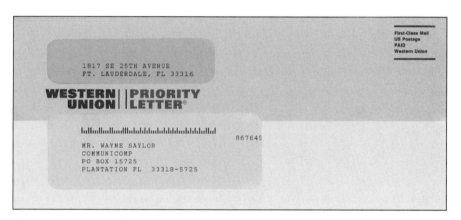

Fig. 5.4a   Western Union, the old warhorse, is still around. And the image of a telegram still spurs people to open a Western Union envelope. This promotional mailing was sent to marketers to prove this is the type of envelope that gets opened. (The letter enclosed is figure 5.4b.)

```
1817 SE 25TH AVENUE                          WESTERN |®
FT. LAUDERDALE, FL 33316                      UNION  |

9825800220311  254103A


|ııllııllıııllıııllllılılılılıılılılılıılıllıllıl        867649
MR. WAYNE SAYLOR
COMMUNICOMP
PO BOX 15725
PLANTATION FL   33318-5725




SEPTEMBER 15

DEAR WAYNE:

YOU OPENED IT...
YOUR CLIENTS AND PROSPECTS WILL OPEN IT...
WE'LL ALL LOOK LIKE HEROES...

TO FIND OUT MORE ABOUT ACHIEVING OUTSTANDING RESULTS WITH THIS HIGH
IMPACT MAILING, CALL CYNTHIA WUMMER AT 954-522-2283.
```

Fig. 5.4b

That makes the question easy: "Will the legend I've put on this envelope induce the recipient to open it?"

Dilettantes, beginners, and even professionals who haven't been privy to the results of envelope-treatment tests tend to ignore envelopes altogether: "All we're talking about is a handful of words, and how important can a handful of words be?"

Others have read somewhere that envelopes with imperative copy pull better than envelopes without copy. So they come bumbling into the arena, with envelope copy guaranteed to induce catalepsy. Or they'll show off all the big words they know. Or they'll art direct it instead of paying attention to the supreme rule of all force-communication, the Clarity Commandment:

> ✎ When you choose words and phrases for force-communication, clarity is paramount. Don't let any other component of the communication mix interfere with it.

The Clarity Commandment doesn't just pertain to envelopes. It pertains to every facet of every component of every message.

Obfuscation + Complication = Negation

An envelope announcing a professional seminar has this legend:

Learn to unravel the mysteries of multiple regression, factor and cluster analysis, and how to apply them on the job—at once.

Sent to a vertical list of statistical analysts, no problem. But this mailing was addressed to me. What's my pre-opening reaction? What's the attitude of the typical recipient?

Incidentally, putting words like *learn* on the envelope can damage response because *learn* seems like work. *Find out* or *discover* are better terms. And *at once*—that's too imperative. The word *fast* has no "I command you" overtone.

New Developments in Envelopes

Is anything new in envelopes? Can anything be new in a medium already peopled with many standard sizes, and after several hundred years of experimentation?

Experimentation hasn't ended . . . certainly not in colors and windows and paper stocks.

"Freemiums" are gift items *enclosed* with a mailing. (See figure 5.5.) When using a freemium, the value of the technique depends on how prominently and dynamically it is presented on the carrier envelope.

Figure 5.2 is an envelope with a premium offer that might appear to be a freemium offer—"See your FREE GIFT INSIDE!" Actually, what's inside is a description of a free gift that comes with a book sent on approval.

A freemium sometimes shows through a second window on the envelope. Because the very nature of mailings requires flatness (unless the mailer goes to unusual packaging), refrigerator magnets, patterns, and iron-ons are among the most popular freemiums.

A typical freemium envelope shows the magnet, with a legend printed on the envelope saying something such as, "Keep the enclosed refrigerator magnet with our compliments." Better: "Keep the enclosed gift with our compliments." We may hate the idea of refrigerator magnets, but we open the envelope to get at the gift, the freemium. And while we're doing it, we read the message.

Staying in sync with the Clarity Commandment, the astute mailer customizes the window to show us the freemium. *Saying* the freemium is inside is in no way as powerful as *showing* us the freemium.

(Instead of a refrigerator magnet, think of a nickel or a dime, and you'll understand why showing it is light-years better than saying it's inside.)

Speaking of Free . . .

If you're after safe envelope copy—not brilliant envelope copy because brilliance has the unpleasant knack of alienating as many people as it attracts—it's hard to go wrong with the barnacled but dependable "Free" or "Private Information" or "Advance Copy Enclosed."

Hard but not impossible.

I'm looking at a double-window envelope, addressed to my wife. Each window has a glassine sleeve, so this mailer—a fund-raiser—spent more than the necessary minimum amount of money. The legend on the envelope: "Your free decal is enclosed."

What's wrong with that? The answer lies in realization of a double mismatch: terminology and target. First, the word *decal* has a zero class quotient. Second, in our age and income bracket, who wants a decal?

Fig. 5.5   This is an actual freemium enclosed in a mailing—an oversized refrigerator magnet, personalized with the name of the person to whom it was sent. The magnet is attached to a descriptive card.

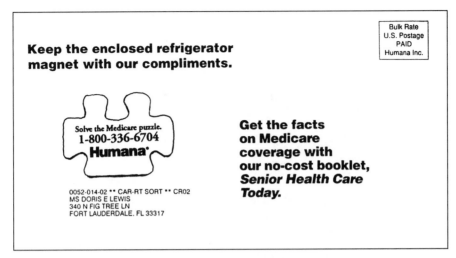

Fig. 5.6   This envelope announces that it has a freemium inside, and the item is clearly visible through a jigsaw-shaped window. Even those who have no use for refrigerator magnets are more likely to open the envelope than they would be if it had no freemium. But disclosing immediately that the freemium is a magnet may have caused this mailing to produce fewer responses than would have been the result of proclaiming "Free gift inside!"

If this had been addressed to Nintendo owners or sign-ups for the Ronald McDonald Breakfast Club, the decal might be a motivator. Kids love to put decals on their bikes and desks and walls. For an upscale sell, "decal" has about as much appeal as "Your imitation cubic zirconium is enclosed."

What substitute legend might this mailer have chosen?

One leaps to mind quickly: "emblem" instead of "decal." That's easy. We're matching terminology to recipient, a basic tenet of communication.

Another substitution becomes available when (or more probably, *if*) we open the envelope. These are the first two paragraphs of the letter:

A shipwrecked sailor was struggling in the water. The shore was near, but his strength was almost spent.

Suddenly there was a friendly presence in the water—a strong, sleek body that buoyed him up, escorted him to shallow water, and saved his life.

What if these two paragraphs, replicated in typewriter face, were on the envelope, with two additional words:

Continued inside.

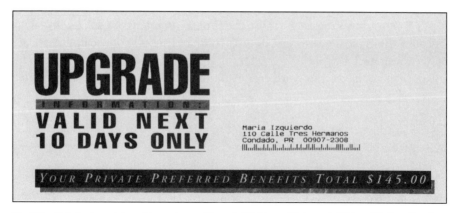

Fig. 5.7 Note the key points on this envelope—"Upgrade,""Valid next 10 days only,""Private,""Preferred"…plus a specific dollar figure. Each adds to the probability that the recipient will open this envelope. (The letter and lift note of this mailing are reproduced as figures 4.2 and 4.3.)

I don't want a load of hate mail from supporters of this organization who do stick those decals on their cars and boats and bikes. My point is absolute. The envelope has to say to the unexpecting recipient, "Open me." And the word *free* says just that. Don't corrupt it with something your target regards as worthless.

When you have that durable word *free* in your pocket and know how to use it (which means even a rudimentary understanding of what causes people to react positively or negatively), you're in a secure psychological area. An example of can't-miss envelope copy from a cigar company:

GIVE THIS MAN A

FREE SPORTS

WATCH AND A BOX

OF *FRESH* CIGARS!

Whoever wrote that, I salute you. You weren't being cute or tricky, and you understood the difference between attracting the reader and blurting at the reader. How many writers would have left out the key and written serviceable but uninspired envelope copy such as . . .

FREE!

SPORTS WATCH

AND A BOX OF CIGARS

This copy loses impact because the typical recipient doesn't believe it . . . because the typical writer just doesn't think of the jolly but scalpel-delicate "Give this man."

A bizarre use of the word *free* is an envelope on which is imprinted:

In Germany,

MEN CHANGE THEIR UNDERWEAR

on an average of

ONCE EVERY 7 DAYS

Immediately under these words, in a circular window, is printed "Free." No, thanks.

The Third and Fourth Rules of Envelope Copy

The trend toward heavy envelope copy has led to overkill . . . which damages response. The Third Rule of Envelope Copy can help avoid overkill:

> ✏ If your offer requires explanation, do not spill your guts on the envelope.

The Fourth Rule of Envelope Copy is founded on a psychological truism: In marketing, asking questions can help formulate attitudes. Questions are as valuable and as underrated a weapon as we marketers have in our arsenal. The rule:

> ✏ When dealing in controversy or when uncertain of the recipient's attitude or prejudices, asking a question on the envelope is less likely to generate antagonism than making a flat, positive statement.

Asking a question on the envelope has power. The question we always have to ask before creating a question for the envelope: "What's the attitude at the moment of opening . . . have we built sufficient interest to overcome hostility or the fear that 'a mailer is breaking and entering my private domain'?"

Figure 5.8 asks a question: "What's the difference between 19.8% and 6.9%?" The question is perfectly logical from this sender—a bank. (The offer is a low-interest credit card.)

Figure 5.9 asks a question aimed perfectly at the company's primary marketing targets: "Why would Leisure Arts give you 4 Leaflets (value to $24.00) FREE? Open right now to find out."

Questions are gaining in popularity, and that's good because questions automatically involve the reader. A popular ploy with publications has been to load up the envelope with a laundry list of questions, assuming that at least one will be provocative enough to induce each recipient to open the envelope. One such envelope had this list of questions:

What do you do if you're locked out of your hotel room—naked?

Why do dogs bark?

Can a man be killed by ants?

How do homing pigeons find their way home?

What is the effect of headache remedies on radishes?

How can you get a free subscription to *Smithsonian* magazine?

Opinions, please: How many recipients think this last question helps get the envelope opened? How many think this question damages the possibility of getting the envelope opened?

I side with the majority, and I'll tell you why: The envelope no longer is provocative. It says too much. We bank robbers have an old saying: Wait until you're *outside* the bank before taking off your mask.

Figure 5.10 asks a bland question: "Do precious gems grow on trees?" The question doesn't quite come off, and from information accompanying this sample, the envelope may have contributed to the mailing not pulling as well as expected.

The Fifth Rule of Envelope Copy

Here's another one-sentence rule that can prevent the negative results of overkill. The Fifth Rule of Envelope Copy:

✐ Saying too much on the envelope can damage response.

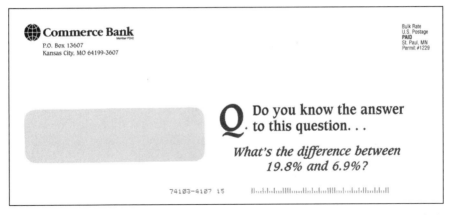

Fig. 5.8   In any type of communication, whether conversation or carrier envelope, asking a question is implicitly reader involving. As structured here, this envelope asks a double question: "Do you know the answer ..." and "What's the difference...."

Fig. 5.9   The word *why* in a question is magical because the reader is forced to participate. This heavily produced envelope also suggests an expiration date, to encourage opening. (Figure 3.17 is the letter inside this envelope.)

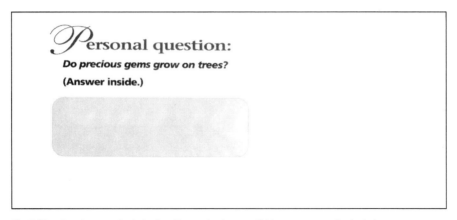

Fig. 5.10   Questions are stimulating, but this question is too artificial to generate much stimulation.

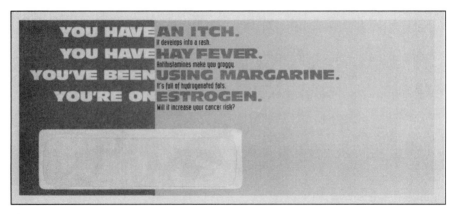

Fig. 5.11   Who can resist opening an envelope with so many personally provocative statements?

Fig. 5.12   For a financial mailing, this envelope is unusually circuslike, with a teaser question, big type, a handwriting look-alike, a rubber stamp, and a picture of a credit card.

What you put on that envelope should encourage the recipient to open it . . . not give away the story inside the envelope.

Example: An envelope has two messages on its face. The first says . . .

_____

Inside: Tax Reduction Kit.

_____

Good copy. Now consider the second piece of copy, an ostensible rubber stamp . . .

_____

Our tax-free funds can help lower your tax bill. See inside.

_____

As you know from previous chapters, I'm a fan of rubber stamps, so I object when a mailer uses them without thinking. This envelope says too much. The rubber stamp wording is *waaaaaayyy* too long. I suggest this mailer put "Inside: Tax Reduction Kit" in a rubber-stamp effect and put that other legend where it belongs—in the wastebasket.

A minor peripheral point: If you're using a rubber-stamp effect, don't just set the type in stencil typeface. Make a real rubber stamp, for three to five dollars. Stamp that thing on plain paper until you get the effect you want, then make a line shot, and it'll look like what it is—a real rubber stamp. If you're printing in two colors, make it 50 percent red, 50 percent black.

Don't draw the conclusion that it's the *number* of words that determines whether or not an envelope says too much. It's the thrust.

Fig. 5.13   The envelope is pink, and the typewritten name and address personalize it. This makes the additional legend at left—"Reading your mail's thirsty work"—not only unnecessary but a giveaway that this isn't one-to-one after all. Another problem is "mail's," which suggests a possessive until the reader reaches the next bunch of words and has to re-recognize what the writer meant.

Figure 5.13 is an envelope that misses, not because of the "Bulk Rate" stamp which many will accept *as a stamp*, but because of the unnecessary extra legend:

_____

Reading your mail's

thirsty work.

Good thing there's

free water inside.

_____

Pity. That extra message, even though it's in a typewriter face, takes off the mask before the robber is safely outside the bank.

How a Database Can Enhance Envelope Copy

I'll make a point here in favor of the database, which I often attack because it's so misused and abused. The more certain you are of exactly who your target is, the more specifics you can pile onto the envelope.

That's because your database isolates those whose (a) professional credentials or (b) specified field of interest or (c) prior buying habits qualify them for a closely targeted envelope message.

After all, *exclusivity* is one of the great motivators of our time. Specifics and exclusivity entwine well together.

Speaking of exclusivity . . .

Words like *preferred* and *priority* have as much impact as *personal* in today's marketplace, with the exception of a handwritten envelope marked "Personal." They also avoid the twin dangers accompanying "Personal": objection to an assumption of a relationship, and recognition of "Personal" as an attention-getting ploy.

Challenging the Recipient

How far should an envelope challenge go? What's the difference between these three legends, all of which really say the same thing?

- Enclosed: Quick test
- Enclosed: Quick quiz
- Your opinion, please

Our role as rudimentary psychologists is never on the line as much as when we're figuring out what, if anything, to put on that envelope. Who are our targets? The problem we face is that our most sophisticated targets, the ones most able to buy what we're selling, are the ones most likely to resent being asked to take a test. The difference between a test and a quiz is light-years. A test puts the tester on a plane far above the testee, who fears being shown up as a fool.

So *quiz* is safe and *opinion* and *ballot* are even safer, because *opinion* and *ballot* put the person to whom you're writing in a position of supremacy. Which would you rather do, vote or take a test?

A fund-raising organization puts on its envelope:

You have been selected to participate in an important survey on America's National Parks.

What if the envelope had said, "You have been selected to participate in a test regarding America's National Parks"? The typical recipient would cry, "Why me?"

Sophisticated recipients know this envelope copy is a ploy to get the envelope opened so they will be exposed to a fund-raising message. Less sophisticated recipients' interest can be piqued because they feel opinions mean something. The mailer can't lose because knowing the purpose doesn't kill off the possibility of response.

But envelope copy that's obviously self-serving runs a far more dangerous course. An organization dedicated to the preservation of wildlife has this on the envelope:

May we list you as a grass roots supporter of protection for endangered wildlife? ❑ Yes … ❑ No.

A half-wit oyster could see through this one.

Speed Formats

"Speed formats" openly intend to establish a *trompe l'oeil* (fool the eye) effect. They aren't as popular as they were in the early 1990s because of a rule we've already discussed—*Sameness equals boredom; overuse equals abuse.* But they haven't disappeared, and the very nature of waning means they'll wax again. By crying "Urgent!" (with hidden third-class mail indicia), speed formats can be an effective way of crying "Wolf!"

(See part II of this book for a description of "The cry of 'Wolf!' "— number 64—and "the cry of 'Fire!' "—number 14—as letter openings.)

Speed formats have a fast burnout rate. A little psychological rule: The more exciting a message is, the faster it wears out.

Do the Enclosures Back Up the Promise on the Envelope?

The more exciting the message on the envelope, the more likely it is to violate the Sixth Rule of Envelope Copy:

> ✏ When readers think you are not telling the truth about one point, they extend that opinion to include your entire sales argument. They reject even those statements which are true.

An example of violating the sixth rule is an envelope housing an offer for compact disks. On the envelope is this wording:

Due to the exclusive nature of this special membership offer, please respond immediately.

Okay, they've used some trigger words—*exclusive* and *special* and *immediately*. They had a free shot at *charter* but didn't use it. Now, what makes me think this is just another mundane offer to sell me some CDs or videos?

In the upper right corner is the betrayal: "Bulk rate." How can an exclusive special be offered in bulk? Mailers have options for that upper right corner, including a bulk-rate stamp many will accept as a regular stamp. Keep the pieces in sync.

Worse is the one that says "Personal and Confidential"—and up in that deadly corner, even though it's a stamp, is "Bulk Rate."

I've had mailings with "Personal and Confidential" addressed to "H. G. Lewis or current resident." An insurance company sent one, marked "Important," just to "Resident."

Don't waste the word *important*. It's not only cheap, thoughtless, chest-thumping writing, but it isn't effective selling. We're in the Age of Skepticism, remember?

The Seventh and Eighth Rules of Envelope Copy

Wild claims of superiority are the basis of the Seventh Rule of Envelope Copy. The seventh is a key that can unlock a lot of response for you, if you've been wondering why your communication just doesn't seem to connect:

> ✏ Even if your claim of superiority is true, it means nothing to the reader unless it relates to him. Don't thump out "Me Tarzan!" unless the person reading your communication is Jane.

The Eighth Rule of Envelope Copy should give you pause if you've been inclined to empty the basket of superlatives, or to scream "Wolf!" or "Fire!" on the envelope when no wolf is in the neighborhood and the only fire is in the fireplace:

> ✏ Calling something "important" when your best readers will know it isn't important will cost you some business you otherwise might have had.

The envelope shown in figure 5.14 says, "IMPORTANT: SUBSCRIPTION NOTICE ENCLOSED." Obviously a renewal is important to the publication; to the subscriber, the very word *important* may damage a fragile relationship.

Save that word *important* for something important. Figure 5.15 justifies the word by adding "Employee materials," the entire legend in a rubber stamp.

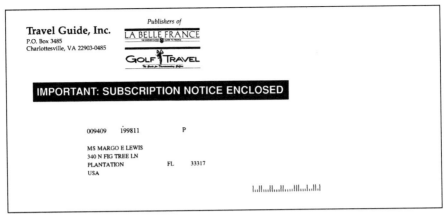

Fig. 5.14 One reason for the decline in the importance of the word *important* is overuse. The equations hold: *Sameness equals boredom; overuse equals abuse.* Is a subscription notice, in fact, "important"? You can see how the message contributes to dulling the recipient's reaction to any use of the word *important*.

Fig. 5.15 To any employee, a message from management absolutely qualifies as "Important." Putting the message in a rubber stamp adds to the timeliness.

Fig. 5.16   The cartoon and personalization seen through the envelope window add brightness and individuality.

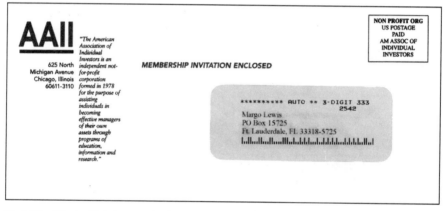

Fig. 5.17   "Membership invitation enclosed" is logical envelope copy, but the legend accompanying it offers no reason to join this organization. Still, the Association has used this same envelope copy for years, which suggests they have tested against it and this version pulls best, or that without testing they like it the way it is.

Does Humor Work on Envelopes?

I'm usually not a fan of humor, but my disdain doesn't extend to envelopes. Why? Because of the overriding Second Rule of Envelope Copy: *The only purpose of an outer envelope is to get the recipient to open it.*

An overnight courier service gets lighthearted . . . and you can see how this lightheartedness generates a receptive mood:

Stepping barefoot on a bee.

Trusting a salesman who says 'Trust me.'

Giving your important shipments to a carrier who doesn't know where those shipments are every single minute.

Then the tiny punchline:

Name three ways to get stung.

Actually, that third bullet is weak because it loses its humor, is too long, and makes a more trivial point than losing a shipment or being late.

The Ninth Rule of Envelope Copy

The Ninth Rule of Envelope Copy is somewhat more abstruse than any of the other eight:

> ✏️ Don't imply a demand for a commitment on the envelope.

An example is an envelope that says:

Introducing the socially responsible Visa Card.

I don't want a socially responsible Visa Card. That means every derelict in town will knock at my door, asking to use my card. This wording is a turnoff. Compare it with this:

_____

Something wonderful is about to happen to your phone line. Now there's a long-distance phone company that helps you save forests, animals, rivers and children—just by talking on the telephone. And it won't cost you a penny more.

_____

See the difference? The second example is a parallel message, but disarming rather than challenging to the point of annoyance . . . except to those who won't respond to this type of message regardless of the goad.

Conclusion

If you accept the cosmic validity of the Second Rule of Envelope Copy— *The only purpose of an outer envelope is to get the recipient to open it*— you automatically shove the egomaniacal component of your creativity into a corner because you force yourself into the *recipient's* position.

This means you'll subordinate all those clever ideas that revolve around in-the-office "How clever you are" reactions, thunderbolts hurled from Mount Olympus, overproduction for no purpose, and any other decision as to what should be on the envelope *other than one directly related to getting that envelope opened.* That's why the Second Rule of Envelope Copy is truly the Cardinal Rule.

Please think that way. Why? Because then the person who gets your piece of mail might actually open it and see the letter inside.

6

The Newest Medium: E-Mail

Some of the traditional rules of letter-writing apply to e-mail, the brash newcomer to the ranks of force-communication. Some, but not all.

Analyze e-mail just as you analyze any other correspondence. Who is reading it? Under what circumstances and with what preset state of mind?

Quickly you arrive at the unmistakable difference, the First Law of Internet Communication:

✐ Stop your target in his or her tracks.

In that respect, e-mail parallels radio more than any other medium. A radio commercial, not sought out by the target individual, either grabs or misses.

And e-mail has an implicit advantage over conventional Website marketing: To achieve a transaction on the Web, the prospect has to come to you; to achieve a transaction by e-mail, you go to the customer.

Oh, certainly, as is true of any medium, overaggressive marketing can result in objections, complaints, and even legal actions. The smart marketer is aggressive . . . but not *over*aggressive.

Four Major E-Mail Selling Techniques

What can an e-mail message do to prevent a quick mouse-click escape? Four major techniques exist:

1. Make a mad promise.
2. Ask a provocative question.
3. Tell an obvious lie.
4. Offer something free and seem to mean it.

Subj: **Hey, thanks for the input!**
Date: 9/4 4:37:12 PM Pacific Daylight Time
From: Katieb493745d@gte.net
Reply-to: Katieb493745d@gte.net
To: Havenmeyers4349tr@user.com

Are You in Debt? If So, We've Got Some Extremely Good News For You...

We Have Lenders That Will Loan You up to 125% the Value of Your Home... Which Means There is Absolutely NO Equity Required From You!

And Even Better, There are NEVER Any Upfront Fees or Advances on Your Part.

Dear Homeowner,

We are a professional referral agency. Our goal is to provide homeowners with lenders that fit your specific situation. We have hundreds of lenders throughout the U.S. that offer the lowest possible interest rates which means... <u>One Super Low Monthly Payment.</u>

Utilize the loan for whatever you want:

> —> **A New Car**
> —> **New Business**
> —> **College Tuition**
> —> **Taxes**
> —> **Credit Cards**
> —> **Vacation**
> —> **Home Improvements**

> —> **Or Anything Else You Want... The Choice is YOURS!**

For FREE Detailed Information... <u>Simply Click Here and go to Our Website</u>

Or type... <u>http://206.132.179.167/gregory235/refi98/mi</u> into your browser and press enter.

Thanks for your time and we know that we can help you obtain the money you deserve.

The Friendly Staff at Coast to Coast Financial

The mailing list that you are being mailed from was filtered against the Global Remove List at <u>http://remove-list.com</u>

If you wish to be removed from our mailing list, please go to <u>http://remove-list.com</u> and add your name to their Global Remove List. This will automatically block you from receiving any e-mail from us or any other ethical bulk e-mailer in the future.

Fig. 6.1   Here is an e-mail message that uses none of the techniques available to a marketer, maximizing the use of e-mail as a distinct medium. Good or bad? Both. To those for whom the message has significance, a lighthearted approach would be a mistake. To those who have no prior thought of a negotiation, a teaser might spur readership where this straightforward message doesn't.

Subj: **Increase Sales Dramatically NOW!   AD:**
Date: 9/3 1:16:33 AM Pacific Daylight Time
From: emsgroup@nwweb.net

=.=
This message complies with the proposed United States
Federal requirements for commercial e-mail bill, Section 301.

For additional info see:
http://www.senate.gov/~murkowski/commercialemail/EMailAmendText.html

Required Sender Information:

The EMS Group
PO Box 273
Yarmouth, ME 04096
888-315-4354
SL ID: 1173

Per Section 301, Paragraph (a)(2)(C) of S. 1618, further
transmissions to you by the sender of this e-mail may be
stopped at NO COST to you by sending a reply to this e-mail
address. mailto:emsgroup@nwweb.net?Subject=CANCEL
=.=

NOW AVAILABLE TO THE GENERAL PUBLIC
THE CREATORS OF A REVOLUTION IN THE DIRECT MAIL INDUSTRY
THE ORIGINAL, DIRECT EMAIL SERVER PROGRAM
THE ONLY RELIABLE AND LEGAL PROGRAM ON THE MARKET

If you've been trying to advertise your legitimate product or service on
the internet, but have been frustrated by the difficulties, you now have a
solution. Have you purchased more than one program to send your mail? And
none of them work! Do you do frequent searches on the internet for new mail
programs, hoping that the *next* one will work for you? Or, are you lucky
enough to just start the complex sorting through endless claims and
contradictions? If so, you may join the growing number of happy users of
our Internet Mail Server Program, who have only needed to buy one program,
and who are easily advertising their product on the internet.

Until we introduced a new way to send mail, those people interested in
advertising through direct mail on the internet used mail programs on one
of two ways, 1) they used ISP's resources that they didn't pay for, or 2)
they used a bulk friendly server and sent the mail through the server.

Stealing resources from an ISP is illegal, and we neither practice nor
condone this. Besides it being a poor way to run your business, it won't
work either, as most ISPs have put up blocks or delete this mass mail sent
to their servers. Fortunately, it's not necessary either. Bulk friendly
servers no longer exist because of complaints to the backbone provider, who
shuts down the before you ever see a day of service, server , usually
within 24 hours.

To solve these problems, we developed an entirely new way to deliver email.
Although you may have seen the imitations, which incidentally, DO NOT WORK,
you may not have seen our product, which we have not aggressively
advertised until now. The programmer has simply been too busy developing

Fig. 6.2   To the pugnacious marketer the opening, announcing compliance with proposed e-mail regulations, is deadly. But look what this marketer is selling: e-mail. The reader is more likely to find the offer credible … provided the reader gets beyond the opening.

A mad promise might be, "Unless you really don't want to live to age 100, go ahead and ignore me." Please don't say "Ignore *this message.*" That's advertising. You aren't advertising. You're sending a one-to-one communication.

Another example of the mad promise: "A week from today at this same hour, you could be counting an extra $1,000 that didn't exist ten seconds ago." Please don't say "Next week." That's too indefinite. It's "A week from today at this same hour." That's specific. In e-mail, the rule doubles in validity: *Specifics outpull generalizations.*

A provocative question often can be preceded by a command: "Consider this" or "Do you have the guts to ask yourself this question?" Structuring a provocative question is easy enough *if you know who your targets are.*

Suppose, for example, they're seniors. A provocative question might be, "Do you want to wait until they slash away *all* your benefits?" or "Just because they call you Grandpa, does that have to mean you aren't a stud?"

To a working woman, a provocative question might be, "Why does the person at the next desk have three more hours of free time every day than you do?" or "Yes, you're overworked and underpaid. So what?"

To a student, a provocative question might be, "Are you willing to settle for an entry-level job?" To a middle-level manager, the single word "Stuck?" To a mail-order buyer, "Did you know you could have bought it for less?" (The technique doesn't require any knowledge of what "it" might be; the question provokes, and that is its purpose.)

"Haven't you wanted to" is a boilerplate provocative opening that usually forces ongoing readership. The positive version, worth cross-testing, is "You've wanted to."

You can see that some people might be insulted by a provocative question. Of course. If the question doesn't ride the edge, it isn't provocative.

Telling an obvious lie succeeds only when the lie is obvious. No, that isn't a truism; it's a caution against telling a lie the reader may accept as truth.

So "I'm going to give you all the money you can carry in two hands. No, make that three hands" or "I'm going to give you a gazillion dollars" is an obvious lie. "I'm going to give you $50,000" is more specific, and being more specific runs the risk of immediate acceptance as truth . . . which means you later generate annoyed rejection.

Other obvious lies: "You might as well give up"; "I know where you were last night"; "Your sex life stinks"; "I've told you once and I'll tell you again: The earth is flat"; "The President wants your advice"; "Two gorgeous girls want to meet you, but you have to choose, right now"; "You asked me for this and I finally have it for you." Get the idea?

Subj: **Find out what "They" don't want you to know!**
Date: 9/6 6:28:37 PM Pacific Daylight Time
From: jgonzo@owntheweb.com

Dear Friend:

If you have already responded to the following announcement a few
days ago, that means your package is already on its way and it
should be arriving soon! If you have not responded to this before,
please pay attention to it now. This is very important!!!

!!!
!!!
!!!

IMPORTANT ANNOUNCEMENT
IMPORTANT ANNOUNCEMENT

==
==

Your future May Depend on it !

!!!
!!!
!!!

Before you know about this 'Important Announcement', you must
first read the following 'Editorial Excerpts' from some important
publications in the United States:

NEW YORK TIMES: "In concluding our review of Financial
organizations to effect change in the 90's, special attention
should be called to a California based organization, 'WORLD
CURRENCY CARTEL'. Members of this organization are amassing
hundred of millions of dollars in the currency market using a very
LEGAL method which has NEVER been divulged to the general public.
While their purpose is not yet known, their presence has most
certainly been felt".

NBC NIGHTLY NEWS: "Members of 'World Currency Cartel', who always
keep a low profile, are considered to be some of the most
wealthiest people in North America".

More excerpts later, but first let us give you this very
"IMPORTANT ANNOUNCEMENT":

==
==
==
==

We are glad to announce that for the first time and for a very
short period of time, WORLD CURRENCY CARTEL will instruct a
LIMITED number of people worldwide on 'HOW TO CONVERT $25 INTO
ONE HUNDRED OF LEGAL CURRENCY'. We will transact the first
conversion for you, after that you can easily and quickly do this

Fig. 6.3   The heading on this e-mail message parallels the provocative envelope copy we see in mailed messages. Note that the first sentence assumes a response to a previous message. This, too, is a technique adapted from regular mail. "Important announcement" damages the impact somewhat because it removes the bond the first sentence had established with the recipient.

Subj: **Dear Mr. Lewis**
Date: 9/14 4:21:43 PM Pacific Daylight Time
From: GHameroff4186
To: HGLEWIS1

I wanted to take a minute to say hello. My name is Evelyn Hameroff and I am Partner in a marketing company. We have been in business on the Internet for over 2 years now. We can help you promote your services, products, and web site if you have one (if not we can help you create one and maintain a great internet presence).

We are offering a special this month on Press Releases. 25 cents for each press release we send, with a minimum of 100 press releases. 100 press releases are $25. 500 press releases are $125. We can send them out to radio stations, TV stations, magazines, newspapers, and other media contacts. We can send them out to one state or all 50 states. We can announce your upcoming speaking engagement or just announce your services.

We can help you write and edit your press release to fit industry guidelines. Press releases are great to promote upcoming events, company news, or any other information you want publicized. We carefully choose who we send the press releases to based on the industry you are in. This could be a great service to your clients.

We are also developing an author's showcase directory that will be completed by September 30. The site is located at http://www.promote-yourself.com/authors.html We already have 15 authors that will be listed in the showcase and are looking to have more listed by opening. The cost to be listed in the directory is only $50 a year. The fee covers all pertinent info about the author including book(s) names and how to order them. The fee also entitles authors the ability to post press releases on our site and one free pr distribution to 100 media contacts.

To be listed in the directory, send $50 along with all important author info, a picture of the book(s) if you want them on the page and any other info you want included to:

Brown & Associates
3559 Greentree Drive
Memphis, TN 38128

We can also handle other public relation duties such as booking engagements, helping promote your books and services by making calls, sending faxes, etc.

We can also help you get more exposure for your web site(if you have one).

Are you getting the response you expected from your web site? If not, our advertising and marketing services can help boost traffic and response rate on your site.

Our services include:

Free Web site Evaluation - Just ask and we'll do it for you.

Fig. 6.4   Mirroring a personal message, this e-mail demands readership. The approach is purely commercial, but the recipient is likely to read it because of the opening. The offer is clear, direct, and best of all, specific.

Subj: **RE: BULLETIN: HOT INTERNET STOCK**
Date: 7/20 5:12:08 PM Pacific Daylight Time
From: interstock_0034@kedumim.co.il
To: interstock_0034@kedumim.co.il

THE NEXT YAHOO?!!

Maxnet, Inc.

Symbol: M X N T

Price: 1 1/2

Maxnet is predicted to go "as high as $15-$20 share" according
to a lead Internet stock analyst from Stockhelper.com.

Utilizing next generation proprietary "search spider" technology
incorporated into its Webphonebook.com division, Maxnet may
become one of the primary "hubs" to the internet.

Web Phone Book "search" is more user-friendly and efficacious
than Yahoo or Excite; and technophiles believe they are at least
12 months ahead on the "curve".

This analyst believes, and we quote, "Maxnet is the next $50 Internet
stock currently trading at $1", according to the Stockhelper.com
newsletter.

For further information on M X N T go to:
http://quote.yahoo.com/

Fig. 6.5   Stock market tips are common e-mail subjects. Here we have not only a tip, but a "Hot Internet Stock."
Medium and message match. Probably the intention is to attract individuals who aren't typical stock market investors.
Some of the hype would never be permitted in other media.

A lot of marketers confuse offering something free with telling an obvious lie. Their "Free" turns out on quick analysis to be an outrageous lie, and the result is damage to all other marketers who actually are offering something free.

If you offer something free, think before you write your e-mail message, "What can I say that will maximize the value of whatever it is to the person who reads my e-mail?" That's the key: offering maximized, optimized value without lapsing into an obvious lie.

Don't assume that these four major techniques are your only avenues. You have unlimited choices, ranging from "A personal message to [ONLINE NAME]" to "Marie wants you to know this."

Don't Forget the Lead-In Line.

The lead-in line—sometimes called "Subject"—ostensibly tells you who is sending the message and why. Here is where we see the most duplicity.

An e-mail message will be from "Audrey" or from "Your next-door neighbor" or from a no-name "At last we're getting together again." The technique is designed to avoid having the recipient delete the message without reading it. If the message is from Audio Book Releases and your target wouldn't be interested in audio books unless he or she read the actual message, you'd have more success sending it from "Your Book Pal" or "We Exchanged Addresses at the Library" than you would by sending it from "Audio Book Releases."

The Value of Timeliness

Remember where you are: you're online, reaching your target when he or she is geared for an instant reaction. So no matter what your offer is or which technique, these or any other, you use, apply the Rule of E-Mail Timeliness:

✏️ Include an absolute expiration date.

That means you'd specify, for example, the offer expires at midnight, September 30. Note: It isn't September 30. It's *midnight*, September 30, which somehow seems more definite and certainly has greater verisimilitude.

The objection some marketers raise to a specific date is that some folks don't look at their e-mail every day or even every week. Quite true; but it's also true that the less often someone looks at e-mail, the less likely that person is to be a good prospect.

And what if someone responds after your artificial deadline? You have the option of sending a happily congratulatory e-mail in return, saying that even though the response was late you're honoring it.

Basic Tips, Squared

Some basic tips for letter-writing, outlined in chapter 2, don't just apply to e-mail—they're *edicts* when composing e-mail.

But they're also enslaved by the medium itself. So an absolute for typed or printed letters—keep your first sentence short—may be subjugated to one of the major techniques described in this chapter. The ultimate effectiveness is a combination, such as "Keep your first sentence short" and "Ask a provocative question." Not easy? Work on it. Not possible? Then ask the provocative question.

That compromise doesn't apply to the second tip, *No paragraphs longer than seven lines*. A five-line maximum is even better. And don't mislead yourself by having five lines of Arial condensed type on an overlong screen line.

Another must is the fifth tip, *Don't sneak up on the reader*. In e-mail, sneaking up on the reader is pure hara-kiri. Come out with guns blazing. Inscribe this tip on your forehead when composing e-mail.

Your personal technology may not allow handwriting; but you can use color, multiple fonts, and screaming type size. Can you overdo it? Certainly. But boredom is a worse curse.

Some of the tips for conventional letters can damage you. A P.S., for example, can seem far more artificial in e-mail than in conventional mail. Handle with care, or use a click-through instead. (If you use a click-through, the rules start all over again.)

Stay abreast of current technology. You might be able to insert marginal notes or a stick-on note. Holding attention is a matter far more crucial in e-mail than in conventional mail.

Tying e-mail to another appeal—Joke of the Day, Bargain of the Day—can develop the magical word, *rapport*. The simple litmus test: If you were reading the e-mail message instead of writing it, would it hold your interest? Would it spur a phone call or an answer or a click-through? Yes? Okay, you're in business.

Subj: **Get money stuffing mail!!!**
Date: 7/20   6:19:39 PM Pacific Daylight Time
From: yan234@sprynet.com

Dear Future Associate,

You Can Work At Home & Set Your Own Hours. Start earning Big
Money in a short time

                            NO Newspaper Advertising!

Your job will be to stuff and mail envelopes for our company. You
will receive $2.00 for each and every envelope you stuff and mail
out.

Just follow our simple instructions and you will be making money
as easy as
1... 2... 3

For example stuff and mail 200 envelopes and you will receive
$400.00. Stuff and mail 400 and you will receive $800.00. Stuff
and mail 500 and you will receive $1,000 and more

Never before has there been an easier way to make money from
home!

Our Company's Home Mailing Program is designed for people with
little or no experience and provides simple, step by step
instructions.

There is no prior experience or special skills necessary on your
part, Just stuffing envelopes.

We need the help of honest and reliable home workers like you.
Because we are overloaded with work and have more than our staff
can handle. We have now expanded our mailing program and are
expecting to reach millions more with our offers throughout the
US and Canada.

Our system of stuffing and mailing envelopes is very simple and
easy to do!
You will not be required to buy envelopes or postage stamps.

We will gladly furnish all circulars at no cost to you. We assure
you that as a participant in our program you will never have to
mail anything objective or offensive.

There are no quotas to meet, and there no contracts to sign. You
can work as much, or as little as you want. Payment for each
envelope you send out is Guaranteed!

Here is what you will receive when you get your first Package.
Inside you will find 100 envelopes, 100 labels and 100 sales
letters ready to stuff and mail

As soon as you are done with stuffing and mailing these first

Fig. 6.6   Some may find humor in an e-mail offer suggesting profits from snail-mail. The offer itself demands credulity, perhaps bordering on gullibility: "Stuff and mail 200 envelopes for our company. You will receive $2.00 for each and every envelope you stuff and mail out." The hook? Deep in the text is a $35 "Registration Fee." Is this legitimate? One has to invest $35 to find out.

Two Notes About E-Mail

1. In the list of one hundred openings described in chapters 8 through 11, those marked with an asterisk (*) are most applicable to e-mail.

2. To launch a serious e-mail campaign, the most prudent course probably is to work with an e-mail supplier. Some, at press time, are:

   - BonusMail (www.bonusmail.com)
   - DeliverE (www.delivere.com)
   - Emaginet (www.emaginet.com)
   - Media Synergy (www.mediasynergy.com)

   Some conventional list companies that also offer e-mail:

   - Worldata (www.worldata.com)
   - American List Counsel (www.amlist.com)
   - Axiom Direct Media (www.directmedia.com)

100 Letter Openings That Will Work Every Time

Part II of this book isn't about letter-*writing*; it's about letter *openings*. After a brief chapter outlining the basic rules for opening letters, you have an extensive four-chapter library of one hundred—yes, *one hundred*—letter openings designed to grab attention and start the sizzle, for *any* circumstance.

(Note: "Any" circumstance includes e-mail. Those openings that work for e-mail are indicated with an asterisk.)

Every writer knows the one Great Truth of Direct-Response Letter-Writing:

> ✎ When reading begins, you're at point-blank range, and you'll never again have that big an advantage over the reader. So: FIRE!

This is why the choice of openings—the first one, two, or three paragraphs—has such a profound effect on response. And the power of the opening applies to mass mailings of two million pieces and also (often more crucially) to a single letter to a key business prospect.

The advantage of having a full library of letter openings parallels having a full wardrobe. You choose this outfit for this event and that outfit for another event. Your attire always matches who you are, who you're supposed to be, and what your hosts are wearing.

Note: Because this section is exclusively about *openings*, you won't see complete letters reproduced, unless the point is the relationship between openings and the rest of the letter.

Will you use every one of the one hundred listed in this part of the book? Probably not. But as you use them, you'll begin to experiment and revise and tweak. You'll develop your own "masterpieces" tailored to the individual position and image you project.

Two ultimate benefits of this library of one hundred openings:

1. Sorting through these openings forces you to analyze the three-way relationship—you, what you're writing about, and your target.
2. The very process of analyzing *who* and *what* prevents you from the tired sameness typical of the output of so many other writers.

And let's hope for a third benefit: those other writers are your competitors.

7

The Importance of the Opening

"Do they really read beyond the opening?"

That question justifies this book.

Too often, your brilliant quips on page 3 go unread because your not-so-brilliant overline or Johnson Box or printed imperative at the top of page 1 or your first two paragraphs of text weren't all that brilliant.

People skip-read.

They'll read the overline, if one exists. They'll read the P.S., if one exists. They'll look at the first couple of paragraphs. Then they'll decide whether to read the letter or not.

Many, many times, curious observers outside our industry ask, "Do you really think people read all the way through a four-page letter?" My own standard answer, in three little words: "I don't care."

And I don't. I care about response, not analysis. Anyone who has seen the results of competitive mailings has seen too many instances of conflicting results to make a flat statement about letter length, except with unconvincing bravado.

Six-page letters have far outpulled four-page letters; two-page letters have far outpulled four-page letters. Two-paragraph letters can demolish an eight-page epic.

Which proves what?

Nothing much. One useful result is recognition that testing letter length for each individual offer pays off.

More to the point: Changing the opening—the first few paragraphs—has the capacity of generating a huge increase (or decrease) in response, often far more profound than letter length. Don't believe it? Test a couple of these openings against each other, without having a preconceived prejudice as to which will pull better.

Changing the opening will surely change your mind.

The Three-Way Matchup: Message . . . Target . . . Motivator

If a single rule can apply to the total concept of letter openings, that rule is . . .

> ✏ Match the opening to both the target and your chosen motivator, and the reader will positively read beyond the opening.

How many pet openings do you have? All of us tend to run on tracks, especially when we find an opening that works for us or reflects our opinion of what our personality is.

From a virtually limitless storehouse of openings, I've chosen one hundred I regard as (1) easy to construct and (2) not yet clichés. In the next four chapters we'll take a look at each and examine their benefits and disadvantages.

Why? Because a three-way matchup—(1) what you're saying (message), (2) who your reader is (target), and (3) the reason for responding now (motivator)—when done with any professionalism (which means your persona matches these), will result in a more powerful response than any haphazard choice of openings might generate. And it's the opening that either performs or ignores the matchup.

In Favor of Provocative Openings

In any list of rules for letter-writing, one key rule applies 100 percent to the remainder of this book:

> ✏ Fire your biggest gun first.

But modify that rule with the governor on the throttle, an equally valid caution:

> ✏ Credibility is the key, opening the door to persuasion.

So, should the opening always be provocative?

This is the type of question the professional letter writer faces, internally or externally. It's the result of saturation—overawareness of apparent sameness in message-creating philosophy.

The routine answer to that question would be "Yes" for two reasons:

First, the writer (and whoever supervises or produces his or her writings) requires extraordinary discipline to obliterate a writer-as-writer reaction to the words. We see each letter fifty to one hundred times before it's printed; the recipient (with luck) sees it once.

So the reader doesn't share our feeling of sameness . . . unless the same day's mail has brought a similar letter. With one hundred openings listed here, and hundreds more beyond these, the odds are in our favor.

Second, a nonprovocative opening implicitly is intellectual; and in any cerebral battle, emotion will whale the tar out of intellect. A provocative opening demands ongoing reaction. Why not go with the higher percentage?

When Does a Letter Actually Begin?

The first words of about a third of today's sales letters aren't the traditional beginning—"Dear Friend" or one of its latter-day surrogates. The message begins with an overline or a Johnson Box or a hunk of type, sometimes occupying half a page or more.

Are these devices good or bad? Do they help or impede the selling power of the letter?

A broad opinion: They help if they tease the reader into the letter; they hurt if they betray the letter's intent without first justifying why we want money or action.

Have you tested the same letter with and without an overline, Johnson Box, or chunk of type? If you have, you know what works . . . for *this* letter to *this* target at *this* time. Fact always is better than speculation as a criterion of what to do in our brutal battle of wits with those people out there.

Are There Really a Hundred Effective Ways to Begin a Sales Letter?

One hundred? Oh, no. The number is well above two hundred. Maybe five hundred. Maybe one thousand. But the question isn't valid for professional communicators because it leaves out the key word—*effective*.

Without that word, any of us has a thousand ways to begin a sales letter. But the professional recognizes the difference between a way to begin a sales letter and an *effective* way to begin a sales letter.

The library of one hundred letter openings described in the next four chapters isn't supposed to be an encyclopedia; it's a reminder. If we recognize how fragmentary even one hundred openings are, we also recognize how many choices we have.

Do These Openings Apply to E-Mail?

Some do. Some don't. To make it easy, those I regard as applicable to e-mail are indicated with an asterisk.

E-mail is the archetype of a problem much direct-mail faces: If the recipient recognizes the message as uninvited and irrelevant, click goes the mouse and the message is deleted before the sales argument can begin.

That's why trickery has surfaced. Mild example: "Subject: Your membership has been approved." Severe example: "Subject: Hey, thanks for the input."

That "Subject," or whatever header your format dictates, parallels not just the overline but the envelope of a conventional letter. It's the determinant: Will the individual read on?

Why Limit Yourself to One Hundred?

Why, indeed? This group of one hundred should qualify itself as a minigroup, because anyone who has started his or her own list of ways to begin a letter will testify: one hundred isn't even halfway home.

The caution I want to superimpose: Don't let a mad desire to be "different" lead you to strange, bizarre letter openings which may be different . . . but stink. "That which is different = that which is good"— what an ugly equation!

So every one of the ways to begin a sales letter described in this group of one hundred is a logical component of the communication mix. Not one of them is supposed to startle the reader without also motivating the reader.

What if having a list of *specific* openings increases the possibility a competitor might use the same one you do?

Possibility? So what. Actual occurrence? Not likely.

My point: Sameness of letter opening isn't likely to be anywhere near as probable a factor as sameness of offer. So worry about dullness and lack of dynamism based on a "running on tracks" mindless hammering at the keyboard instead of wringing your hands over what your competition might do.

Creativity isn't limited to lifting an entire document from a template, the way you might pick up a legal form from a computer disk of standardized forms. The creative process is alive and well . . . and those who either depend on incessant repeats of the same theme, or pick up someone else's letter and change only the names, are doomed to the eternal damnation of coming in second.

This may not reassure you if you're afraid another mailer may use the same opening you do. More reassuring: Every one of these openings—and the hundreds of others not included in this series—has been used before any of us was born.

Your advantage: No previous mailer has used them as effectively as you will.

Subtle Differences Can Be BIG Differences.

A suggestion: Don't test two similar openings against each other. For example, I wouldn't test number 8, "I have a free gift for you," against number 10, "I have something good for you." I wouldn't test number 2, "Ask a provocative question," against number 3, "What if . . ." Why not? Because I won't learn as much as I would testing number 8 against number 2. Broader strokes yield broader information. Let the refinements come later.

The Benefit of Multiple Options

Having multiple options is a benefit in almost every endeavor—buying goods and services . . . evaluating job opportunities . . . choosing a permanent mate . . . calling for a run or pass . . . deciding where to sit at a movie . . . and, yes, beginning a sales letter.

Which to use? The choice of openers is crucial because if you're wrong, the reader may never reach the core of your selling argument. It's parallel to walking up to an amusement park ride—a spectacular, thrilling ride—but the entrance is shabby, or the carnival barker hasn't shaved, or a passerby you don't even know says the ride isn't so hot, or the ride is enclosed in a tent and no sign gives you a clue about its capacity for exhilaration. You pass.

That's what readers do. They pass. BUT—readers aren't bugs in a bottle, a homogenized mass of ectoplasm. Some respond to one stimulus and others to another. Matching the message to the target is the peculiar edge the alert letter writer has over the journeyman letter writer.

The very act of selection goads us into nonautomatic decision-making. We have to evaluate. So a major benefit of being able to choose from a number of letter openings is the enhanced possibility that we'll match the message to the recipient.

Another benefit is more subtle: Selection interferes with our natural tendency to run on tracks, to use a standard opening. Placing personal comfort above a commitment to communicate at maximum thrust inevitably reduces response. Even a 1 percent loss of response we might have had if we'd shifted our concern away from "I like to do it this way" (or worse, "We've always done it this way") is a minor disaster.

Minor? Sorry. *Disaster* parallels *uniqueness* and *pregnancy*; it exists or it doesn't, without shades of gray.

So having two options means having a greater possibility of matching the message to the target. Having one hundred means an almost absolute probability of matching the message to the target.

As you note and evaluate letter openings, you'll undoubtedly see some similar to others. Similar but not identical . . . as number 16, "Because you did that, we're going to do this" is similar but not identical to number 17, "Because you are who you are, you may get special attention," or number 36, "Because you're 'A' you're also 'B.'" Or as number 14, "The cry of 'Fire!'" is similar but not identical to number 64, "The cry of 'Wolf!'" (Someone yells or prints "Fire!" and those who hear or read may not feel threatened by *that* fire; someone yells or prints "Wolf!" and it means the wolf is stalking *you*.)

Are the differences subtle and unnoticeable? Sometimes they may be subtle and unnoticeable to us as we write them; but the results will differ. We all know the letter is the ideal component for a test. Letters hold the motivators; and other than price, motivators are as logical a test as we can mount.

8

The First 25 Ways to Start a Letter

In this chapter:

(An asterisk means applicable to e-mail.)

1. *If you're like me . . .**

2. *Ask a provocative question.**

3. *What if . . .**

4. *Suggest a cataclysmic decision.**

5. *I [We] need help.*

6. *Congratulations!**

7. *I invite you . . .*

8. *I have a free gift for you.**

9. *As you know . . .*

10. *I have something good for you.**

11. *A specific episode narrative*

12. *Private invitation**

13. *We don't know each other, but it's time we did.*

14. *The cry of "Fire!"**

15. *What I want you to do is . . .**

16. *Because you did that, we're going to do this.**

17. *Because you are who you are, you may get special attention.*

18. *Stroke, stroke—You're a rare bird.* *

19. *Here's what the experts say.*

20. *Why are we doing this?* *

21. *This is disgusting and you're the one to fix it.* *

22. *We've got bad news . . . and we've got good news.* *

23. *Good news!* *

24. *Are you paying too much?*

25. *Did you know . . .* or *Do you know . . .*

The first twenty-five are the most common ways to start a sales letter—old and not-so-old dependables.

If you limit yourself to these you'll still have a lifetime of variety because they cover the key psychological approaches—happy, sad . . . aggressive, pleading . . . sophisticated . . . straightforward. This is a tight grab bag of guaranteed-useful openings.

We'll start with my personal favorite, one which can't miss if you're determined to proclaim affinity with the reader and have that reader accept your relationship.

1.   IF YOU'RE LIKE ME . . .

My high regard for this opening stems from two bases: First, it strides across all barriers of consumer-business, highbrow-lowbrow. Second, it establishes immediate rapport. This works to soften receptivity for messages from an anonymous signatory; better yet, it adds an arm-across-the-shoulder "buddy binder" to a communication signed by a recognizable power name.

I sometimes use "If you're like I am" instead of "If you're like me." Why? "If you're like I am" seems just a tad less presumptuous than "If you're like me" because it's a tad less all-inclusive.

Usually, what follows "If you're like me" is an automatic "you" or, to complete a parallel, "you're." You can see why this opening is implicitly reader-involving.

I take a parental view toward this opening, and I'm torn between statesmanship, directing me to share it with those who haven't yet sampled its joys, and proprietorship, predicting application of the deadly rule: *Overuse equals abuse.* Statesmanship wins because I suspect, from my own incoming mail, word is already out.

A letter from a scuba-diving organization begins:

Dear Diving Enthusiast:

You and I are part of a remarkable group.

Someone who's never been on a scuba dive could never understand it.

See the exclusivity building here? See how much stronger this opening is than "You're part of a remarkable group"?

A variation on the you-and-I theme is "The source from which I got your name tells me. . . ." This opening isn't as convivial nor as personal because it separates writer and reader instead of welding them together; the writer runs the risk of antagonizing readers instead of drawing them into the net. The value of this variation is its sidestepping of circumstances in which the reader thinks, "Who the hell is he to think I'm like him?"

A recent letter circulated within the communication community begins:

Dear Direct Marketing Colleague:

The source of your name given to Bob Stone and me indicates to us that you're obviously deeply involved in direct marketing and want to continue learning about it.

I don't like that word *learn* because, sent to professionals, this approach suggests the writer thinks they aren't quite professional; but the concept is arresting.

2. ASK A PROVOCATIVE QUESTION.

This one isn't as automatic as the first suggested letter opening because it doesn't indicate what the question is. Nor does it help point out that the question depends on what we're selling.

I'm guessing that thousands of sales-letter writers *sense* the value of an interrogative opening . . . but don't recognize the qualifier, *provocative*. Some uses of this opening are ludicrous; others are preposterous. What destroys their value is their disregard for the reader's own experiential background.

Lack of understanding leads to reader rejection because the writer opens the letter with a question whose relevance the reader dismisses without analysis. For example:

If I open a letter with, "Do you know the name of the ninth incarnation of Vishnu?" your response has to be (a) "Are you nuts?" (b) "Who cares?" or (c) "Something is wrong with you, and if I did know the name of the ninth incarnation of Vishnu there'd be something wrong with me."

**Financial
Direct**

——— HELPING YOU ———
DO MORE
TO SAVE FOR YOUR RETIREMENT
PRIVILEGED ASSETS
CALL 1-800-549-5602

Herschell G. Lewis
340 N. Fig Tree Ln.
Plantation, FL 33317-2561

Dear Mr. Lewis:

If you're like many Americans, you're probably looking forward to a long and enjoyable retirement. That's a pleasant thought, until you realize how much money you'll need to finance those non working years. It's more important than ever to plan carefully and conservatively to ensure that you don't outlive your retirement savings.

Not long ago, I wrote to you extending an invitation to participate in Privileged Assets. I'm contacting you again because I strongly believe you should consider this opportunity.

PRIVILEGED ASSETS® HELPS MAKE RETIREMENT SAVING EASY

As a Platinum Card® member, saving for retirement can be easy with Privileged Assets, a tax-deferred annuity that can provide a secure, convenient way to help you save for retirement. Advantages include:

    USE YOUR PLATINUM CARD • To make saving simple, your monthly contribution will be automatically billed to your Platinum Card account and credited to your Privileged Assets annuity when your payment is received.

    GUARANTEED PRINCIPAL AND EARNINGS • Some portion of your retirement portfolio should be secure to protect against stock market volatility. With a Privileged Assets annuity, your principal and earnings are fully guaranteed by American Partners Life when held to maturity. (See *More About Privileged Assets*).

    GUARANTEED LIFETIME RETIREMENT INCOME • With Privileged Assets, you can choose an option that provides regular, guaranteed payments for the rest of your life. And you can take advantage of this benefit at any time without incurring withdrawal fees. It's nice to know you won't outlast your retirement savings — no matter how long you live.

    TAX-DEFERRED EARNINGS — YOUR MONEY GROWS FASTER • The tax-deferred status of your Privileged Assets annuity allows your money to grow without being eroded by taxes each year. This means your money grows more quickly and to greater sums than it would in a taxable investment paying the same interest rate.

    ATTRACTIVE 6.5% FIRST YEAR RATE • When you apply by November 30, 1998, you'll earn one of the most attractive annuity rates in the nation — 6.5% for one year from the date of enrollment (4.5% base rate + 2% first year added rate). In addition, we'll continue the 2% added rate in the second year.

ENROLL IN PRIVILEGED ASSETS TODAY

To start your Privileged Assets annuity, simply call 1-800-549-5602* or return the application below. We'll automatically bill your Platinum Card each month in the amount you choose, to help you close the gap in your retirement savings.

Sincerely,

Brian Kleinberg
Executive Vice President-Financial Direct
American Partners Life Insurance Company

P.S. Call 1-800-549-5602 today or return your application by November 30, 1998 to secure the 6.5% first year yield.
Phone enrollments are not allowed in Kentucky.

PL.
2CSG

LF8/98
AF8/98

TEAR ALONG THIS EDGE AND RETURN APPLICATION IN ENVELOPE PROVIDED.

Fig. 8.1 (letter opening number 1) "If you're like many Americans" is a variation of "If you're like me." In this instance it's more apt because a recipient may look at the signature and conclude, "I'm not like you." Consider versions and adaptations of each of the one hundred letter openings in these pages, and you'll quickly expand your own list to five hundred.

US MONITOR

IS YOUR MAIL DELIVERED?
HOW LONG DOES IT TAKE TO BE DELIVERED?
IS YOUR LIST AND DATABASE PROTECTED AGAINST UNAUTHORIZED USE?

US MONITOR HAS THE ANSWERS!

Dear Direct Marketer:

Mail delivery and list protection have always been important - but today they are more important than ever!

HERE'S HOW OUR SERVICE WORKS FOR YOU:

You are given a unique decoy name for the cities you choose. The decoy name is incorporated into your mailing list. When mail addressed to the decoy name is received by our agents, the date is noted on the envelope. Each piece is returned daily, unopened by first class mail. You learn if your mail was delivered, how long it takes to be delivered and if the use of your list was authorized.

WHO CAN USE THIS SERVICE?

STANDARD MAILERS (A):

According to U.S. Postal Service regulations, mail in this classification is distributed only after higher priority mail has been processed. Many Standard A mailers find there are times their mail is delayed. A delay disrupts any direct mail operation. For example, delayed response can make a successful direct mail package appear to be a failure. Based on faulty evidence, test results become meaningless ... a sound direct mail program may be discarded...sales and profits suffer. However, if you know how long it takes for your mail to be delivered, you can take steps to analyze returns properly and get a true picture.

It's a check on your lettershop operation - it's important to learn if all inserts have been included in your mail piece and in the proper order.

The service lets you know which BMCs move mail faster and the best time to mail.

FIRST CLASS MAILERS:

The business world moves fast and the USPS plays a major role in its economy. Correspondence, orders, inquiries, quotations, shipping information, contracts, invoices, corrections, checks, and a host of other important mail matter must be delivered on time. Otherwise, many dollars and valuable goodwill can be lost. When you know how long it takes for your mail to be delivered, you can plan mailing schedules to allow for delays and help insure on time deliveries.

(OVER ,PLEASE)

Fig. 8.2 (letter opening number 2) The provocative questions are in the pre-greeting header. This header isn't quite a Johnson Box and is too "headline-ish" to be an overline. But to someone in the direct-marketing industry, the questions do qualify as provocative.

SOUTH PLAINS MORTGAGE COMPANY
Expect more from the Nations Leader

3101 Maguire, Suite 259
Orlando, Florida 32803
407-898-1501 • 1-888-550-NOTE(6683)

Mr. Herschell Lewis
340 N Fig Tree Ln
Ft Lauderdale, FL 33317

Dear Mr. Lewis:

Are you tired of being the banker on the $180,000 real estate note you are carrying in Florida? Are collecting payments, checking on the taxes and insurance, hoping the borrower will pay, and filing all of the government forms, not what you expected when you sold the property?

Instead of carrying the note, would having **cash** be better? Payments frequently get spent and not turned into an investment like a lumpsum amount.

South Plains Mortgage will purchase your note for **cash**. We take care of all of the headaches and risk. No more filing forms, collecting payments, worrying about the property burning and many other situations that could happen.

What's more, now is the time the note is worth the most. When interest rates are low, notes bring the maximum. Now is the time to get the cash for investing, paying bills, paying for college expenses, buying an RV travel trailer, or just being relieved of the responsibilities.

Best of all, we can purchase your note with a minimal amount of effort. It takes just a short time to get the cash, because we handle all of the paperwork for you. <u>The time to do it is now!!</u>

As a special for the next 30 days, South Plains Mortgage will pay all of the seller's closing costs on all residential note purchases. This can amount to $1,500 or more depending on the size of the note. This bonus makes now the time to act.

So call today to turn your paper into the **cash** that is owed you!

Sincerely,

Joe DiLuzio
Regional Vice President

P.S.　If you would like a quote on the value of your note, call in Orlando **(407) 898-1501** or toll free at **1 (888) 550-NOTE (6683)**. There is no cost or obligation, and we can give it to you over the phone.

©South Plains Mortgage Company. 1993 "MET FL 5-11-98 26613"

Fig. 8.3　(letter opening number 2) This letter opens with a powerfully provocative question. If the respondent doesn't reply, a logical follow-up would be number 56 (chapter 10), "I'm surprised I haven't heard from you."

Now, suppose I open that same letter with, "Why do I think you might know the name of the ninth incarnation of Vishnu?" I've added the element of *provocation*. You're involved even though you haven't the foggiest notion where I'm heading. (Neither of us has the foggiest notion what the name of the ninth incarnation of Vishnu is.)

Would "Why should you know the name of the ninth incarnation of Vishnu?" be as on target? Certainly not. You at once penetrate my veil: I'm taking a superior position and I'm selling something, both positions perilous in establishing rapport.

Questions are easy, and that may be why they rank number one as misused openers. A letter from a trade magazine opens with a double question:

HAVE YOU NOTICED IT?

Dear *Business Marketing* Reader:

Have you noticed the major commitment that *Business Marketing* has made to help you do your job better.

The lack of a question mark is the letter writer's, not mine. But that isn't the major flaw here. What's wrong is the thrust of the questions: they're totally, baldly self-serving. The all-capped first question grabs the reader; the second question takes off the mask too soon. This opening parallels the windbag dinner partner who says, "I've talked about myself long enough. Now let's talk about you. What do *you* think of me?"

3. WHAT IF . . .

"What if" openings are often the instruments of choice for a "touchstone" (tying your concept to another the reader pre-accepts) opening:

- "What if you had bought Miami Beach property in the 1920s?"
- "What if you could go back to the day you graduated from college?"
- "What if you had been in the audience at Gettysburg in 1863 when Lincoln gave his speech?"

"What if" also fits a "hurl down the gauntlet" approach:

- "What if I could prove you can make a thousand dollars before sundown today?"
- "What if you could double your reading speed?"

FOR IMMEDIATE RESULTS
CALL: Marsha Friedman
        727-443-7115

MANAGEMENT
SERVICES
A PUBLICITY FIRM

No-Risk P.R.
Guaranteed results
Or you don't pay

What if you could get first-class publicity -- television and talk radio shows that deliver high audience numbers -- with zero financial risk?

If you've ever dealt with public relations companies, you know they'd just laugh at such a proposal. You know there's always a steep up-front charge and monthly retainer fee. Plus you typically have to sign up for a long contract -- even though you don't know whether they can deliver on their promises.

As you know, Event Management Services has a completely different approach to publicity.

Introducing "No Risk P.R."

The risk is on us. Either we deliver, or you don't pay.

Publicity can make or break a project. For example, publishing industry insiders, lawyers, doctors, non-profit organizations, and corporations have used Event Management Services -- with great success.

One of the firm's clients, Benjamin Dover, publisher and best-selling author of consumer-oriented books said, "Using radio and TV to sell my books was the major difference between succeeding and failing. The media was an integral link in the chain of success for publicizing my books, and of course, for creating profit!"

Client Dr. Ross Hauser saw a 25% increase in his book sales *and his practice* as a result of his appearances on television and radio.

Another client, Dr. Arnold Goldstein, founder of E-Z Legal Forms and best-selling author of numerous financial books said, "Dollar for dollar, talk radio interviews have shown a much better return than our advertising."

Marketing consultants, as well as ad agencies and even other PR firms, use Event Management Services because we deliver results.

Guaranteed results. Or you don't pay.

PLEASE TURN OVER FOR FREE, LIMITED-TIME OFFER

519 Cleveland Street, Suite 205
Clearwater, Florida 33755
813-443-7115 Fax 443-0835

Fig. 8.4   (letter opening number 3) "What if" is a challenger, which gives it great value in a business service ambience. See figures 8.5 and 8.6 for variations.

71411-7/98

Dear Friend,

Working for a large company can qualify you for group discounts on benefits. But what if you don't work for a large company? The absence of a connection to a large group can be detrimental to your pocketbook when it comes to buying health insurance coverage and other important services for yourself, your company and your family.

That is why I am writing to you today.

If you are self-employed, a small-business owner or an employee of a small company, you are not alone in your need to save money in both your business and personal life. The Alliance for Affordable Services can provide the buying power to meet this need.

To meet the needs of Americans just like you, the Alliance for Affordable Services has surveyed thousands of its Members. The results of these surveys have informed us about products and services that you want. As a result, the Alliance uses the power of group purchasing to offer you:

- $1,500 per year in major airline and cruise discounts deducted from the best available fares!
- $500 per year in grocery coupons on products that the member chooses!
- A way for the self-employed to legally deduct 100% of health insurance premiums if qualified!
- A credit card processing rate of 1.59%!
- Free bad check collection!
- Low-interest, fixed-rate Visa and MasterCard!
- Affordable, customized health insurance for individuals!*
- $30,000 guaranteed line of credit!
- 7.9¢ rate on long distance phone calls!
- $50,000 in guaranteed college funding for each of the member's children!

When you connect with the Alliance, your buying power improves immediately.

I urge you to return the reply card in the enclosed postage-paid envelope right away to learn how you can join in the savings. If you have any questions, you can also request information by calling our toll-free number 1-800-366-7818.

Cordially,

Vincent Roazzi
Director of Marketing and Development
Alliance for Affordable Services

P.S. I'm personally convinced that the Alliance for Affordable Services is the answer to reducing cost and improving your buying power. Return the enclosed reply card today for more information.

*Underwritten by Mid-West National Life Insurance Company of Tennessee. Home office: Nashville, TN. An insurance agent may contact you.

ALLIANCE FOR AFFORDABLE **SERVICES**

Alliance for Affordable Services
P.O. Box 869024 • Plano, TX 75086
1-800-366-7818 • www.affordableservices.org

M/MWNATL-118

Fig. 8.5 (letter opening number 3) The "What if" in this letter follows a "setup" sentence. The value of this variation is that it enables the writer to use the opening where the situation has to be explained to clarify a possibility of change.

5900 Hollis Street, R2, Emeryville, CA 94068-2008

Increase your ink and air this coming year—guaranteed!
No-risk trial subscription—at the lowest available price.

AUTO
Margot Lewis   89BPJ
Communicomp
340 N Fig Tree Ln
Plantation, FL   33317-2561
|ıllıılllıııllıııllllıılıılılılıılllıııllllılılıılıııllll

Dear Public Relations Professional:

If you could <u>double</u> the positive media coverage you score for your company in the coming year, what would that mean for your organization . . . and your career?

I suspect you both would profit immeasurably . . . since increased ink and air in major media translates into tens of thousands of dollars for your company and greater recognition for you.

Here's good news: I know a way you can achieve such dramatic increases in positive media coverage <u>right now</u>—with <u>no risk</u>.

It's called *Bulldog Reporter*—the insider media intelligence newsletter that tells you exactly how to grab the attention of influential journalists . . . and place more stories with them, immediately.

Bulldog Reporter gives you personal access to top editors, reporters, producers, bookers and bureau chiefs—and lets them tell you <u>in their own words</u> precisely how to pitch them. I'm totally confident this insider information will translate directly into more coverage for you and your company this coming year.

I'm so sure *Bulldog Reporter* works because I hear amazing success stories every week from subscribers—stories like these:

• Fenton Communications' Laura Burstein learns in *Bulldog* that reporter Laura Tangley is soon to join *U.S. News and World Report* and notes Tangley's interest in science topics. Burstein invites her to breakfast—a week before Tangley joins the magazine. Her pitch results in a two-page story. She reports, "*Bulldog* keeps me ahead of the curve."

• After reading a *Bulldog* interview with *The Washington Post* reporter David Segal on exactly what he's looking for in a story, Lauren Kapp with Ein Communications sees a perfect match with her client, attorney Wayne Chen, and pitches Segal. *Bulldog*'s tip turns into gold when her client is featured prominently in Segal's column.

• Melissa Rubenstein of Rubenstein Associates discovers in *Bulldog* a superb placement possibility for her hard-to-pitch client's anti-snoring nose drops. After reading about CNBC executive producer Andy Segal's particular criteria for stories, she pitches him her idea. She's rewarded by an

(over, please . . . .)

Fig. 8.6   (letter opening number 3) The word *what* doesn't begin the letter, although it is a key word in the first sentence. A "What if" opening obviously requires a question mark at its end.

Obviously the word *you* is a significant factor in a "What if" opening. Without *you*, the reader has the option of translating "What if" as "So what?"—"What if every member of Congress were to resign?" (Yeah, I know: good idea.)

4. SUGGEST A CATACLYSMIC DECISION.

This one bursts with power; but as the automobile commercials say, don't try this at home. It's the first one in this group requiring the professional laying on of hands.

At the fingertips of an amateur or dilettante writer, cataclysm can degenerate into comedy. "The decision you make today can . . ." is a grabber *if* the recipient of your message at once agrees with two pre-canned conclusions: First, you're in a position to judge and guarantee. Second, the decision is possible and logical.

A fund-raising organization has this cataclysm as its opening:

Dear Friend,

I've enclosed a Life or Death Seed Catalog for you.

Okay, what's wrong with that? Right! We just can't think of a seed catalog as a life or death determinant. We'll explore this same example more fully in the next chapter, in a discussion of number 29, "I've enclosed."

The same organization follows the formula more logically—if with a mildly contrived device—in this opening:

In the ten seconds it took you to open and begin to read this letter, five children died from the effects of malnutrition or disease somewhere in the world.

I'd have left off "somewhere in the world," which shifts the reader somewhat out of the arena. And, yes, the opening is a mite trite. But it grabs.

Cataclysmic declarations should have two mechanical components: a cutoff date and a suggestion of exclusivity. If the reader concludes the entire world has the opportunity to profit from the identical decision, the argument doesn't work because the cataclysm is too universal to generate a head of steam.

5. I [WE] NEED HELP.

At one time a generic fund-raising opening, this suffers from overuse and sociological evolution (devolution?). Among fund-raisers it's just as popular as ever, even though the impact isn't as formidable as it once was. Its use is actually growing because it no longer is the exclusive property of fund-raising.

"We need help" flourished during the 1950 to 1980 period—a kinder, gentler time when guilt was a more automatic motivator than it has become in the self-centered decades since. Many of today's old-line donors are holdovers from "We need help" recruitment campaigns of fifteen to thirty years ago.

Oh, sure, fund-raisers still use "We need help," and it still pulls well enough, for some, to maintain position. That's one reason it's on the list. But another reason is the spillover from fund-raising to commerce. A paradox! Business mailers have discovered need for dominance as a burgeoning motivator. By appealing to this need for dominance . . . by putting their target in a position of make-or-break supremacy . . . shrewd mailers have picked up the slack.

Few commercial mailings use "We need help," because today's consumers don't buy from weaklings. Instead, the mailers use a form of primitive psychology we all recognize when it's used on somebody else and seldom recognize when it's used on us:

- "You're the one person in thousands who can. . . ."
- "I want your opinion on something. Will you tell me what you really think?"
- "I admit: I need a favor from you."

6. Congratulations!

In for a penny, in for a pound: If you're using that single word, *congratulations,* I suggest following with an exclamation point, not a period. A calm congratulation has its uses, but calm doesn't match the single word. Mogul-to-mogul might be, "I congratulate you." That's not exclamatory. The single word *is* exclamatory, which means you use it only if what follows justifies the exclamation.

A letter to one of my decoy names begins:

Dear H. Gordon,

Congratulations! It's my great pleasure to welcome you to all the benefits and privileges of a Columbia House Club membership.

Your Pre-Approved MusiCard means you can receive our best offer to first-time members—not available through newspaper or magazine ads—but reserved for a select group of music lovers like you.

I'd never use the indefinite article *a* to describe the membership. I'd say "your Columbia House Club membership" or plain "Columbia House membership," not "*a* Columbia House Club membership." But this letter does maintain its congratulatory character. It adds automatic impact by capitalizing "Pre-Approved MusiCard" (and here the writer quite properly uses "Your"). Capitalization adds validation.

But "first-time members"? If they have any kind of database they've suppressed lapsed members, goniff members, and users of stolen credit cards; so if they want to build rapport with me, why not maintain the tone of invitation?

Anyway, the point isn't merciless dissection of a cold-list letter. It's recognition of "Congratulations!" as a dynamic opener, with the caution that you can't hit and run with it.

A properly used "Congratulations!" letter, from a credit-card company, came to my wife:

Dear Margo E. Lewis:

Congratulations! Because of the exemplary way you have handled your account you qualify for our new low variable rate on your Norwest credit card account. It's our way of saying "Thank you" and to show you how much we value your business.

The pitch is the standard credit-card "Transfer other balances to this account" sales argument, but couching it in a congratulatory message makes it both more readable and more palatable.

7.　I INVITE YOU . . .

"I invite you" is the first cousin—no, closer than that, the sibling—of "Congratulations!"

A point we all know (anticipating opening number 9): The invitation has to follow through *as an invitation*. No, this doesn't mean locking into an invitation-size format and including an engraved enclosure . . . although some of the more thoughtful invitations do this. It does mean keeping the tone invitational throughout the letter, never lapsing into hard sell or going out of character.

I have a letter from a publication which begins:

Dear Nominee Elect:

It is my pleasure, to inform you that you have been elected as an Associate Member of the American Museum of Natural History.

NATIONAL
GEOGRAPHIC
Video

1145 17th Street N.W.
Washington, D.C. 20036-4688 U.S.A.

Save $15 on your first video, and receive a FREE gift!

Journey to the forbidding Arctic
where few humans have ever dared to go...
where a vast ocean lies locked in the
uncompromising cold of winter.

And witness the coming of a great force
that will conquer this frozen sea....

Dear Friend,

When spring overtakes the Arctic, it awakens a world of motion, danger, and glorious life. You're invited to experience this dramatic transformation in Arctic Kingdom: *Life At The Edge.*

For nearly six months, the polar north endures frigid darkness. But in summer, as the Earth's axis tips, the region is pointed sunward. The ice cracks and shifts, forming new pathways to the open sea. And as the sunlight powers an explosion of Arctic life, <u>crowds of animals gather for a feast</u>.

Arctic Kingdom is yours to explore
<u>FREE for 10 days</u> as your introduction to
the WORLD'S LAST GREAT PLACES...
a spectacular series from National Geographic Video.

You'll watch a mother polar bear prowling the ice for her first meal in four months! <u>She can sniff out a seal half a mile away.</u>

At the edge of the ice, beluga whales click and call as they hunt cod. Walruses haul out of the sea to rest after a meal of clams. And <u>the largest Arctic animal arrives to feed on the smallest</u>!

<u>As a special bonus</u>, this video includes an exclusive 25-minute program, Freeze Frame: An Arctic Adventure, absolutely <u>free</u>. In a unique switch, you'll go behind the scenes to film the filmmakers as they shoot Arctic Kingdom! You'll experience all they faced -- a rugged lifestyle, daunting weather, and <u>very</u> real danger. In all, you get an exciting <u>85 minutes of adventure</u>!

And, to help you track your journeys, we'll send you a <u>FREE National Geographic *World Map*</u> if you decide to keep Arctic Kingdom!

Each program in the series will transport you to wild realms that remain in the province of nature -- <u>places you won't find on the itineraries of even the most adventurous travelers</u>.

All selections in the WORLD'S LAST GREAT PLACES carry the

Fig. 8.7   (letter opening number 7) An invitation can take many forms. This classic invitation letter says to the reader, "You're invited to experience ..." after a lyrical pre-greeting message.

We would request that you return the enclosed invitation as soon as possible, indicating whether or not you will be accepting this election. Your temporary Associate identification card is enclosed. You may sign it and begin using it immediately.

Except for the comma in the first sentence and the factorylike phrase "identification card" instead of "membership card" and the "Mother, may I?" tone of "You may sign it," this is a model of its type. One clever touch: moving into the conditional to avoid the appearance of pressure—"We would request" instead of the more imperative "We suggest."

Text of the letter does point out benefits other than the opportunity to get the magazine, such as free admission to the museum and various discounts; and it closes with a reaffirmation of its point: "We put a great deal of care and thought into the election process . . . ." Even knowing the ploy, who can resist an invitation that stays in character?

8.   I HAVE A FREE GIFT FOR YOU.

Over a long period of years, advertisers and marketers have agreed that "free gift" is a redundancy, and all have agreed it works. So free gift it is.

Okay, what *is* a free gift? Two schools of thought on this. One is the voice of utter integrity: it's free only if it's free. The other is the voice of sales logic: it's free if you don't pay extra for it.

Neither of these addresses the matter from the proper point of view—reader reaction. We have another mini-rule:

> ✎ A free gift as a letter opening has impact in direct ratio to the reader's recognition of the value of that gift.

I bring this up because we all damage future impact of the much-scarred phrase "free gift" by calling a sample issue of a magazine a free gift. It isn't. It's a free *issue* or a free *sample* or a free *look*. A token outside the arena of what we're selling is a gift.

A magazine renewal letter states in an eighteen-point overline:

Here's a free gift for you.

The letter is well written, except for a mechanical decision with which I don't agree: Paragraphs aren't indented. And a curiosity: Except for the aristocratic putoff "We would now like to reward you for your loyalty," the gift is buried in the text. After the overline, it isn't mentioned until the fourth paragraph. Good or bad?

If you want to <u>save</u> your company <u>thousands</u> <u>of</u> <u>dollars</u>...
If you want to <u>greatly</u> <u>improve</u> your company's <u>productivity</u>...
If you want to make the jobs of travelers and travel arrangers in
your company <u>much, much easier</u>...mail the enclosed card.
It brings you OAG® Travel Information System™, with no obligation.
It's absolutely...

Dear Executive,

The revolutionary OAG® Travel Information System™ is a comprehensive software package that contains OAG's FlightDisk®
and OAG's HotelDisk™. It's an essential business solution
for companies who want to control their third largest
expense — *travel*...

   ...And now OAG® Travel Information System™ is available
   in a LAN (Local Area Network) and Intranet version!
   It's guaranteed to bring travel savings to where it
   matters most — <u>your company's bottom line</u>.

Example: If your company has 95% domestic travel and 5%
international travel...

   ...you can save your company $24,236...$48,472...
   $484,723...$969,445...depending on how many people in
   your company travel.

See for yourself: you have the exclusive opportunity to
receive a limited-time trial of OAG® Travel Information
System™ — <u>free</u>. There is absolutely no obligation.

           The world's #1 source of travel information...
               created by Official Airline Guides.

   <u>It's true! OAG® Travel Information System™ gives you</u>
   <u>instant access to the same flight information the FAA</u>
   <u>and all airline reservation systems use to create their</u>
   <u>schedules</u>. <u>You'll have access to over 600,000 flights</u>
   <u>and 65,000 hotels</u>.

           A much, much better way to control T&E expenses.

Whether your company has 3...30...300...3,000 or more
travelers...you will be amazed at <u>how much money</u>
<u>OAG® Travel Information System™ can save you</u>. With OAG®
Travel Information System™ you give <u>every</u> traveler...and
<u>every</u> travel arranger in your company the power to reduce
T&E expenses and readily communicate corporate travel policies.

                                        (over, please)

Fig. 8.8   (letter opening number 8) Lots of "If" phrases here, but the key is "FREE." Do you think impact suffers because "FREE" follows a challenge instead of preceding it?

Get your hands on

FREE

trial issue of

FAST COMPANY

You'll never let go.

Dear Business Professional:

Get out the highlighter, the scissors, the notepad, the routing envelopes. Your free trial issue of *Fast Company* is just a reply card away!

Fast Company is unlike any business publication you've ever known. As revolutionary as the new face of business it reports on. Don't expect a magazine that lulls you to sleep on the train. Or merely offers you "perspective." This is front burner stuff all the way. Intelligence you can act on, pass along, and profit from. *Today.*

Fast Company attracts a special kind of reader. One who isn't content just to know what's happening...but *makes* things happen. Sound like someone you know?

A couple of caveats. Don't lend *Fast Company* to anyone; you'll never get it back. And never let your rivals get their hands on it. For obvious reasons.

Just for requesting your FREE TRIAL ISSUE, we'll send your custom-designed *Fast Company* analog watch — made in fashionable and water-resistant acrylic plastic for comfortable wear —absolutely free with our thanks.

That's all I'll say. Let the magazine speak. If you like *Fast Company*, I'll send 9 more issues (10 in all). If you don't, simply write "Cancel" on your bill, return it and owe nothing. Your FREE TRIAL ISSUE and FREE WATCH are yours to keep regardless. Just be sure to send the enclosed "Free Gift/ Free Trial Issue Request" in the postage-paid envelope to receive your copy.

Then roll up your sleeves. And get to work.

Sincerely,

Pat. Hagerty

Patrick Hagerty
Publisher

P.S. I hope you enjoy the enclosed free gift, "My Favorite Bookmarks" — highlights from one of *Fast Company*'s most popular features. Don't miss out on the rest of *Fast Company*. Send for your free trial issue today!

FC-L27

Fig. 8.9   (letter opening number 8) Note the unusual treatment of "FREE" above the greeting. In this letter, the free gift other than the magazine is left hanging until the fifth paragraph. A good decision, or not?

 Lucent Technologies
Bell Labs Innovations

 FREE Phone system installation
No leasing payments for 3 months
On-site phone system analysis

When it comes to communications solutions, Lucent Technologies speaks your language.

Dear Executive:

Free. Gratis. Za Darmo. No matter how you say it, you'll be saving up to thousands of dollars on a Lucent Technologies Small Business Phone System—the name that stands for Bell Labs innovations, quality and reliability all over the world.

Free installation—now through March 31.

It is our best offer ever! Now small businesses can hook up with our state-of-the-art communications technology *for free.* When you buy or lease a Lucent Technologies Small Business Phone System through March 31, *the entire installation costs you absolutely nothing*—all you pay for is the equipment and wiring.

We'll install the control unit *for free*, the desk phones *for free*—we'll even install your voice messaging system *for free*. And programming...testing...training—*we'll do all that for free, too*. It's a limited-time offer that can *save your business up to thousands of dollars*—and that's just the beginning!

No payments for three months—with our special leasing arrangement.

You can also take advantage of a special lease offer through AT&T Credit and pay nothing for three months.* Which means your phone system will be installed, up and running and helping your business be more productive—before you've spent a penny. Just as important, you'll have our 24-hour service and support agreement—peace of mind in any language.

Free phone system analysis—for all your communications needs.

We want you to be certain that the technology you're investing in today will serve your needs as your business grows. That's why before we sell you anything, we provide a professional on-site evaluation. We'll answer your questions, analyze your communications needs, and custom-design a phone system that not only fits your budget, but also positions your business for the future. We'll even show you how you can afford applications that boost productivity, like voice mail and messaging, and computer telephone integration. And we'll provide you with a complete customized analysis in writing.

So don't wait—find out how your business can save up to thousands of dollars on a Lucent Technologies Phone System! Simply mail or fax the enclosed reply card or call today: **1 800 833-2233, ext. 188.**

Lucent Technologies. We speak your language. And now through March 31, we're talking *"free"!*

Sincerely,

Pat Reily
Small Business Communications Systems
Vice President

AT&T
Lucent Technologies - formerly the communications systems and technology units of AT&T

P.S. Just say the word before March 31—for free installation and up to thousands of dollars in savings!

*Subject to credit approval.
NOTE: This offer cannot be combined with any other equipment offer.
©1997 Lucent Technologies

TALKA

Smart solutions for small business from Lucent Technologies

Fig. 8.10   (letter opening number 8) Despite the intrusion of a "When it comes to" cliché, the word *free* is omnipresent in this bright letter. Emphasizing a free offer is never a mistake.

min's New Media Report

News, strategies and tactics to grow your online publishing and new media business

                    Who's grabbing eyeballs ...
                     How are they doing it ...
              Where's their revenue coming from ...
              ... and how can you get your hands on
                       their business plans?
                          For FREE?

Dear Executive,

    <u>The answer is</u>, you can get all this strategic
business information in the pages of *min's New
Media Report* ... and even better, <u>you can get it
free for the next 3 months.</u>

    Take a look at the special **Digest Issue** I've
enclosed, packed with actual articles and charts
from recent issues of *min's New Media Report.*

    You'll see first-hand the tactics and business
models your competitors are using to break through
the online clutter and build solid revenue streams
for their sites ...

    <u>Top Headline News</u> (see p. 1 of the **Digest**) —
here's an article I thought you'd find useful
on working with portals to drive traffic to
your own site. This is a thorny issue among
online publishers and as the editor puts it,
*"The engines have the eyeballs, while the
sites have the content, so how can you avoid
cannibalizing your own products?"* See our
analysis, and get more top news like this in
every issue of *min's New Media Report;*

    <u>Box Scores chart</u> (see p. 3 of the **Digest**) —
this is our monthly data report on top

                                    Over, please

Fig. 8.11   (letter opening number 8) "FREE" is the payoff in a Johnson Box effect above the greeting and has a quick payoff in the first sentence. Might you have handwritten "For FREE?" in the pre-greeting text?

I'm not privy to the results and I don't know whether this subscription renewal letter is a "control" (winner that has staved off other approaches testing against it) that survived an onslaught by challengers. Yes, I *do* understand the nature of thanking the subscriber before banging away at the gift. Ah, but I *don't* understand using "Here's a free gift for you!" in eighteen-point Garamond, then holding back on what it is (a shoe bag set—nice!) until paragraph 4.

One compromise, using the combination of "free gift" to gain attention and then expostulating on the main issue before getting to the gift in the body of the letter: a hand-scrawled circle around that fourth paragraph.

9.　AS YOU KNOW . . .

One of the classic ways of establishing rapport is telling readers something they already know . . . or think they should know.

"As you know" is one of the great argumentative ploys of our time. You can use it without fear to drive an imperative all the way to the insult border because those three little words say to the reader, "You and I are knowledge confrères."

The psychological value of "As you know" goes beyond artificial comradeship. The reader is supposed to think, "I *do* know," and depending on how professionally the message is transmitted, the reader's previously nonexistent position is established and polarized.

So "As you know" enables opinion to masquerade as fact. It can sell where a bald imperative can't.

And, in bumbling hands, it can turn off the reader before the real point of the message ever gets under way.

A letter from one of the Australian Lottery publications begins:

Dear Subscriber:

The midnight hour has arrived. As you know, last year, the Mailing Rates raised dramatically. We, at the Lotto Advisor decided to bite the bullet and hold off passing along this increased cost to you, but all that is about to end.

Punctuation problems aside, do you see what's wrong with this use of "As you know"? The writer wastes it on a point the reader has to regard as trivial and without mutual import.

A credit-card company drops "As" but uses the device:

Dear H. G. Lewis: [I hate that impersonal personalization.]

You know that motivating your company's top performers can have a crucial impact on the bottom line, especially in today's competitive market.

Again the writer wastes the device because "As you know" as an opener has to tie itself to the firing of a big gun. This generalization is at best a self-serving little gun.

10.   I HAVE SOMETHING GOOD FOR YOU.

This one is dangerous if the opening makes the promise and the text becomes a letdown as in the following fund-raising letter sent to me by my friend Bob Dunhill of Dunhill International List Company:

Dear Mr. Dunhill:

Bill is a student here at Cumberland College. And, he is probably going to save you money on your federal income tax return. Incredible? But true. Please let me explain.

Well, the explanation, on page 2, is that Bill is going to save Bob Dunhill money because if we help him go to college by making a contribution Bill won't be a tax burden. You know what this is like? It parallels the fellow who kept a bank from being robbed. He changed his mind.

Another example of this opening is an eight-page document—printed, not typed—with the subtly condescending overline, "How to Get The Life You Want!" (I should say insulting, not condescending, because it was addressed to me, and I already have the life I want.) To list and database companies I repeat the old saw: Garbage in, garbage out. The letter begins:

Dear Friend,

My name is Virginia Lloyd and I have something valuable to give you. This letter is very important to you because it details how you can dramatically improve your life, in every way that you want.

First, let me tell you that I am a successful author, businesswoman, and mother. If you wish, I can furnish you with my complete personal references and business credentials.

The letter goes on to tell me she transformed her life twenty-two years ago from bad debt and bad health to financial freedom and vitality.

*Isn't it time to wave good-bye to
expensive credit card rates?*

DEAR MARK X. JENNEMANN:

   As the old saying goes, I'm making you an offer you can't refuse. (A better way of
putting it: I'm making you an offer you shouldn't refuse.)

   I'll tell you why:

   I'm offering you the opportunity to acquire a Commerce Advantage MasterCard® at one
of the lowest interest rates you've ever had the good fortune to enjoy – an incredible
6.9% APR!* And that very low rate is guaranteed for the first six months. All this
with no annual fee.

   Just one catch: This offer is open until 7/15/96. So, if you're going to take me
up on this deal, do it now. Don't stick this notice in a desk drawer intending to
"get to it later." That's the surest way to miss out.

   What are you currently paying in credit card rates? I'll wager it's higher – maybe
a lot higher – than 6.9% APR. In fact, as of this writing, the Discover® card charges
17.15%. The GM® card charges 18.65% and AT&T 17.40%†. Smart financial management calls
for you to get this Card, use it to pay off those high-interest balances, and start
saving on anything and everything you buy, right now!

   You'll continue saving month after month, even after the introductory period,
because you'll enjoy a super-low interest rate, – currently 13.85% APR.**

   Want some other reasons you should have a Commerce Advantage MasterCard (aside from
the rate)? I'll name a few (please read carefully, because we're talking money here):

   How's this? If you transfer your balances from any other card to your new Commerce
Advantage MasterCard, you won't pay one cent in balance transfer fees. And remember,
there is no annual fee! That's a happy difference, isn't it?

   I've also enclosed a handy chart to give you an idea of how much you can save
by switching to the Card that carries the prestige of Commerce Bank and the logic of
smart money management.

                         (more benefits on back...)   CL

Fig. 8.12   (letter opening number 10) Note the impact of this "I have something good for you" opening. Also, note the inventive modification of the approach and the reading ease.

From HAMMOND GROVES

3885 41st Street, Vero Beach, Florida 32967

A full season of the world's finest oranges and grapefruit has already been reserved for you at Hammond Groves.

Confirm your reservation now and you'll receive FREE shipping and a FREE gift!

Dear Friend:

Greetings from Florida's Indian River region! Wish you were here to smell the indescribable sweetness of the citrus blossoms in our groves. It's an aroma that refreshes you mind, body and soul!

But quite frankly, even the fragrance doesn't compare with the flavor of the resulting fruit. Our oranges and grapefruit are sweet and juicy beyond your wildest dreams. To prove it, <u>I'll pay for a full season of shipping charges on</u> Tom's Pride™ *Best of the Best* citrus!

Oranges and Grapefruit
so sweet they'll sour you on supermarket citrus

One taste of Tom's Pride *Best of the Best* citrus and you just might wonder if you're sampling an all-new and entirely different kind of fruit. Bursting with juice, it's that much sweeter and more delicious than an ordinary orange or grapefruit. You'll vow to never settle for supermarket citrus again!

And you'll never need to! Because <u>a full season of this superlative citrus has already been reserved for you at Hammond Groves.</u>

Just imagine! You'll be sipping fresh orange and grapefruit juice all winter long...delighting holiday guests with the world's best Navel Oranges...enjoying succulent Honeybell Tangelos for dessert...sharing a heart-smart snack of Temple Oranges with your Valentine...chasing the winter blues away with refreshing Ruby Red Grapefruit...and welcoming spring with tender and juicy Valencias.

Since the supply of Tom's Pride *Best of the Best* citrus is always limited, I can only offer a specially selected group of people <u>the chance to enjoy grove-fresh deliveries of my finest oranges and grapefruit from mid-November through late May.</u> This year, you are among the fortunate few.

Enjoy the top 10% of our crop

Here in the Indian River region of Florida, growing superior citrus is easy. After all, nature's given us the edge--with mineral rich soil and gentle Gulf Stream breezes.

However, my goal has always been to grow the best citrus in an area

Free Gift when you reserve by 10/31/98

(Over, please)

Fig. 8.13 (letter opening number 10) This isn't a particularly strong example of "I have something good for you." Why? Possibly because the introduction is too poetic and lengthy to build quick acceptance that, yes, this is good for me. Compare the rhetoric with the conviviality of figure 8.12.

Dear Music Lover,

You've probably been listening to the radio all your life. But if you've never heard the Bose® Wave® radio, you may not realize how much more enjoyable your listening experience could be.

The Wave radio delivers stereo sound that's rich, full, and natural. Sound that's so realistic, it's almost like you're at a live performance, hearing your favorite music the way it was *meant* to be heard. And with a choice of colors — imperial white or graphite gray — the Wave radio will not only fill an entire room with sound, it will fit into any room's decor.

It's hard to imagine just how lifelike the Wave radio sounds. The truth is, you really have to experience it for yourself. That's why I'd like to invite you to hear the Wave radio in your own home, with absolutely no obligation.

Here's how easy it is to take advantage of our risk-free offer:

- Order the Wave radio in the next 30 days.

- We'll pay for the shipping — a $15 value — and deliver it right to your door.

- Enjoy listening to it in your home.

- If you are not completely satisfied, simply call us toll free within 30 days. We'll refund the entire purchase price and arrange to have the Wave radio picked up and returned to us at no charge to you. *There's absolutely no risk.*

You also have the option of making twelve interest-free payments.

- When you order your Wave radio, you can choose to pay the $349 in full or make twelve monthly payments of $29.08* with this once-a-year offer.

To begin enjoying one right away, simply fill out and return the enclosed order form, or call us toll free at 1-800-249-2673, 24 hours a day, 7 days a week. And get ready to hear music like you've never heard before.

Best regards,

Steve Kingsbury

Steve Kingsbury
Director, Consumer Direct Division

P.S. Remember, to take advantage of this risk-free offer, you must order within 30 days.
    For information on all our products: www.bose.com/rdmb

Steve Kingsbury

Director

Consumer Direct Division

Bose Corporation

The Mountain

Framingham

Massachusetts

01701-9168

BOSE®

* First payment to include applicable sales tax. ©1998 Bose Corporation. Covered by patent rights issued and/or pending. Installment payment plan and free shipping offers not to be combined with any other offer. Installment payment plan available on credit card orders only. Prices and/or payment plan are subject to change without notice.

♻ Printed On Recycled Paper

Fig. 8.14   (letter opening number 10) This opening is something of a hybrid——"Look what you've missed" as a lead-in to "I have something good for you." Selling speaker sound isn't easy because sound has a zero visualization quotient.

Lady, you may be a successful author, but you aren't a successful sales-letter writer. This technique is about twenty years out of fashion . . . and even then, those who wrote classic "I transformed my life and so can you" letters didn't beg the issue and weaken their image by offering references—*references*, for God's sake—before even making a point.

11. A SPECIFIC EPISODE NARRATIVE

Fund-raisers know three communication truths too many writers of conventional sales messages either ignore or don't discern:

1. Episodes outpull statistics.
2. Examples are more credible than exhortation.
3. Coupling examples *with* exhortation geometrically expands the emotional impact of a message.

Outside the fund-raising arena even the giants stumble over that tricky third truth. They unearth esoteric or confusing examples the typical reader can't penetrate; or they become shrill, fearing any message short of screaming on paper won't penetrate the reader's apathy.

Difficulty of execution isn't germane to *this* list of openings. If we limit ourselves to the basic concept—a specific episode narrative—professionalism requires no more than finding an episode which makes your point for you.

A flawed example from (where else?) the world of fund-raising:

Dear Friend,

Unlike most kids, 12-year-old Patrick J.* rarely looks forward to the end of a school day.

That's because his journey home is often a terrifying one. Clutching his books tightly in his hands, Patrick runs at top speed through his South Bronx neighborhood, fearful of getting caught in the crossfire of a drug deal gone bad, or terrorized by a street gang....

I warned you it was flawed. That asterisk is *deadly*. I'll interrupt my own narrative to repeat the easiest rule ever offered to a communicator, the Asterisk Exception:

> ✏ When should you use asterisks in a direct-response message? Never.

(This asterisk referral at the end of the letter is predictable: "Names have been changed to protect individual privacy." Ugh.)

Herschell Lewis
340 N. Fig Tree Ln.
Plantation, FL 33317-2561
IıIIıııIIııIIıııIIIIıııIıIıIıIIıIIıııIIIıIıIIIıııIıIıI

You'll Want to Sample a Half Case
of Our Award-Winning Wine,
Direct from Our Vineyards to You...
at a Saving of Over 35%.

Dear Herschell Lewis,

Over three decades ago, our winery's founder came home to Sonoma County
from a sojourn in France. His dream was to purchase vineyard land that
equalled what he saw in Europe... and his dream came true in the
Russian River Valley. Since 1959, we've grown, blended, aged and
bottled award-winning premium wines from these vineyards and offered
them to discriminating consumers through our direct purchase program.

That's why we're revealing one of America's best-kept wine secrets to
you... and encouraging you to enjoy a selection of our fine wines direct
from Windsor Vineyards, <u>at a special introductory saving of over 35%</u>.

Try our most popular sampler case--consisting of six full-size bottles
of premium varietal wines--<u>for just $36--a special introductory saving
of 35%</u>. We're so sure that you'll enjoy these exceptional wines that
we'll give you an additional $7.00 discount on your next order. Simply
indicate your acceptance on your personal order form and we'll send
your $7.00 discount coupon when we send your wine.

> Every bottle of Windsor Vineyards wine has a rich heritage of
> almost 40 years of winemaking excellence. <u>In fact, we've received
> more awards for quality than any other winery in America</u>.
>
> In 1997, Windsor Vineyards was named <u>"Golden Winery of the Year"
> by the California State Fair</u>, because Windsor won more awards for
> excellence than any other winery in the fair's wine tasting
> competition. You'll want to try the wines that brought us awards
> like these, from rich red Cabernet to creamy golden Chardonnay to
> our light, refreshing Riesling.

How can we sell such good wines at such fair prices? Because, as the
oldest direct-to-the-consumer winery in the United States, we only sell
directly to you, the consumer. Our mission is to offer a quality wine
experience to every household in America. We've been creating and
marketing fine wines since 1959, but you won't see our wine on a
restaurant wine list or on the shelf at your grocery store. Only
because we sell direct can we afford to sell our wine at such
tremendous savings.

                         In addition...

Windsor Vineyards of Florida
P.O. Box 6128 • Fort Lauderdale • FL 33310

Fig. 8.15   (letter opening number 11) A specific episode narrative succeeds if it intrigues the reader. How about this one? To a wine lover … and wine lovers are the singular targets … it succeeds, but only partially because specificity is muddy.

Some of the terminology is arm's length, too. Each of these suppresses emotional impact: *clutching*; *crossfire*. An episode has to grab and shake. Any one of us might have humanized that opening. And since they've changed the name anyway, it doesn't have to be the formal "Patrick." Suggested rewrite:

Bobby is 12. Every day he's afraid to go home from school.

One of his friends was shot dead crossing the street, when a drug deal went bad and a random bullet smashed through his neck. Bobby himself was lucky one day when he was able to get away with just a torn shirt, from a street gang that wanted his schoolbooks—to sell for drug money.

So Bobby runs home … literally for his life….

The concept works, even when execution is weak. When execution has some bite, the concept has great power . . . because if you create an episode the reader can envision, you've drawn the reader into your emotional net.

Oh, another mini-rule:

> ✏️ Present-tense episodes have more wallop than past-tense episodes.

12.   PRIVATE INVITATION

How do you get somebody who never heard of you before to feel specially chosen for the signal honor of hearing from you?

Exclusivity is one of the five great motivators of our strange era (the others, remember, are fear, greed, guilt, and need for approval). It's the easiest of the great motivators to construct, and "Private invitation" is one of the most logical manipulations of exclusivity because being one of the chosen few is a universal grabber.

A private invitation has significant differences from "You're a very special person," which emphasizes stroking beyond emphasizing the offer.

A classic "Private invitation" opening is this letter:

A Private Message to a Very Special Person

Dear Friend,

This private invitation is going out to just a handful of people, yourself included. I hope you'll accept my invitation. And even if you decide not to, I want to send you a gift … ABSOLUTELY FREE….

ASM/M8127/0C

CERTIFIED COURIER SERVICES, INC.
SECURED DELIVERY PROFESSIONALS

BC-28

...ICES, INC.   SECURED DELIVERY PROFESSIONALS

JEFFREY R. REDER
PRESIDENT & CEO

HAWTHORNE, NEW YORK 10532

```
AUTO ************ 3-DIGIT 333
M8141-2Y          00391
|..||..||..||....||||....|.|.|.|.|..||....|||.||..|.|.|
Margo Lewis
340 N. Fig Tree Lane
Ft Lauderdale, FL  33317-2561
```

To Margo Lewis,

Because of the important nature of this correspondence, and the need to maintain strict security precautions during prize delivery, Reader's Digest Assistant Treasurer, W.H. Magill, has asked me to contact a selected list of individuals today. Your name is on that list.

My name is Jeffrey Reder. I am enclosing my business card (along with Mr. Magill's) to introduce myself as the President and CEO of CERTIFIED COURIER SERVICES, specialists in secured courier delivery.

We have been instructed to inform you that two (2) official Prize Entry Cards have just been dispatched to your Ft Lauderdale residence. These documents should arrive within three to five days, in a red envelope, from Reader's Digest.

> It would be my distinct pleasure to learn that you may have already won $23,500.00.

Your immediate action, however, is essential. Watch your mailbox, and return your entry documents to Reader's Digest as soon as they arrive. In the event yours is the winning number, CERTIFIED COURIER SERVICES will handle all security arrangements for the delivery of your prize, and one of our bonded agents would soon be in transit to your home.

Please tear off the attached SECURITY AGENT AUTHORIZATION slip and keep it in a safe place. You will be asked to give this form to our agent (or show him any other valid form of identification) before he can release your $23,500.00 to you if you are the winner.

In the meantime, my very best wishes to you and your family. I hope CERTIFIED COURIER SERVICES will be knocking at your front door in just a few short weeks. Please return your documents to Reader's Digest as soon as you receive them.

Jeffrey R. Reder

Jeffrey R. Reder
President and CEO

(over, please)

DETACH HERE AND KEEP IN A SAFE PLACE

CORPORATE HEADQUARTERS • HAWTHORNE, NEW YORK 10532

Fig. 8.16 (letter opening number 12) A private invitation achieves verisimilitude only if the reader is immediately convinced of the exclusivity factor. To validate the impression of exclusivity, enclosing a business card with this letter is inspired.

I don't know what "yourself included" is doing there, but you get the idea: "You're one of the chosen few." This letter stays in character, continuing the stroking with "I believe you're someone who travels well, eats in fine restaurants—and appreciates the difference between dinner at a four-star restaurant and a hamburger on the run."

The power of private invitation exclusivity, when well-handled, lies in its ability to cause recipients to think they have to live up to your expectations of them.

13. WE DON'T KNOW EACH OTHER, BUT IT'S TIME WE DID.

This one is dangerous because you're at the mercy of both the recipient's background and mood of the moment. "We don't know each other, but it's time we did" is just as likely to generate "Who the hell do you think you are?" as "Yeah, you're right."

This opening has value as a precursor to a follow-up phone call. It has the guts any assumptive opening commands. It also works when the writer can throw in a third name known to the recipient.

An example of "We don't know each other, but it's time we did":

Dear Mr. Lewis:

YOU DON'T KNOW ME, BUT …

I've been asked by Terry Winter, Vice President of Uniprop, Inc., to contact you regarding your investment in one of their Manufactured Home Community programs. I believe, the firm that set this up for you is not now handling Uniprop investments. There are, Mr. Lewis, some potentially very important developments shaping up that you should know about. Communication between us over the next few months will be very important....

You guessed it. The writer is a financial planner. The major fault with this letter isn't its failure to indent paragraphs nor the strange comma after "believe"; no, this letter builds a reef and then runs aground on it by ignoring the one rule a "We don't know each other, but it's time we did" letter has to follow:

> ✏ After claiming a need for relationship, immediately explain why.

Incidentally, I wouldn't know Terry Winter if I fell over him.

14. THE CRY OF "FIRE!"

"Fire!" differs from "Wolf!" (number 64, chapter 10) in just one respect: the issue is broader. A wolf can eat you (yes, dear fellow environmentalists, I know we've never had a recorded case of a wolf eating a human being), but a fire can wipe out a whole town.

The problem with "The cry of 'Fire!'" isn't that it'll start a panic inside a crowded theater; it's that the cry demands a statesmanlike attitude and we're wallowing in "Me"-ness. From greedy politicians to self-centered jocks, our society has turned away from issues affecting anybody but Me.

Still, it's comforting to know that somebody cares. Dedication is so rare today we should honor it by responding—which I did to this cry of "Fire!" (strange overuse of hyphens and capitalizing "Schools" are the writer's doing, not mine):

Dear Friend,

America's Schools are in crisis!

Twenty-two percent of all first, second, and third grade students fall-behind their age groups!

Each year, more than five-hundred thousand children fall-behind, or fail, *in first grade alone*!

The cause is a worthy one, so I hope the rapport-killing statistic "Twenty-two percent" didn't maim its impact.

15. WHAT I WANT YOU TO DO IS . . .

This one is delicate. Written with delicacy and finesse, it achieves that wonderful connection, *rapport*; written with a heavy-handed bludgeon, it alienates the reader.

An excellent example of this approach is a letter which, following a too-lengthy Johnson Box, has this superior beginning:

Dear Viewer,

Just for a minute, I want you to forget everything you've ever learned about American history.

Because I want to take you back—400 years and more—and make the story of North America *come alive* for you and your family....

Visualize that letter with a more pedestrian opening. This writer makes the demand both soft and logical, an indication of a professional at work.

AT&T Universal Card

The enclosed check is yours to use as you want.
And when you cash it, you'll be entitled
to receive even more money-back privileges!

You deserve this money back...

Dear Herschell Lewis,

You've been a very loyal AT&T Universal Card member since 1990. And now you're entitled
to exclusive money-back privileges — starting with the enclosed $5.00 check.

Simply cash or deposit your check, and you'll also receive a new **Money-Back Card** to use
<u>absolutely free</u> for the next three months. So you can receive cash back on things you buy.

This is not a credit card — it's a savings card. Use it with your AT&T Universal Card to get exclusive
money-back privileges through the Buyers Advantage® program. Cashing this check automatically
enrolls you in this program and entitles you to —

- money back when items you buy go on sale within 60 days,

- refunds when you return even final sale items within 60 days,

- rebates on repairs to just about every household appliance
  you own — no matter how old, and

- the same money-back and replacement protection your
  manufacturers' U.S. warranties provide — extended to a full
  two years from the date of purchase!*

The **Money-Back Card** from Buyers Advantage is yours without any cost whatsoever for the
next three months. So you can check out how much money it saves you, <u>without paying a cent</u>. Use it
as much as you like — to collect cash refunds on returns and sale items — up to $250 per item and $1,000
annually* — and get 20% back on repair bills — up to $100 on each item. Then, no matter how much
you've saved and how much cash you've received from Buyers Advantage, <u>you won't pay anything at all
unless you continue your membership.</u>

(Over, please)

Fig. 8.17 (letter opening numbers 16 and 17) Both 16 and 17 are "Because you" openings. This letter combines the two cousins in its first two paragraphs.

16. BECAUSE YOU DID THAT, WE'RE GOING TO DO THIS.

This opening can be a powerhouse when you use it properly because, unlike "I have a free gift for you" or "I have something good for you," this offer ties itself into a positive action your target has accomplished. The tie-in adds both credibility and rapport.

A letter addressed to my son (and my coauthor of *Selling on the Net*) began:

Dear Robert Lewis:

Because of your company's growing commitment to the Windows environment, I'd like to send, for your evaluation, a free copy of Correct Grammar for Windows.

Now, what if this letter had begun, "I have a free copy of Correct Grammar for Windows for you"? Neither rationale nor reader involvement would have been as powerful.

Often, levels of power stem from the amount of information we have about the target. So don't discard the "I have a free copy of Correct Grammar for Windows for you" opening; rather, make a substitution when you have enough information to replace it with this opening. "I have a free copy of Correct Grammar for Windows for you" has its uses . . . for example, a retail store wielding *Correct Grammar* as an incentive. In such a circumstance, "Because you did that, we're going to do this" would be presumptuous.

Only partly parallel to "Because you did that, we're going to do this" is . . .

17. BECAUSE YOU ARE WHO YOU ARE, YOU MAY GET SPECIAL ATTENTION.

Note that word *may*; it's the huge separator from number 16.

This one is just as close to number 12, "Private invitation," as it is to number 16. In fact, an example in my file has an invitation above the overline:

You are invited to apply for a free subscription.

Please reply by [DATE].

Dear Computer Professional,

Your position suggests that you may qualify for a complimentary subscription to *InfoWorld*....

You can see the difference: Conditions peek slyly through tiny holes in the invitation. I'm invited to *apply*. Any applicant is implicitly on a lower plane than the person to whom he or she applies. So this isn't a genuine

MediaMap

We Got You Covered.

215 First Street
Cambridge
Massachusetts
02142
888.624.1620
617.374.9300
Fax: 617.374.9345
www.mediamap.com

When you work with
MediaMap, you're in good company...

AG Communication Systems
Agnew Carter McCarthy
Alexander Communications, Inc.
Ameritech
Andersen Consulting
AT&T
BSMG Worldwide
Brodeur Porter Novelli
Burson-Marsteller
Carlson Company
CARE
Compaq
Cone Communications
Copithorne & Bellows
Creamer Dickson Basford
Cunningham Communication
Dow Jones & Co., Inc.
Dreyer's and Edy's Grand Ice
Cream
Dura Pharmaceuticals
Edelman Public Relations
Worldwide
EDS
Fisher Rosemount
Fleishman Hillard, Inc.
Frank Russell Company
Fujitsu
Gateway
GCI Group
Golin Harris
Hewlett Packard
Hill & Knowlton
Intel
John Hancock Mutual Life
Insurance
Ketchum Public Relations
Knight-Ridder New Media
KVO-Karakas, VanSickle and
Ouellette
Lois Paul and Partners
Makovsky & Co.
Manning, Selvage & Lee, Inc.
Metropolitan Life Insurance
Microsoft
Miller/Shandwick Technologies
Ogilvy Adams & Rinehart
Parker Nichols & Co.
Pioneer Funds Distributor, Inc.
Porter Novelli International
PR Newswire
Rubenstein & Associates
Ruder Finn
Rourke MS&L
Scudder & Kamper Investment
Schwartz Communications
Thompson Financial Services
Waggener Edstrom
The Weber Group
Ziff-Davis
and 1,200 more...

Get More and Better Press Coverage!
To get a FREE MediaMap PR Research Report, a FREE software
Demo disk, and a $50 voucher, Just call 888-624-1620.

August 28

Ms. Margot E Lewis
COMMUNICOMP
340 N Fig Tree Ln
Plantation, FL 33317-2561

Dear Margot,

As a PR professional, you are eligible to receive a FREE MediaMap Research Report
and a FREE software demo disk. Respond by September 30 and get a $50 voucher
good towards a purchase of MediaMap products and services. Find out how MediaMap
clients use our "different kind of media research" combined with MediaMap PR Software to
achieve better PR results in less time. In short, MediaMap clients get more and better press
coverage with less effort.

Detailed, Accurate Information about Reporters...
WORK SMARTER, GET MORE INK.
MediaMap provides 1,200+ agencies, corporate PR organizations, and associations with
incredibly detailed and accurate information about the media in key markets. This research is
coupled with the breadth of coverage from Bacon's to provide you with a very different kind
of media intelligence solution. Reporters will more often take the time to listen because you
have taken the time to understand what they really want (before you get on the phone).
Respond now and get a free MediaMap Research Report and a free software demo disk.
The Research Report gives you essential:

- Tips on working with the publication.
- Inside information on reporters' areas of coverage.
- Recommendations on the best method for contacting the editors.
- Editorial calendars for all publications that issue them.

The software demo disk introduces the power of MediaMap's customized PR database
software, which features:

- List building and maintenance.
- Editorial calendar tracking.
- Note sharing among users.
- Mail merging, labels, and e-mail dissemination at the touch of a button.

(over)

Fig. 8.18　(letter opening number 17) *As* isn't a potent first word of a letter, but this is a clear example of number 17,
"Because you are who you are, you may get special attention."

"invitation" any more than a note from a club or a human resources director or a college, agreeing to look over your application, is an invitation.

See that word *may* lurking in the first sentence? It makes the offer equivocal . . . which is what we want to do if we aren't certain of the applicant's credentials. This publication, like all controlled-circulation publications, analyzes the application and then sends one of two messages: either number 16, which we just discussed; or a "We're sorry, but . . ." letter rejecting the applicant and "inviting" him or her to become a paid subscriber.

18.   STROKE, STROKE—YOU'RE A RARE BIRD.

If you think many sales letters begin with flattery, you're right. After all, every one of these samples is based on the hope of doing business, and flattery does outpull insults, doesn't it?

A "Stroke, stroke" opening can become treacly and oleaginous. I don't recommend it on the executive level because if the recipient immediately pierces the phoniness you're better off sending a bald offer without a letter. "You're a rare bird" works best among the less sophisticated.

So this example, which combines stroking with an obvious lack of information about the recipient, is the wrong way to begin this particular sales pitch:

Chief Executive Officer

Communicomp

Dear Executive:

You are a member of a company made up of high achievers. As such, you know how a little recognition goes a long way to encourage ever-greater levels of performance.

Citation Directories, Ltd. is offering your company yet another way to reward employees for outstanding accomplishments—in the professional arena as well as within your community. **And, the cost to you is 15 minutes of your time.**

We publish **Citation's Who's Who Registry of Rising Young Americans**, an annual directory dedicated to recognizing those individuals with superior potential for contributing to the future of American business. . . .

What's wrong here isn't the vanity aspect of a directory that, if every recipient used all five nomination blanks, could fill a five-foot shelf. No problem with that, from a promotional point of view. No, the problem lies in using *this* approach for *this* recipient.

0002047-03

Alfred F. Kelly, Jr.
Executive Vice President
and General Manager

Margo E. Lewis
340 N Fig Tree Ln.
Plantation, FL 33317-2561

Dear Margo E. Lewis,

In an age when athletes jump from team to team and consumers switch brands just as
fast, your loyalty to American Express is something we have never taken for granted.
And never will.

As an American Express® Cardmember since 1978, you have my deepest thanks for your
ongoing commitment to our company. What's more, I want to make a personal pledge to
you that we will continue to make your membership more useful, more relevant, and more
exciting in the years ahead.

As we celebrate the 40th anniversary of the original American Express Card, we're thankful we have Cardmembers like you. And as an expression of our gratitude, we have added
2,500 *Membership Rewards*® points to your *Membership Rewards* account.

I realize that the market continues to provide you with other choices. But I am committed
to making sure that American Express Card membership always provides you with
increasingly unique benefits and a level of personal service and responsiveness that simply
doesn't exist with any other charge or credit card.

Once again, thank you for sharing the past 20 years with us. We look forward to
sharing many more.

Sincerely,

Alfred F. Kelly, Jr.

Alfred F. Kelly, Jr.
Member Since '81

AMERICAN EXPRESS Cards

PL 7/98

Fig. 8.19   (letter opening number 18) Can you overstroke a reader? Maybe, but not easily. Flattery, provided the reader doesn't think he or she is being patronized, can't miss.

0035215-30

Alfred F Kelly, Jr.
Executive Vice President
and General Manager

Herschell G. Lewis
340 N Fig Tree Ln.
Plantation, FL 33317-2561

Dear Herschell G. Lewis,

In an age when athletes jump from team to team and consumers switch brands just as
fast, your loyalty to American Express is something we have never taken for granted.
And never will.

As an American Express® Cardmember since 1966, you have my deepest thanks for your
ongoing commitment to our company. What's more, I want to make a personal pledge to
you that we will continue to make your membership more useful, more relevant, and more
exciting in the years ahead.

As we celebrate the 40th anniversary of the original American Express Card, we're thankful
to have Cardmembers like you. I realize that the market continues to provide you with other
choices. But I am committed to making sure that American Express Card membership
always provides you with increasingly unique benefits and a level of personal service and
responsiveness that simply doesn't exist with any other charge or credit card.

Once again, thank you for sharing the past 32 years with us. We look forward to sharing
many more.

Sincerely,

Alfred F. Kelly, Jr.
Member Since '81

AMERICAN EXPRESS Cards

PL 7/98

Fig. 8.20 (letter opening number 18) Compare this letter with figure 8.19. See the difference? This one doesn't supplement the stroking with "Membership Rewards®" points, even though the individual has been a Cardmember twelve years longer than the other Cardmember. Is a puzzlement.

If you say, "But the sender couldn't know who would be the letter recipient," I reply, "Exactly." That's why a "Stroke, stroke—You're a Rare Bird" opening is dangerous when mailed at random. Save this one for those who either (a) will believe they're rare birds or (b) will believe you have a genuine reason to know they're rare birds.

19. HERE'S WHAT THE EXPERTS SAY.

This is a no-nonsense opening, and that's why I like it for business-to-business mailings. Sometimes it appears cold-blooded because it gets directly to the point; this means the writer has to consider not only who gets this message but what the state of mind probably will be at the time of receipt.

One danger: "Here's what the experts say" too often is followed by self-applause without substance. If that's your approach then *don't* inflict it on business-mail recipients. Dedicate applause without substance only to consumers—preferably downscale ones, at that. Heed this warning, relative to business targets: Unless what the experts say relates to the reader, don't waste your paper.

Here's a typical "Here's what the experts say" opening. Note that it jumps in without prelude; with a prelude, it isn't this type of opening:

Dear Windows Resource Kit owner:

Windows User Magazine voted it the **Best Windows Utility of the year**.

PC Magazine says it's " . . . essential . . . hard to imagine running Windows without it."

PC Computing says it's " . . . a lean and mean program-launching machine that should be found on every Windows user's computer. . . ."

See that third encomium? " . . . program-launching machine"? This is a specific, which gives the reader some meat to chew.

20. WHY ARE WE DOING THIS?

"Why are we doing this?" belongs to a group of openings which hurl down the gauntlet in front of the reader. Rather than establishing conviviality with an opening such as "I have a question for you," or "As you know," this one *assumes* the recipient starts reading with an apathetic or adversarial attitude . . . and therein lies its strength.

A "Why are we doing this?" opening often is tied to a seemingly incredible admission, accusation, offer, or gift. And, I submit, it's one best left untouched by dilettantes. Like opening number 4, "Suggest a

THE BUSINESS OF TECHNOLOGY

*"God gave me the stubbornness of a mule
and a fairly keen scent"*

Albert Einstein

Dear Technology Executive,

When I came across this quote from Albert Einstein the other day my first thought was how much it reminded me of *Red Herring* and its readers.

If you could back them into a corner most *Herring* readers would sound as off-handed about what they've accomplished as Einstein does. But their collective résumé reads like a who's who of technology and innovation. And more than a handful of them will gladly tell you that the *Herring* is their favorite read.

So, on the theory that there are a few more readers out there like them, I'm writing to invite you to sample the *Herring* at no risk whatsoever.

A magazine unlike any other.

If there had been a magazine like the *Herring* on the stands back in 1993, I doubt I'd be writing this letter.

But there wasn't. So Tony Perkins and Chris Alden, who know a business opportunity when they see one, emptied their piggy banks, rented an office and started putting their vision between covers.

<u>From the beginning their focus was absolutely clear: to cover the business of technology and innovation in ways it wasn't being covered. The *Herring* was to be a magazine with global perspective, written for industry professionals and investors who needed reliable information and informed analysis on the business.</u>

I think they wanted to publish the kind of magazine they'd subscribe to themselves...mule-stubborn in its pursuit of the news...with the "fairly keen scent" Einstein spoke of. It would be first with the news because it would report on companies still in their incubation stage.

Fig. 8.21 (letter opening number 19) The effectiveness of "Here's what the experts say" is in direct ratio to the reader's acceptance of those quoted as experts. Who can quarrel with Albert Einstein?

cataclysmic decision," "Why are we doing this?" demands the professional laying on of hands.

An example of this type of opening, in which a shiny new penny was glued to the letter:

Dear Mr. Johnson,

Why have I enclosed this FREE penny?

Because it represents the introduction of a NEW Medicare Supplement Insurance Policy that completely eliminates every penny of your out-of-pocket doctor expenses for all Medicare covered services. . . .

I'd have dropped the underlining as used and saved it for every penny to point up the parallel with the free coin.

21.   THIS IS DISGUSTING AND YOU'RE THE ONE TO FIX IT.

As you evaluate this opening, you have to think of what's wrong, not what's right. Yes, yes, positives usually outsell negatives; but *guilt* is a potent motivator, and looking back at opening number 5, "We need help" or opening number 14, "Fire!," we've approached but not equaled this one—guilt PLUS anger. Wow!

Opening number 21 is aptly numbered because it's geared to the twenty-first century. Its strength comes from anger, not a plea. We don't have a kinder, gentler society; your dog has to eat their dog. What this opening has is guts, and we admire guts.

An example of this opening is a letter from an environmentally aimed fund-raising group. The letter begins (regrettably after a far too long typed three-paragraph overline which diminishes its impact):

Dear Friend,

Our world is drowning in filth. Garbage covers the land, and toxins seep into our groundwater and our homes. Our cities sprawl beneath skies awash with a brown haze. . . .

This writer starts with guts and shifts to poetry. Uh-uh. You don't set a charge of dynamite and then pull out the wire. "Our cities sprawl beneath skies awash with a brown haze" isn't gritty enough to qualify for this opening.

Understand, please: The writer may not have wanted a full-scale "This is disgusting and you're the one to fix it" opening. If he or she had, the wording might have been . . .

Our world is drowning in filth. It's up to troubled citizens like you to do something about the garbage in the streets, the drinking water poisoned by chemicals, the smog that half blinds you and deposits ugly black soot on your windows....

If I had my druthers, I'd pick our opening over theirs because the key to making anger work for you is *staying in character*. (That's true of every role we actors play. Stanley Kowalski doesn't say, "Oh, what a rogue and peasant slave am I.")

22. WE'VE GOT BAD NEWS . . . AND WE'VE GOT GOOD NEWS.

I like this one because it's an irresistible grabber. Every one of us has had this phone call: "I've got good news for you and bad news for you. Which do you want first?"

In a letter opening, we usually go just one way: bad news first. Why? Because stating a problem, then giving the solution, is far more potent that stating the solution, then explaining what the solution covers.

The exception: when the bad news brings relief.

A classic example of the "bad news first" opening is a letter from a paper company (compare it with the "good news first" counterexample in the analysis of opening number 23):

The bad news is ...

I'm sure you've heard many bad news/good news stories over the years. Well, here's a bad news/good news story that can be quite beneficial for you.

The bad news is Weyerhaeuser no longer manufactures Cougar Laser Opaque. The good news is we've replaced it with not one, but two new guaranteed laser compatible papers....

The disappearance of Cougar Laser Opaque is hardly life threatening. That's why this opening works. It pulls pedestrian information out of the "so what" muck and tags it with a magic wand.

23. GOOD NEWS!

This opening isn't at all related to the one we just explored. "Good news!" is a one-string fiddle, a straightforward pitch. The reader recognizes it as a pitch from the first handful of words.

If "We've got bad news . . . and we've got good news" is a rocket among openers, "Good news!" is a sturdy bicycle. "Bad news/good news" requires sophistication from both writer and reader; "Good news!" operates on an uncomplicated plane.

ACUITY

Herschell G. Lewis
C.E.O.
Commincomp
340 N.Fig Tree Ln.
Plantation, FL 33317

Dear Herschell G.,

Have you heard the great news? WebCenter 2.0 from Acuity Corporation has been named . . .

** 1998 C@ll Center Solutions Editors' Choice **

WebCenter was recognized for "providing companies with a comprehensive Web call center solution that integrates with existing technologies." First the Internet changed the way companies do business, and now the Internet is now changing the way companies interact with their customers. WebCenter is leading the way! WebCenter delivers a complete solution for web-based customer interaction; enabling companies to slash support costs through self-service and improve customer satisfaction through live Internet help.

> *"Between now and the year 2000, companies that implement Internet-based service will slash their call-center labor costs by 43%. Without Internet solutions, the same labor costs would likely rise by 3%."*
> **-- Forrester Research Inc.**

WebCenter delivers dramatic return on investment with increased customer choice, intimacy, and satisfaction. Don't be left behind as Acuity and WebCenter pave the way for web-based customer interaction.

> *"It's about reinventing customer service and being very responsive and seamless. The ability to provide support in the same medium as the product is really satisfying."*
> **--Rick Washburn, Managing Director of Executive Automation, Charles Schwab & Co., an Acuity customer**

Included with this letter is the article from *C@ll Center Solutions* magazine describing WebCenter. Call now or visit our website to receive a FREE WebCenter Whitepaper and an Acuity T-shirt! You can contact us at 888.242.8669 or http://www.acuity.com/webcenter/803.

Sincerely,

Dean Cruse
Vice-President of Marketing
Acuity Corporation

11190 Metric Blvd

Building Seven

Austin, Texas 78758

512 425 2200

fax 512 719 8225

www.acuity.com

a Delaware Corporation

Fig. 8.22   (letter opening number 23) Good news is always welcome. This example typifies the difference between number 10, "I have something good for you" and "Good news!" Just one giant problem here: good news for *whom*?

The benefit of "Good news!" is its universality. The danger of "Good news" is using it and then falling flat with self-serving information that may be good news for the message sender but not for the message recipient.

An easy rule to follow: As you write the first paragraph following your proclamation of good news, ask yourself, dispassionately and cold-bloodedly, "If I were getting this instead of sending it, would I think it's good news?"

A laser-personalized letter from a university begins . . .

Dear Mr. Lewis:

Do you want to hear some *good* news?

Twenty-three months ago we got a very special person, Dr. Denis Waitley, on the calendar. If you know of him, you probably will want to skip the rest of this letter and simply call in for your tickets for the November 20 Florida International University "Lessons in Leadership" program....

See what I mean? Yes, I've heard of Denis Waitley. No, I can't "hear" some good news by reading a letter. And yes, yes, yes, the "Good news!" opening is a misfit for this communication. This letter should have tied the information to another opening. Even the one we just discussed, "We've got bad news . . . and we've got good news," would work better, using the "good first" exception. Our version might begin like this:

Dear Mr. Lewis, [I prefer commas.]

I've got good news . . . and I've got bad news.

The good news is that we've been able to convince the renowned Dr. Denis Waitley to present his "Lessons in Leadership" program here, November 20. The bad news is that seats are *very* limited.

The example points up the difference between opening number 22 and opening number 23.

24. ARE YOU PAYING TOO MUCH?

This opening is loaded with power because it combines absolute one-to-one personalization, an immediate reader-involving question, and an appeal to greed.

This recognition should lead to a second recognition—whatever follows is a *comparative* pitch. If you want to be gentlemanly or ladylike, this opening is not for you.

Here's an example of the "Are you paying too much?" opening. It's an execrable example. Can you tell why?

Dear Mr. Sax:

Are you paying too much for your life insurance?

The Multifunding Agency has made arrangements to offer term[*] life insurance at a substantially reduced rate. This outstanding opportunity is available to non-smoking clients[**] who also qualify as select health risks....

The first line is a grabber, a classic use of this opening. But ugh! Asterisks all over the place . . . immediate lapsing into obvious puffery ("outstanding opportunity") . . . referring to the targets as "select health risks."

For heaven's sake, with this or *any* opening, STAY IN CHARACTER. If you or I had written the letter, we'd have maintained the tone and pace of the gauntlet-hurling opening:

Dear Mr. Sax,

Are you paying too much for your life insurance?

You bet you are, if you're paying more than the rates you'll see on this page. You wouldn't knowingly over-pay for a car or a magazine or a computer. Why overpay for insurance? . . .

The opening of a letter is a supercharged Harley-Davidson. You wouldn't use a Harley as an exercycle. Open up that throttle and barrel down the highway.

25.   Did you know . . . *or* Do you know . . .

"Did you know" is another question opening that's implicitly reader-involving. It's one of the easiest openings to construct . . . and that means it's one of the most misused.

The writer who starts a letter with "Did you know" or "Do you know" has to be sure to key whatever follows to the reader as fact, not puffery. And even though present tense ordinarily outpulls past tense, for this opening "Did you know" is usually more appropriate for two reasons: (1) Logic says this is information the reader didn't have before and now will have; (2) "Do you know" is more quizlike, giving the writer an Olympian position the reader may dislike.

An example of this opening:

Dear Business Reader . . .

Did you know that *Investor's Business Daily* is now the "Hottest Business Newspaper in America"?

It's all new with 68 features added in just the last 12 months (we've even changed the name) . . . subscriptions and advertising are up, while older Wall Street publications are down. . . .

———————————

This letter would be stronger if it had observed the rule of "Did you know" openings and followed those three words with fact, not puffery. Example:

———————————

Did you know *Investor's Business Daily* subscriptions and advertising are *up* . . . and the older Wall Street publications are *down*?

———————————

That's the batch for this chapter. Openings 26 to 50 are in chapter 9.

9

25 More Ways to Start a Letter— Openings 26 to 50

In this chapter:

(An asterisk means applicable to e-mail.)

26. *Have you ever wished . . .*

27. *You're in trouble [You and I are in trouble], and this is what you'd better do.* *

28. *Why do they . . .* or *Why don't they . . .*

29. *I've enclosed . . .*

30. *Here's the sermon for today.*

31. *We've missed you.* *

32. *We're solving your tough problem.* *

33. *This is short and sweet.* *

34. *Believe it or not.*

35. *I know who you are.* *

36. *Because you're "A" you're also "B."*

37. *Historical buildup*

38. *You just might be (and probably are) . . .* *

39. *I'll get right to the point.*

40. *These are critical times.*

41. Visualize this scenario. *

42. If you like that, you'll love this. *

43. Whether you do this . . . or do that . . .

44. The classic quotation

45. I have to tell you the truth. *

46. You're important to us. *

47. Now you can . . . or At last! *

48. They think I'm nuts! *

49. Before you do that, do this.

50. Wouldn't it be lovely if . . .

The second twenty-five are workmanlike ways to start a sales letter. Properly used, they're all reader involving. Another benefit: most are relatively easy to create.

26.   HAVE YOU EVER WISHED . . .

This lyrical opening can penetrate defenses which leap into position against more hard-boiled attacks.

In use, too often even the most professional practitioners shoot a coat of dulling spray over "Have you ever wished" by having an introduction so long, tedious, or dynamic the opening itself becomes ancillary instead of primary—a harsh switching of gears.

Don't do that. Harshness destroys wistfulness.

I'm looking at a letter selling computer software. The actual letter begins:

Dear Friend,

Have you ever wished that you could produce incredible looking documents, construct bigger than life posters, build dazzling looking slide presentations—or even touch-up photographs and drawings, just like a world class graphic artist might do?

A workmanlike job—although I'd have hyphenated "incredible-looking," "bigger-than-life," and "world-class," taken the hyphen out of "touch up," and dumped the weak "looking" after "dazzling." These are tweakings, not objections. The opening does stand up.

P R E N T I C E   H A L L
Business & Professional Publishing
240 Frisch Court • Paramus, NJ 07652
A division of Simon & Schuster • http://www.phdirect.com

Mr. Herschell G. Lewis
Communicorp, Inc.
P.O. Box 15725
Ft Lauderdale, FL 33318-5725
lıllıılllıılllıuıllllılılılılıuıılılılılıuıllllılıllıl

Proven advertising strategies
and techniques <u>guaranteed</u> to
<u>increase</u> <u>sales</u> and make it
<u>faster</u> and <u>easier</u> to create ads.
Use them <u>FREE</u> for 30 days!

Dear Mr. Lewis:

Have you ever wished for a "magic formula" that would enable you to produce powerful ads <u>guaranteed</u> to produce results, every time? A proven process so easy to apply that your ads would practically write and design themselves?

Well, there <u>is</u> such a formula. You'll find it in a powerful resource that condenses an acclaimed advertising expert's six decades of acquired sales wisdom and award-winning ideas into one essential volume that's been hailed as the "bible of modern advertising." Now updated and revised to reflect the challenges of today's competitive marketplace, it's called

TESTED ADVERTISING METHODS
by John Caples, revised by Fred E. Hahn

This best-selling advertising tool takes the time-and-effort-wasting guesswork out of creating ads, streamlining your creative process and turning it into a precise science of predictable -- and profitable -- results. It shows you what works, what doesn't, and why. Most importantly, it's packed with strategies and techniques designed to help you produce <u>more</u> effective ads in <u>less</u> time.

You'll find step-by-step guidelines and creative shortcuts for selling both products and services in any medium, plus methods you can put to work <u>immediately</u> to write a powerful headline ... increase the selling power of your copy ... create layouts that demand attention ... write a first paragraph that hooks the reader ... design small ads that get big results ... and test and improve your ads. You'll also find key words and phrases that boost response ... appeals that inspire action ... tips on fine-tuning offers ... and much more.

**Discover how Easy it Can Be to Create Dynamic Ads that Command Attention
and Demand a Response -- <u>Absolutely FREE for 30 Days</u>!**

I invite you to send for your FREE-trial copy of this new edition of a powerful advertising tool. Simply print your name on the 30-Day FREE-Trial Invitation below, detach it and return it to us in the enclosed postpaid envelope. When your copy arrives, put it to every test you can think of and start creating headlines that attract customers, layouts that grab attention, and copy that produces results. Then, after 30 days, just honor the accompanying invoice. If, however, the book is not <u>everything</u> you thought it would be, return it and pay nothing, owe nothing.

Sincerely,

Richard B Hopkins

Richard B. Hopkins

P.S. Remember, there is absolutely no obligation to buy. Order your 30-day, risk-free copy to examine and use today!

CYA/B

Fig. 9.1 (letter opening number 26) "Have you ever wished" has great power if what follows is loaded with dynamite. What follows here is on the long and involved side, but for the proper targets it qualifies. A more concise opening might have had more punch: "Have you ever wished that your ads could write and design themselves?"

But this opening doesn't start until two-thirds of the way down the page. A batch of rock-'em, sock-'em display type above the greeting shouts:

Now Two *PC Magazine's* Editors' Choice

Award-Winning Software Programs can be yours ...

Get three of the world's easiest to use desktop publishing packages, bundled together **for only $49.95!**

You save $527 off the price [**and on it goes** ...]

A legend above a "Have you ever wished" greeting isn't damaging per se; it's damaging when it's exclamatory. When you're writing a letter, pretend you're in a play. Who are you? Stay in character.

"Have you ever wished" is a natural for travel, investments, fund-raising, and self-improvement. Its most attractive virtue is that it's easy to write.

27.   YOU'RE IN TROUBLE [YOU AND I ARE IN TROUBLE], AND THIS IS WHAT YOU'D BETTER DO.

This opening differs from number 21, "This is disgusting and you're the one to fix it," because "You're in trouble" is a direct accusation of existing involvement instead of a command for post-trouble involvement.

"You're in trouble" or "You and I are in trouble" is loaded with dynamite, and that should be a caution as well as a challenge. The driver of a dynamite truck usually gets a bonus for safe delivery . . . and a funeral for steering into an accident.

As you undoubtedly already concluded, this opening explodes with force when used for fund-raising and politics. The first sentence should include the word *your* or *our*.

A fund-raising letter begins:

Right now, our oceans are in serious trouble. Coral reefs, the marine equivalent of tropical rain forests, are dying. Beaches are fouled by oil spills and wastes. Fisheries are in decline. Many species of sea mammals are in danger of extinction.

Is this an example of opening number 27? Partly. In my opinion the writer decided to soften the opening. Softening also softens personal impact, and softening personal impact reduces response, and that's the way we keep score. We might have opened the letter this way (see page 181):

AT&T

AT&T Universal Card

**Do you know *what's* on
your Credit Report and
who put it there?**

FIND OUT FOR FREE!
**Initial and return the enclosed
Release Form right away.**

Dear AT&T Universal Card Member,

Last month *someone* may have added inaccurate information to *your* Credit Report.

Do you know if they did? Chances are you don't, and that's precisely why I'm writing to you today.

**When you initial and return the enclosed
Release Form, you will receive the materials you need to
obtain a confidential copy of your Credit Report – Free.**

Why is it important for you to see your Credit Report?

Because *other people and organizations* are constantly adding information to it. And, since credit approval is often determined by what your Credit Report says about you, <u>it's important that you review it for accuracy.</u>

Providing you with a **Free** copy of your Credit Report is our way of introducing you to the valuable protection available through PrivacyGuard®.

Knowledge is power. By giving you a **Free** copy of your Credit Report, PrivacyGuard *puts you in the know* about the very personal records available to your employer, insurers, credit card companies, and government agencies -- helping you protect your credit rating.

For the next three months, compliments of PrivacyGuard, you'll now have access to the **4 most important areas** of confidential information about <u>you</u>.

1) <u>**Your Credit Record:**</u> Get a complete picture of your credit status and payment patterns in one easy-to-understand document that combines data from all three national credit bureaus on all your credit cards, mortgages, and loans.

2) <u>**Your Driving Report:**</u> See the official Motor Vehicle Report that helps insurers determine your auto insurance rates, including all reported violations and even out-of-state tickets.

3) <u>**Your Social Security Record:**</u> Know how much you're entitled to at retirement, plus learn about health and death/disability coverage for you and your family.

4) <u>**Your Medical History:**</u> Find out what insurance companies, the government, and other non-medical personnel know about your health -- and exactly who has asked to see your file, if you have one at the Medical Information Bureau.

L2841-1101

(Over, please)

Fig. 9.2   (letter opening number 27) One of the most compelling openings is "You're in trouble, and this is what you'd better do" because this opening is as personal and as promising as you can write. Note the word *may* in the first sentence—an unavoidable weakener, obviously necessary here. A powerful substitute: "Last month, did someone add inaccurate information to your Credit Report?"

Cards

> If you need extra time to pay for a large purchase, you can still use the Card <u>and</u> earn *Membership Rewards* points.

Margo E. Lewis
340 N. Fig Tree Lane
Plantation, FL 33317-2561

Կ␣ll␣ll␣␣ll␣␣ll␣␣llll␣␣ll␣ll␣ll

Dear Ms. Lewis:

Have you ever made a major purchase with another card rather than the American Express® Card because you weren't sure you wanted to pay for it all in one month? If so, you may have sacrificed thousands of valuable *Membership Rewards* program points for the wrong reason—points that could have put you much closer to free travel or other rewards.

You get more payment flexibility and more *Membership Rewards* points.

Just use the form below to sign up for the Special Purchase Account℠ feature of the American Express Card. Once you do, every Card purchase of $350 or more will appear on a special portion of your monthly statement. You will have the option of paying just the minimum due on these special purchases, the entire balance, or any amount in between. As long as you continue to pay your balance in full, you accrue no finance charges.

<u>But whether you choose to pay in full or over time, you'll continue to earn one *Membership Rewards* point for each dollar charged</u> as long as the Card you use is enrolled in the *Membership Rewards* program.

Add 1,250 <u>bonus</u> *Membership Rewards* points to your balance.

Return the form below by November 20 to sign up for the Special Purchase Account. There is no fee to enroll. <u>And there's no pre-set spending limit.</u> As always, your Card purchases are approved based on a variety of factors, including your account history, credit record, and personal resources.

As never before, you'll have added control over when and how quickly to pay. And you'll receive 1,250 bonus *Membership Rewards* points just for enrolling. But that's nothing compared to the thousands more you can earn by comfortably charging your large purchases to the Card.

Sincerely,

Alfred F. Kelly, Jr.

Alfred F. Kelly, Jr.
General Manager, Consumer Cards

SPECIAL PURCHASE ACCOUNT

RMRF-998   RMRL-998   (If you have recently responded, thank you.)   02-11-0158411

Fig. 9.3 (letter opening number 27) This qualifies as a "You're in trouble" opening, but just barely. It's equally close to "You made a mistake." The sender's awareness of corporate image softens the message; a smaller, more aggressive competitor might have been more straightforward.

We're in trouble, you and I. Our oceans are dying. Yes, *dying*. Look at any beach. Chances are it's fouled by oil spills and wastes. Fish can't even breed. Sea mammals? Take a good look while you can because a few years from now they might be added to the melancholy list of extinct species.

Please understand: I'm not criticizing the letter because whoever wrote it didn't write it the way I would have; I'm just explaining how this *semi*-"You're in trouble" opening can be shifted to a full-scale "You're in trouble" opening.

28. WHY DO THEY . . . *OR* WHY DON'T THEY . . .

Don't regard "Why don't they" as a parallel for "Why don't *you*." The difference is immediate and potent: "Why do they" or "Why don't they" places you arm in arm with the message sender; you're co-gripers. "Why don't you" establishes the message sender as either coach or critic.

"Why don't you" is a cousin of an opening we've already discussed, number 15, "What I want you to do is." It's more imperative, which can make it more rejectable.

But "Why do or don't they" has the wonderful capacity to place you, together with the writer, above "those people." Rapport is implicit, ergo instant.

An example of a "Why do or don't they" opening:

Dear Marketing Professional:

Exasperating, aren't they?

I'm talking about human beings. Americans. Consumers. The public. The markets. The crazy-making jury out there you're paid to understand—and whose whims and flights of fancy you're rewarded for predicting.

Just what *do* they want? And what will they want tomorrow?

You can see the immediate advantage of this opening. The reader knows an imperative is on the way, but it's padded and softened and covered with downy feathers.

(As used in this example, the opening loses impact because too much claptrap precedes the greeting. *Before* "Exasperating, aren't they?" we have this text: "Why do people buy what they buy? Two reasons, according to one marketing guru: 'To get what they don't have—and to keep what they've got.'" Marketing guru? Marketing cliché expert is a better title.)

Consider the "Why do or don't they" opening when you want readers to superimpose an attitude they won't reject, or to ridicule a competitor mildly instead of fiercely.

29.   I'VE ENCLOSED . . .

"I've enclosed" is a straightforward, businesslike opening. This makes it a logical beginning for a letter accompanying samples, evidence, or validation.

The opening isn't parallel to number 8, "I have a free gift for you," or number 10, "I have something good for you," each of which specifies benefit *before* naming what's enclosed (or more frequently, promised).

"I've enclosed" gets to the point immediately, so it's more straightforward and less emotional than an opening which states a problem, then offers a solution to that problem. Frankly, I'm puzzled to see fund-raisers using "I've enclosed."

Let's revisit the example from number 4, "Suggest a cataclysmic decision." I'm guessing this opening from a major nonprofit organization was supposed to have an emotional wallop. Remember it?

Dear Friend,

I've enclosed a Life or Death Seed Catalog for you.

I call this the Life or Death Seed Catalog because what you do after looking through the catalog could help save the life of a small child . . . a child like Youssouf.

Youssouf is a little boy who. . . .

Had they asked me, I'd have tied an acknowledgment of the mismatch into the mix:

Dear Friend of [NAME OF ORGANIZATION],

I know it's hard to believe. But what you do with the little seed catalog I've enclosed could literally make the difference between life and death for a helpless child.

Within the "enclosed" framework, explaining *why* immediately establishes a more emotional, more motivational opener. "Why have I enclosed . . . ?" is a variation of number 20, "Why are we doing this?"

Compare the potency if the writer had started the appeal with a "Why" opening:

Why am I sending you a seed catalog . . . and why do we call it the Life or Death Seed Catalog?

Because a few seeds literally might mean the difference between life and death for a little boy. The seeds you buy for him might mean he'll still be alive next year.

But suppose we ignore altogether that unfortunate appellation, "Life or Death Seed Catalog," which before we even get into the letter makes us uncomfortable (not guilty) with an unpleasant challenge—Dracula plants sprouting and blooming only at the stroke of midnight. We're discussing letter openings, not product psychology.

An "If" opening would be completely safe as a substitute:

If you'll buy a few packets of seeds, a little boy in Mali might live another year.

Those seeds are for *him* to plant. If they sprout, he won't starve. It's as simple as that.

Can you see the difference in both impact and rapport the choice of letter openings can make? With such a huge menu, why choose an appetizer the reader finds distasteful?

30.　HERE'S THE SERMON FOR TODAY.

What a dangerous instrument this opening is!

In my opinion, sermons are best left to the clergy. They can get a reaction no outsider could ever induce because they address the Captive Willing Guilty. Anyone who shows up for a religious service expects a sermon and is schooled to respect the person delivering the sermon, if not the content.

But how about sermonizing in a nonsectarian ambience? Will readers think you're making assumptions on their behalf and reject those assumptions, even though they may be true? Worse, will readers doze off during your sermon because they are preconditioned to regard sermons as dull?

Those are the dangers. As an example:

Dear Herschell Lewis:

Making the right decisions on your business travel policies requires a thorough grasp of what's happening in the marketplace. Widely considered the definitive source for information from T&E experts, *The American Express Survey of Business Travel Management can be invaluable in optimizing your travel invest-ment.* Published only once every two years, the Survey gives you an inside look at the travel policies of America's corporations thanks to interviews with over 1300 top travel executives.

Snor-r-r-r-e.

Look at that stultifying opening sentence: "Making the right decisions on your business travel policies requires a thorough grasp of what's happening in the marketplace." Aside from the "Huh?"-inducing rhetoric, the sentence uses the word *policies*, which invites multiple interpretations.

The sermonlike aspect of this opening, unbacked by specifics, turns the reader away. If we had any specifics, we might suggest replacing the sermon with number 19, "Here's what the experts say," the yet-to-come number 65, "Here's the deal," number 79, "You want it. We have it," or even number 94, "Why do you need this?" But we don't have any specifics; so what if, instead of a sermon, the letter opened with a gauntlet-casting question:

Are you making the right management decisions about your company's travel practices? Are you *sure*?

Now you can have an *inside* look at what 1300 other top travel executives are doing....

Sermons do work when the sermonizer and the sermonizee are in sync. For mailings, I suggest saving this approach for continuation or resuscitation of an existing relationship. Example:

Trouble. It's just around the corner. Trouble comes from having to "fly by the seat of your pants" in a tough, competitive business climate. That's what faces you, unless ...

---

31. WE'VE MISSED YOU.

A cliché? You bet. Effective? Usually . . . in two separate directions, geared to the sophistication of the reader.

"We've missed you" as a mass appeal to dormant customers works best within the lower echelons of buyers. An appeal which is recognizably bulk in creative approach isn't state-of-the-art; but to lower levels, or greedy former buyers, it's an old dependable, working like a Heimlich maneuver.

On a business-to-business or executive level, don't you dare let the look of a mass mailing peek through. To these targets, "We've missed you" has to be one-on-one, with a hand-finished look. If you can't do this, don't waste the postage.

Oh, a second qualifier: If you can't tie "We've missed you" to a special resuscitation offer, don't waste the postage.

A video club uses—quite properly—the mass approach, complete with Johnson Box. (As mentioned in chapter 3, I've come to regard Johnson Boxes as *de*personalizers.) A truly personal "We've missed you" to somebody who dropped a negative-option video deal would seem gushy and phony.

Under the Johnson Box is another bulk line, printed in Goudy hand-tooled typeface:

Take Any 6 Movies for 39¢ each

Okay, we now know this isn't going to be a personal "We've missed you." Here's the opening:

Dear H. Gordon:

You're the kind of individual any company would be proud to have as a customer. And we've missed you since you left us. And because of the responsible way you handled your Columbia House membership privileges, you have been selected to receive this special V.I.P. "welcome back" savings offer reserved *exclusively* for special friends of Columbia House....

This is the way to do it, all right. "We've missed you" doesn't generate any commiseration unless it's tied to the opportunity to get *Titanic* for thirty-nine cents.

32. WE'RE SOLVING YOUR TOUGH PROBLEM.

This opening is tricky, because problem-solvers tend to emit a self-serving aura. Result: The person with the problem becomes resentful rather than grateful.

Here's where the writer has to hope either the database is accurate or the message recipient isn't sensitive. Here, too, is an opportunity for light-hearted, nonpreachy solutions to nonthreatening problems.

The handwritten overline on a letter:

Your search for "the perfect gift" is *over!*

Not the stuff awards are made of, but the overline does serve a purpose: it tips off the reader that what follows won't raise hackles. Reading the greeting—"Dear Struggling Holiday Gift Shopper"—we can see how the handwritten overline tempers our reaction to the greeting itself. Proof? Visualize "Dear Struggling Holiday Gift Shopper" without that overline. Presumptuous, isn't it? The overline douses the negative fire.

The letter then begins:

Finding just the right gift for those special people on your holiday gift list can be tough. Especially if they live out of town, certainly if they "have everything," and most assuredly if they're people of discriminating taste.

This year, why not give a truly unique gift ... one they're not likely to find in any store ... a gift that will stimulate, challenge and delight the mind ... one that is *guaranteed* to please every puzzle enthusiast on your list! *Give the gift of membership in the Crossword Puzzles of the Month Club—a gift that keeps on giving all year long!*

SIXTY YEARS

I.C.SYSTEM

July 20

Herschell G. Lewis
President
COMMUNICOMP
340 North Fig Tree Lane
Plantation, FL 33317

Dear Mr. Lewis:

You can't just think about matching the competition, you've got to outwit, outthink and
outgun them at every opportunity.

It's not simple...but there is help. I.C. System has the real-world experience to help you put an
aggressive marketing program into action, and use it wisely to get a jump on the competition.

Our primary objective is to provide intelligent solutions that help our clients realize the highest
profits possible from their direct marketing efforts. We have the resources that will enhance
your ability to defend current markets and attack new ones by focusing on the strengths you
bring to the marketplace. We have the resources and expertise to define customer behavior,
wants and needs that will pinpoint their leading decision-making factors -- issues critical to
your company's success in the months and years ahead. We will help you outmanuever the
competition by finding and using marketing intelligence in every key area.

I.C. System has been in business for sixty years. As the marketing and sales resource in this
area, I am available to help you develop real-world strategies that will work for your
company. Together, we can increase "brand loyalty" with your existing customers, lay claim
to new customers, and increase profitability.

Team up with a business partner that knows the ropes. I welcome the opportunity to introduce
you to the people and services of I.C. System. Please contact me at 651-481-6369 or return the
enclosed business reply card as soon as possible.

Sincerely,

Mark Christiansen

Mark Christiansen
Associate Vice President

I.C. SYSTEM, INC.
444 Highway 96 East • P.O. Box 64226 • St. Paul, Minnesota 55164-0226 • 612/483-0585 • 800/245-8875 • Fax: 612/481-6363
#6103 12/97

Fig. 9.4   (letter opening number 32) When you tell the reader, "We're solving your tough problem," a primary job is
to spell out that problem in negative terms. Does this letter accomplish that? The text writes around the problem it itself
creates, reducing the forcefulness of the message with each succeeding paragraph. Had more specifics been offered, the
letter might have qualified for number 27, "You're in trouble, and this is what you'd better do." Opportunity lost.

Help Desk professionals face more pressure every day.

Lon Hendrickson
Director, Industry
Relations

That's why I'm ready to give you a new software tool proven to help release pressure - a FREE SLA Generator.

Dear Customer Support Colleague:

Service Level Agreements help your organization avoid an unrealistic expectation: support-everything-for-everybody-all-the-time.

SLAs release some of the pressure we all share. Pressure from senior management expectations. Pressure from staffing requirements. Increasing customer demands.

Char LaBounty, the respected expert on service level management, worked with Bendata to bring you this empowering new tool. It helps you design Service Level Agreements that clearly outline your support commitments. And I would like you to have the SLA Generator free.

That's right, there's no cost or obligation connected with this offer. This powerful software tool is yours when you call our toll-free number or return the enclosed reply card.

****

(However, I do have a motive for offering you a free copy of Bendata's SLA Generator.)

****

It provides a realistic sample of how our award-winning Help Desk software tools can put management control back where it belongs. In your hands.

Automating your entire help desk operation:

HEAT™ supports everything you deal with as a Help Desk Manager: call tracking, problem resolution and problem management. And it provides enterprise-level solutions at a workgroup price.

1125 Kelly Johnson Blvd • Colorado Springs, CO 80920 • www.bendata.com

Fig. 9.5   (letter opening number 32) "We're solving your tough problem" is one of the better business-to-business approaches. Be certain, if you use this opening, that the reader identifies with the problem.

2373

ACCELERATED DEBT REDUCTION

HOW DO YOU FACE DEBT?

Dear Mr. Herschel G Lewis:

My company, Accelerated Debt Reduction, Corp. (ADR) can show you how by **eliminating all your debt automatically.** We'll eliminate your consumer debt, mortgage debt, *everything* and not by increasing your monthly payments but in many cases by reducing them. Not by charging you interest because we do not sell loans. How then do we do it?

ADR does the work for you by restructuring your debt and the payments. Then we implement the plan for you until completion.

Imagine being completely **out of debt in an average of 4 to 8 years!** Your earned income could go toward savings, investments or retirement. What would that mean to you or your family?

Debt pushers are out to get you deeper in debt and keep you there. **You want out!** The banks and credit card companies are ready to make more credit available. Mortgage companies have mailed you sample checks and you see debt consolidation offers on TV inviting you literally to keep overpaying. You've been offered easy-to-get credit cards, which only add to your out of control finances. These are ways for the debt pushers to get you further into debt and make more money off of you.

You will **not** get any of these offers from ADR. I know of only one successful way to get you out of debt. If you really want a 21% or 22% return on investment; pay off those consumer loans! That investment is guaranteed.

LIVE STRESS FREE!

ADR puts **you** in control of your finances simply, without pain and with the ongoing gratification of watching yourself successfully get out of debt.

Make the call **1-800-750-2221** and put yourself on the way to building your financial independence. Contact us at **www.adrcorp.com/t1** or by sending the postage free reply mail card. We'll respond quickly and confidentially to your request.

Please, make the call. Start living stress free today.

Respectfully yours,

Andy Schweitzer
Senior Debt Management Consultant

P.S. There is an initial $75.00 application fee. If our analysis does not show a potential of at least $10,000 in interest savings, you will receive a *full* refund. *Guaranteed!* Or if you choose to implement the program, the $75 application fee will be applied towards your ADR program fees. So you actually have nothing to risk!

A Partner of: Debt Acceleration Administered by:

FUTURE FINANCIAL   ADP

3832 N. University Drive, Sunrise, Fl 33345 - 1178 • www.adrcorp.com

Fig. 9.6 (letter opening number 32) The overline states a problem, but obliquely. An unanswerable question always dampens its own effectiveness. Nonetheless, the first sentence of the letter dynamically tells the reader, "We're solving your tough problem."

> **Business Insight® Release 5.0**
> **More Sophisticated Strategies in Less Time.**

Dear Valued Customer: *"Insight for Marketing Excellence!"*

Now that you have established yourself in business wouldn't it be great if you could insure your success? You can go a long way toward that goal with our award-winning software, Business Insight®. Business Insight will assist you in developing a winning marketing strategy. It is the **most comprehensive software tool available to develop and analyze marketing strategy**, and is has just been improved. We guarantee that Business Insight will provide new perspectives of your market and a more effective strategy - **or your money back!**

When we asked some customers what we could do to improve Business Insight, the overwhelming response was to make it **easier to use**. We focused our attention on that task in everything that we changed or created for Release 5.0. Here is how we responded:

The Data Input Process is Faster and Easier
A new "Quick Start" feature allows you to make a first pass evaluation in about two hours. From your answers to about sixty questions, Business Insight forms a "profile" and "assumes" answers in other, more detailed, areas producing a marketing strategy analysis. Then you review the analysis, investigating areas where the analysis is most critical of your success potential. This investigation will probably result in your changing some of the "assumed" answers. By the end of the review you will have a clear understanding of the potential for your offering and can decide if it merits the additional effort to directly answer all of the questions and develop an in-depth marketing strategy. This is a big improvement over the eight to ten hour interview process of the previous versions, allowing you to use the product more often for more scenarios.

The User Interface has been Simplified
The new interface is so intuitive that even if you only use Business Insight occasionally you will be able to pick it up quickly and be productive immediately. Tabs are used to organize the major and minor categories of information so you can find your way at a glance. A progress bar will keep you informed of your input process. Complex menus and toolbars have been simplified. A graphical interface focuses your attention on what to do next. An overall "bottom-line" of the analysis is always just a mouse-click away.

A Single Analysis with Selectable Levels of Detail
Business Insight 5.0 provides a single analysis report, with all segments of the analysis information integrated into one consistent document. It begins with a written analysis that describes your business, product and marketplace and shows how you can integrate current factors into an effective marketing strategy. Charts addressing important marketing concepts show how your enterprise and product or service fit into each concept. A written observation calls to your attention critical conditions or conditions that imply an inconsistency in your strategy. Now you can select the amount of output you want. Business Insight 5.0 provides three levels of integrated analysis which allow you to get a summary, intermediate, or detailed review of the business.

New Sensitivity Analysis
Business Insight 5.0 includes a new feature to quickly evaluate the effects of external changes to the business. Scenarios such as: the emergence of a new technology, the entry of a significant new competitor into your market, or a substantial change in the cost of a critical resource or service can be examined and automatically compared numerically and graphically with the current strategy. This feature allows you to test the sensitivity of your strategy and to evaluate the impact and your response to external events should they occur.

The Comparison Feature has been Expanded
The comparison feature has been expanded to allow you to compare several strategies simultaneously. No longer are you limited to comparing two at a time. Additionally, the comparison content has been greatly enhanced. The eleven key factors are compared along with their detailed elements and charts and graphs to highlight the differences between the cases. Now you can examine several options simultaneously and see the detailed impact of the differences. This will allow you to make the best choice of strategy much more rapidly. You can even compare the strategies of all your competitors with yours in one comparison.

Business Insight 5.0 produces better business strategies is less time.

Fig. 9.7 (letter opening number 32) When telling the reader you're solving a tough problem, which is better—hitting the problem head-on or sliding into it? Power comes from a head-on smash. Compare this soft version with figure 9.5 or even 9.6.

Oh, yeah, it's mushy and generalized and never quite gets into gear. That reflects on the execution, not the concept. If you or I had written that letter, we'd have remembered the purpose of letter opening number 32 and come out swinging, something like this . . .

Dear Struggling Holiday Gift Shopper,

All right, quit struggling. Quit worrying about neckties he may never wear and candies her diet says are a no-no.

Instead, look how easy it is to get *just the right gift*—a gift that tells those special persons on your list you respect their intellect: One entire year's membership in the Crossword Puzzles of the Month Club.

My point: the looser the rhetoric, the harder it is to knock over your target. A tight argument, even for a totally nonsensical notion, demands consideration.

33. THIS IS SHORT AND SWEET.

Overall, in consumer mass mailings most writers I know have had better luck with long letters than with short letters. But I certainly wouldn't quit testing, especially since the heartless Internet Era gives us results which seem to point in both directions.

So "This is short and sweet" is the perfect test vehicle.

Just three cautions:

1. Tell the reader, flat out, your message will be short and sweet.
2. Keep it short and sweet.
3. Keep sentences and paragraphs in character: Short. Terse. Quick.

I treasure a letter that came to me a couple of years ago. On page 2, the writer said, "To make a long story short. . . ." The letter ran six pages.

You be the judge: Does this opening qualify as a classic "short and sweet" approach?

This letter is going to be short and to the point. We don't want to make a big thing out of it. Not yet, anyway.

We'd like to invite you to take advantage of what we call our "no-strings" membership.

This offer extends an unusually generous introduction to you: choose any 4 books for only $1.

How did you vote? I vote no, and I'll tell you why. Even though the sentences are short and the paragraphs are just a couple of lines each, the letter is injected with fat.

Compare the approach with what you or I would have written—a true, genuine, authentic "short and sweet" opening, something like this:

_____

This letter is going to be short and to the point.

Choose any 4 books for only $1. That's it. No strings.

_____

See the difference? Our opening actually *is* short and sweet.

34. BELIEVE IT OR NOT.

The value of "Believe it or not" is its recognition of the Age of Skepticism—the age in which we're wallowing. The very admission builds rapport. The writer says to the reader, "Yes, I know this is hard to believe, but it's true."

For product introductions, especially on a pseudo-breakthrough level, this opening can bring a response when the usual puffery and bombast won't.

What cautions should we observe when we're using "Believe it or not"? Two major ones:

1. Don't misuse this as a phony justification for bending credibility beyond what a skeptic will accept, i.e., wild claims . . . an obviously preposterous discount . . . an unvalidated declaration of superiority.
2. Don't hit and run. Back up your argument so the reader begins to nod, "Yes, this might be true after all."

A computer software company starts with a Johnson Box which discloses the deal: "Announcing a once in a lifetime special sale" *and* "Save 80% for a limited time only" *and* "Get $2,195 worth of the PC world's top rated typefaces for just $49.95." The "Believe it or not" aspect is drowned in a sea of puffery. For analytical purposes let's ignore that (and the peculiar arithmetic—$49.95 is about 2 percent of $2,195, not 20 percent) and look at the letter proper:

_____

Dear PC User:

This is no hype! It's hard to believe, but absolutely true. I want to give you over $2,000 worth of fonts for the amazing low price of only $49.95.

This top rated collection of typefaces is MoreFonts. And, for sure, it is the most important printing bargain of the century.

_____

Reward without risk, with satisfaction guaranteed.
There *is* such a thing.
Enjoy $75 just for giving AT&T a try.
Call I 800 833-0700, ext. 60925.

Dear Herschell Lewis,

I'm sure you didn't wake up this morning thinking, "Maybe it's time to switch phone companies." But ask yourself: Are you really satisfied with your current company?

Well, maybe not. Today MCI, Sprint, and AT&T's calling plan rates are all competitive.

I can prove this to you. All you have to do is give AT&T a try, if only for a couple of months. Which is plenty of time to compare our rates to what you're getting now.

It's so easy to switch.
And the attached $75 check is yours to spend — no matter what!

All you do is sign and cash the check. Then we'll automatically switch you to AT&T Long Distance Service and, if available in your area, AT&T Local Toll Service.* Or, call us today at **I 800 833-0700, ext. 60925,** and we'll switch you *free of charge.* Either way, you can spend the $75 check any way you like. No risk, no hassles. And if you're not satisfied with AT&T after 30 days, we'll switch you back to your previous carrier, for *free.*

Try a simpler calling plan: the AT&T One Rate ® Plus Plan.

I know what you may be thinking: *Everyone* says they're cheaper. Simpler. Sometimes it's hard to know who to choose.

So how's this for simple: a low flat rate of just I0¢ a minute, 24 hours a day, 7 days a week, on all your state-to-state direct-dialed long distance calls from home for just $4.95 a month †. No restrictions. No spending minimum. And you could get a single low rate for local toll calls, too — just call for the specific rate in your area.

Our customers love the freedom AT&T **One Rate Plus** gives them to call whenever they want — with no waiting for rates to go down. You'll love it, too.

Of course, if you have any questions — or want to switch right away — I urge you to call one of my associates at **I 800 833-0700, ext. 60925.** They'll be more than happy to help. They'll even switch you for free.

I hope you give AT&T a try. You really have nothing to lose.

Best regards,

Jo-Anna Kressen

Jo-Anna Kressen
AT&T Marketing Manager

P.S. Remember, you can try AT&T *without risk* — your satisfaction's guaranteed. All you have to do is sign and cash the attached check or call one of my associates at **I 800 833-0700, ext. 60925,** to be switched today. If you call, we'll even switch you for free.

Please see important information on back.

It's all within your reach.   **AT&T**

Fig. 9.8   (letter opening number 34) "Reward without risk, with satisfaction guaranteed. There *is* such a thing." This qualifies as a "Believe it or not" opening, reinforcing itself with a genuine bank check *atop* the letter. (Endorsing the check authorizes a switch in long-distance services.)

NG109-LT1

Call 1-800-881-9919
Fax 1-800-700-2915

**NATIONAL
GEOGRAPHIC**
INTERACTIVE
Distributed by Mindscape Direct
P.O. Box 629000
El Dorado Hills, CA 95762-9983

PROUDLY SPONSORED BY

Kodak
ADVANTIX
System

✱ ✱

*More than a century of exploration and discovery
is reserved and ready for you in this magnificent CD-ROM collection...*

The Complete NATIONAL GEOGRAPHIC
109 Years on CD-ROM... Every page, every issue!

Preview this stunning collection and enjoy your FREE GIFT!

✱ ✱

Dear Fellow Adventurer,

Some things you just have to see to believe, and this is one of them... this is undoubtedly the richest, most rewarding library of information and insights ever captured on CD-ROM and now available as a resource like no other on Earth. A technological treasure that puts the most memorable images and discoveries of the 20th century right at your fingertips.

**Presenting every issue, every page of NATIONAL GEOGRAPHIC magazine
on CD-ROM – it's going to change the way you see the world!**

Specially reserved for your exclusive preview — The Complete NATIONAL GEOGRAPHIC 109 Years on CD-ROM. This magnificent collection allows you to rediscover the world decade by decade, issue by issue. Just click and go – into 109 years of the most compelling voyage of discovery you've ever taken. Search, zoom in, and print out in black and white or color...you have complete access to *every page, every issue* of NATIONAL GEOGRAPHIC magazine!

Tap into amazing destinations (visit China in the '20s, Paris in the '30s, space in the '60s)...you can join the hunt for the pharaohs in Egypt...take flights of fancy by balloon and biplane, railroad journeys into the Orient and river rafts up the Amazon, venture into unexplored forests and undiscovered deserts, into the histories and mysteries revealed in the pages of NATIONAL GEOGRAPHIC magazine.

Join world-class photographers, writers, and naturalists as they discover a world like no other!

Understand how courageous explorers first conquered Mt. Everest. Journey through the lush beauty and perilous dangers of the Nile. Uncover little-known secrets of the wild panda, and stand on the rim of the Grand Canyon. You can relive these and thousands of other compelling stories reported over the past 109 years in NATIONAL GEOGRAPHIC magazine. Best of all, you'll do it in the comfort of your own home.

Please continue to other side

NG109-LT1

Fig. 9.9   (letter opening number 34) Here is a pure "Believe it or not" opening: "Some things you just have to see to believe, and this is one of them...." A question might be, Wouldn't this exact line be a more provocative heading than the thin "More than a century ..." text? "Believe it or not" openings, along with the cries of "Fire!" and "Wolf!" demand an explosive approach.

Nope. This letter doesn't qualify because it violates both cautions. It doesn't justify credibility, and it hits and runs.

Hey, don't write slop such as "And, for sure, it is the most important printing bargain of the century." Don't use "amazing" and expect it to stick without rhetorical glue. That isn't copywriting, it's just word-grabbing. And as long as we're being picky, why not indent the paragraphs?

You or I would have opened the letter this way:

Dear PC User:

If I told you I'm going to give you more than $2,000 worth of fonts for $49.95, you'd probably think, "This guy is lying."

I'm not lying, and I'm about to prove it.

Actually, the offer is more credible if the company is offering $700 worth of fonts. And as it turns out, on page 2 the writer admits, "This award-winning program sells for the extremely low price of $149.95 in most computer stores." Huh?

The logic of this argument is neither our problem nor our subject. We just want the pieces of a sales argument to be in sync. If you tell the reader what you're about to say is incredible, don't make "This is incredible" your only credible statement.

35. I KNOW WHO YOU ARE.

Danger! This isn't parallel to opening number 1, "If you're like me," or number 17, "Because you are who you are, you may get special attention." This is Zeus hurling thunderbolts from Mount Olympus.

The key to an Olympian position is the reader's acceptance of you as Zeus. "I know who you are" is a terrific guilt-generator when the reader either is preconditioned to accept apparent judgment, or the writer is adept enough to create that acceptance.

Two examples:

I know all about you. Yes, I do.

I know you'd like to be a world traveler. I know you'd like to enjoy the good life. I know you sometimes aren't quite able to enjoy all the good things of life you deserve.

That's about to change.

Experts agree, the key to success in
any direct mail promotion is having...

The right mailing list!

LIMITED TIME OFFER!

SAVE $50!

Return the enclosed
$50 voucher when you order
the **DIRECT MARKETING
LIST SOURCE®**
and pay only $399.
Act Now...Offer expires
October 16, 1998

Reach the right audience—no matter who you're
targeting—with the **Direct Marketing List Source**.
(We used it to find you!)

Dear Direct Marketer:

We knew you'd open the envelope of this package and want to read this message.

How did we know?

Because we used the right mailing list...a list targeted to people like you—those
interested in increasing the pulling power of their direct mail.

Every mailing you do from now on will have this pulling power, as long as you
understand one thing:

> **Your mailing list is the single most important part of any direct
> marketing promotion. If you're missing the target, it doesn't matter
> what you are selling or how powerful your message is!**

Selecting the right list can result in breakthrough response rates...and you can't
say that about any other single component of a direct marketing promotion.
Direct mail authority Herschell Gordon Lewis said it best:

> **"Determining lists is the decision that will make the greatest difference
> in the pulling power of a piece of direct mail. Poor copy won't completely
> ruin a mailing the way poor list selection can."**

Fig. 9.10   (letter opening number 35) Telling the reader "I know who you are" can be dangerous if the point is made
without flattery. This letter uses the opening properly.

You're someone who really appreciates fine dining. Like you, our customers are also discriminating fine food lovers. But since we couldn't find your name on our lists, I'm sending you the enclosed certificate to introduce you to the unique pleasures of Vermont's cuisines.

Both examples are flawed. In the first, using "you'd" instead of "you" nails the recipient as a loser. Even losers resent being called a loser by somebody who's trying to sell them something.

The second is nonthreatening and convivial; but why make the flat statement, "You're someone who really appreciates fine dining," then say, ". . . we couldn't find your name on our lists." The reader may reinterpret the first statement as speculation. An easy way to avoid the paradox: "The source from which your name came to us suggests you're someone who really appreciates fine dining."

36.   BECAUSE YOU'RE "A" YOU'RE ALSO "B."

This one isn't easy and isn't often interchangeable with other openings, even number 17, "Because you are who you are, you may get special attention." It's best used when adopting a patriarchal position because it implicitly places the writer on a judgmental plane.

Okay, quick question: which of the previous thirty-five openings is closest to this one?

If your choice is number 9, "As you know," we're in sync. "As you know" is an assumptive opener, more convivial (and therefore more peer-positioned) than this one. The relationship suggests a choice: (1) If after writing an "As you know" opening you think it's too weak, switch to this one. (2) If after writing a "Because you're 'A' you're also 'B' " opening you think it's too condescending, switch to "As you know."

An example of this opening is a letter from a nonprofit organization pitching an internal motor club:

Dear Member,

As a driver, you know all about the problems that can arise when you're on the road. Your Association membership includes eligibility for the AARP Motoring Plan among its member benefits to offer you peace of mind while driving and dependable help when you need it.

A good match. Members give their association a "Big Daddy" image, and the letter reflects this paternal benevolence. A more commercial group might have begun the message more promotionally: "As you know, when you're on the road you can run into a sudden problem at any moment."

GE Financial Assurance
Colonial Penn Insurance

Executive Offices
P.O. Box 1990
Valley Forge, PA 19482

LD-0056-898

************ECRLOT**C-023
Margo E. Lewis
340 N Fig Tree Ln.
Ft Lauderdale, FL 33317-2561
|..||..||..||....|||..|.|.|.|.|..||....||..||||....|.|.|

Your car may easily pass a careful inspection...But can your <u>car insurance</u>?

If you're not sure, let us give you a <u>FREE</u> Inspection of your current coverage along with a Rate Quote...It's quick and easy, and it may save you <u>hundreds every year</u>.

CALL NOW: 1-800-445-0821

Dear Margo E. Lewis:

Because you're a safe driver, you probably take the time to make sure your cars are properly inspected. You have the brakes checked. You make sure the lights and signals work properly, and so on. But when was the last time you had your <u>car insurance inspected</u>?

A Quick Inspection And Rate Quote Could Bring Substantial Savings

At Colonial Penn, we specialize in insuring safe drivers for much lower premiums. <u>You may qualify for savings of $200, $300, or more every year</u>! We'd like to show you just how much you can save, with one quick phone call.

We'll quickly inspect the coverage you have now, and quote you a rate for the <u>same coverage</u> at rates that are often <u>much less</u>. There's no cost and no obligation for your FREE Inspection and Rate Quote.

How Can We Offer Such Low Premiums? There's No Middleman, We Have Exceptionally Low Operating Expenses, And We Offer Numerous Money-Saving Discounts

With Colonial Penn, you deal directly with us insuring your cars. And because there is no middleman or agent, we can keep our costs lower. We also do all that we can to keep our operating expenses down. In fact, our operating expenses are among the lowest in the auto insurance industry. And we are pleased to pass the savings on to you.

We also offer many discounts to help you save even more money. These discounts are available <u>in addition</u> to our already low rates:

- **Safe Driver Discount** — Provides up to an additional 10% savings each year if you and all other operators on the policy have a clean driving record.
- **Multi-Car Discount** — Brings up to an additional 25% savings on each car if you insure more than one car with us.
- **Defensive Driver Discount** — For up to an additional 10% savings if you take an Approved Accident Prevention Course.
- **Safety Features Discounts** — Earn even more savings if you have safety devices such as airbags, anti-lock brakes, daytime running lights, and automatic seat belts.
- **Retirement Discount** — Allows up to an additional 5-15% savings for drivers 55 and over who are retired.
- **Deluxe Discount** — For extra savings of up to 10% if you carry liability limits of $100,000/$300,000, insure more than one vehicle and carry collision coverage on at least one vehicle. (Deluxe Discount not available in addition to Retirement Discount)

We bring good things to life.

Priority #: PKX9LDF

Fig. 9.11 (letter opening number 36) A "Because you're 'A' you're also 'B' " opening isn't for beginners; this letter is highly professional. The text at the top is somewhat cluttered and, by making a blurry point, may impede readership rather than spurring it.

**Special Rates Available only
to Discover® Cardmembers**

Discover Savers' Account 5.06%.* APY
Annual Percentage Yield (APY)
is for a $5,000 minimum deposit
opened with new money.**

Discover Card CD Account 6.00%* APY
Annual Percentage Yield (APY) is
for a 1-year, $5,000 CD Account.**

****************ECRLOT**C-023
Herschell G. Lewis
Margo Lewis
340 N. Fig Tree Ln
Plantation FL 33317-2561

Dear Herschell G. Lewis:

As a Discover® Cardmember, you understand value. And you want your savings to work
as hard as you do.

That's why you should know about two great ways to make your money grow:
our Discover Savers' and Discover Card Certificate of Deposit Accounts.

They're available <u>exclusively</u> to Discover Cardmembers, and designed to help you reach
your personal investment goals, whether they include retirement ... starting a college fund ...
or saving for a new car or a bigger home.

Competitive rates
Both Discover Savers' and Discover Card CD Accounts offer you attractive interest rates
on a variety of deposit amounts (see rate charts below). And when you open a new Account,
you enjoy our high New Account Premier Interest Rate for the first 30 days!**

Worry-free investments
You can also count on security. Discover Card CD and Savers' Accounts are offered by
Greenwood Trust Company and <u>insured by the FDIC for up to $100,000 per depositor</u>.

Exclusive Cardmember benefits
Our Accounts also give you the benefits you deserve, including helpful customer service,
convenient ATM access to your funds (Savers' Account only), on-line account statements
at our web site (www.discovercard.com) and much more.

So now's the time to start making your money grow! To open an Account, simply complete the
enclosed Account Opening Form and mail it with your initial deposit. Put your money to work
toward your goals <u>today</u>.

Sincerely,

J. Nathan Hill
President, Greenwood Trust Company

*APYs are accurate as of 07/21/98 - 07/27/98.
**See Important Disclosures on back.

Fig. 9.12   (letter opening number 36) "Because you're 'A' you're also 'B'" is an automatic connector with *exclusivity*.
Here, apparently because the reader holds a specific credit card he also is entitled to a special rate. The multitude of asterisks damages the message immeasurably.

37.   HISTORICAL BUILDUP

I like narrative openings, but by golly they'd better be bright. Many letters, especially those four or more pages long, get into a historical buildup—but not at the outset. Beginning with history requires both talent and guts because without an exquisite mixture of both, your reader is long gone before you've reached the year 1962.

The classic historical buildup embarks with something like "It all began with . . . " and includes at least one detail the reader already knows. Starting out that way *demands* a payoff before the reader asks, "So what?" Crucial to a historical buildup is the transition to *sell*. History per se doesn't sell; it opens the curtains.

Take a look at this historical buildup opening, plus the paragraph that follows:

Dear Colleague:

It started quietly with a simple affinity card. Then came the frequent flier cards, corporate cards, and now tiered pricing and a host of powerful enhancements offered by the big non-bank card players—from discounts on long distance phone service to rebates on cars.

Like top executives in network television coping with the market fragmentation created by cable, astute executives in the credit card industry know they are witnessing a fundamental market change that affects *everyone* in the business—CEOs, product managers, marketers, finance and operations executives, even collections specialists.

Successful? Anything but. This is a snore-maker because after the enticing first four words, the message starts to leak impact out its sides. The second paragraph is a naked laundry list of everybody the writer wants to snare.

Match this same opening—"It started quietly with . . ."—to a genuine buildup and you'll have a readable, response-producing letter.

38.   YOU JUST MIGHT BE (AND PROBABLY ARE) . . .

This opening is a favorite of sweepstakes promoters. Because sweepstakes have such power, more and more marketers (and fund-raisers, too) are hooking their tails onto this high-flying promotional kite.

The difference between "will be" and "might be" is profound but often concealed. At the fingertips of an expert wordsmith, a properly structured "You just might be" opening *implies* the second half—"and probably are"—without running afoul of the spiderweb of legal restrictions.

Typical of this beginning is a letter with a provocative overline and ongoing amplification:

You may already have won a brand new Lincoln, An exotic 7-day Caribbean vacation, A convenient pocket-sized cellular phone, or A relaxing Florida getaway.

Dear Florida Business Leader,

As part of an unprecedented promotion exclusively for Florida executives, you may have already won any one of these prizes—or more!

Imagine if you will . . .

. . . Watching the countryside roll effortlessly by as the exhilarating power and elegance of a brand new Lincoln Sedan heeds your beck and call.

The letter avoids the pitfall into which so many pretenders tumble—leaving Shangri-la too soon. Whatever you're selling, restrain the urge to pitch until you've painted a winning scene.

(Phrases such as "unprecedented promotion" and a dangling "or more" are touches of weakness, marching in place.)

39.   I'LL GET RIGHT TO THE POINT.

"I'll get right to the point" parallels number 33, "This is short and sweet," only in its promise of directness. The two differ in emotional thrust because "This is short and sweet" smiles and "I'll get right to the point" doesn't. The difference underscores the value of each. (The yet-to-come number 92, "I won't waste your time," makes a different promise altogether.)

A letter from a publication begins, "My message is short"; but it's all business, which shifts it into the "I'll get right to the point" category:

My message is short . . .

. . . because it's simple. Here are three important reasons why you should get your own subscription to *Advertising Age* now.

1. *To get ahead in business. Ad Age* is read regularly by more executives than . . .

I sense some confusion hovering about the first line—"My message is short because it's simple." That word *simple* is dangerous when used to influence professionals. Mightn't this letter have generated greater rapport by staying with a "This is short and sweet" attitude?

40.   THESE ARE CRITICAL TIMES.

Here's one that in less-than-expert hands can appear ludicrous. The writer has to be able to convince the reader that these *are* critical times, relative to

NO MORE RENEWAL NOTICES

Dear Subscriber:

I'll get right to the point.

Your subscription to THE WALL STREET JOURNAL is up for renewal now.

And if you reply today, this is the last renewal notice you'll receive. No follow-ups. And your subscription will continue without interruption.

<u>Renewing promptly is to your advantage</u>.

You can renew right away at the Journal's subscription rates. And it pays to renew long term. With a two-year renewal, you pay just $124 for your second year of the Journal -- a full $51 off our one-year price of $175.

When you renew for two years, the Journal costs just 59 cents a day -- and your savings will be locked in for a full 24 months, no matter what happens to the newsstand price or subscription rates.

As you can see, our renewal policy is as straightforward as it can be. By renewing now, you avoid a series of last-minute reminders -- less paperwork. Best of all, you will be certain of receiving every issue -- no interruption in service.

Simply tell us on the enclosed form which subscription term you prefer. Then mail the form back with payment in the enclosed reply envelope.

Thank you.

Sincerely,

William E. Casey Jr.

William E. Casey, Jr.
Vice President/Circulation

WEC:fbg

P.S. Another benefit to your subscription: a special rate for The Wall Street Journal Interactive Edition, a 24 hour, 7 day a week complement to the Journal on the World Wide Web. To take advantage of this offer, register at http://wsj.com

THE WALL STREET JOURNAL.

200 BURNETT ROAD, CHICOPEE, MA 01020

DOWJONES

JL016

Fig. 9.13 (letter opening number 39) This letter begins right on target—"I'll get right to the point." And it does. Too many such letters make that statement and then ramble away from the point. For renewals, continuity-program resuscitations, and quick offers of close-out merchandise, this approach has muscle.

the reader's own experiential background. Otherwise we've just cried, "Fire!" or "Wolf!" less competently than a professional cry of "Fire!" or "Wolf!"

Don't assume this opening is reserved for politics or religion or loathsome diseases. It has a surprising universality. But recognize, too, the necessity for being able to read and burrow into the reader's background.

A letter has this typed overline and opening:

At no other time in recent history has it been more important for you and your family to understand the world around you.

Dear Member,

In recent times, the world has witnessed extraordinary changes:

- the dramatic dissolution of the Soviet Union—and emergence of the Commonwealth of Independent States....

Weak? Yes. The overline exemplifies what's wrong with so, so many overlines. The writer just doesn't understand, care, or have the ability to cope with this fact of selling in print: the purpose of an overline is to initiate reader salivation. Limp clichés such as "At no other time in recent history has it been more important for you and your family to understand the world around you" leave the reader with a dry emotional socket.

The purpose of this letter was to sell an atlas. Why couldn't the overline have had some guts, such as "Uh-oh. I'll bet your atlas still has a map of the Soviet Union and Zaire, and not of Belarus, Uzbekistan, and Congo"?

The writer is in control . . . but only until the reader rises up in wrath, slumps down in apathy, or (joy!) lifts pen or phone.

41.   VISUALIZE THIS SCENARIO.

I have a love-hate relationship with this sophisticated opening. When absolutely targeted, it's dynamite; when askew, it's stupid. When tightly structured, it's arresting; when larded with the fat of inconsequential details, it's tedious.

That's because an absolutely targeted opening harpoons readers within their own experiential backgrounds, and a mis-hit leaves readers completely outside the message.

An example of "Visualize this scenario" is this opening of an eight-page letter:

Dear Entrepreneur,

It's early morning, before your employees come in . . .

You unlock the door to your business, turn off the alarm and step inside. You pause for a moment to look around.

You take pride in the business you've created here. Every paper clip, desk, typewriter, machine, car and truck is yours (well, maybe the bank's too!).

But it's *your* business. Its success depends solely on your wits. You call the shots, no one else.

You slide behind your desk and settle back in your chair. You're looking forward to the day!

———————————

Ugh!

Reread just the first two short paragraphs. Don't you get the feeling we're selling security devices? We aren't.

Reread the entire opening. Do you yet have any idea what we're selling? I don't. Actually, the opening persists for more than a page.

A total mis-hit: What entrepreneur has the time to wade through treacle?

The last paragraph on page 2 tells the reader what's for sale—a book. By that time any entrepreneur worth a nickel is exasperated. (For that matter, any entrepreneur who takes pride in his paper clips probably rattles when he shakes his head.)

Above the greeting is this legend:

———————————

If you're running your own business (or plan to soon) I'll send you the SUCCESSFUL BUSINESS MANAGE-MENT *Starter Set—free of charge.*

———————————

Does this save it? In my opinion it compounds the felony because any wallop the opening might have had disappears in this betrayal of suspense. It's parallel to a mystery movie which opens with one of the characters telling the audience, "You'll be surprised when you find out I'm the murderer."

Tightened and oiled, this could have been a forceful, reader-grabbing opening.

42.   IF YOU LIKE THAT, YOU'LL LOVE THIS.

How reader involving this one can be! Notice, please, I said "can be," not "is." In a major respect this beginning parallels number 41, "Visualize this scenario"—reader involvement depending squarely on relevance.

Suppose I say to you, not knowing what pleases your palate, "If you like squid, you'll love octopus." Not only are my parameters too narrow (and too squishy), but by selecting the wrong parallel I can destroy your latent positive response.

Too often, users of this opening water it down by *generalizing* the first half of the parallel. It still works, but the strength doesn't come within light-years of the same opening which brings up specifics. An example:

Dear Friend,

If you're fascinated by the people and things that make America so interesting and unique, then you're going to **love** *SMITHSONIAN Magazine!*

See what happened? How can *anybody* be fascinated by "people and things"? What people? What things? Later on in the letter, the writer does begin to specify. Why not fire when at point-blank range? A suggested rewrite, based on examples from within this same letter:

If you're fascinated by the Pennsylvania archaeological digs that show humans may have reached our continent well before the traditionally accepted date of 115,000 years ago ... if you chuckle over teenage scientists creating acid rain and showing how headache remedies affect radishes ... you're going to love *SMITHSONIAN Magazine,* where every month brings hundreds of engrossing, riveting stories and articles.

Now, I grant you these aren't blockbusters, but they're what I found buried in the letter. A half dozen issues of the magazine probably would have yielded more savory grist for the word-mill.

43.   Whether you do this . . . or do that . . .

The best way to describe this boilerplate opening is "serviceable." It's a workmanlike old dependable, one you'll call on when you're writing an umbrella letter to a polyglot group of readers.

"Whether you do this . . . or do that" says whatever you're selling covers a multitude of circumstances, a broad spectrum of situations that surely include the reader.

A typical example of this opening:

Dear Reader,

Whether you administer the business travel of 10 employees or 1,000 you can benefit from the most complete information source on corporate business travel: *CORPORATE TRAVEL* magazine.

Obviously this semi-targeted opening has less energy than a totally targeted opening. But two compensations: (1) This one works where the target can't be pinpointed; (2) this opening doesn't require changing the message as you change lists.

Shrink Away Prostate Problems Without Drugs or Surgery

A new therapy alleviates all prostate-related ailments. The doctors have proven it's safe — and that it works. This is for every man who...

Dr. Leonard Haimes, M.D.
As seen on NBC's "Today" show.

✔ *can't "make it through the night..."* ___

✔ *cherishes his sex life...*

✔ *cringes at the thought of having to wear diapers...*

✔ *fears prostate cancer (one in six American men develop this dreaded killer)...*

✔ *considers prostate surgery and its devastating effects unacceptable...*

Start getting relief in <u>just 15 days</u>!

Dear friend:

    Whether you want to slash your risk of being the one of every six males who will get prostate cancer...want to end those sleep-disturbing nightly visits to the bathroom...or rid yourself of the side effects (and dangers) of the expensive prescription drug you're taking for benign prostate enlargement (BPH)...

    ...even if you're a healthy male in your 40s with no obvious signs of prostate problems yet...

    ...this letter can change your life!

    If you don't mind, I'd like to share a "man-to-man" note we received recently from Thomas T., a man in his 50s: (It's on file in our office)

        "Since my mid 40s, I'd been getting up two, sometimes three times a night to go the bathroom. When I got divorced, I started keeping a urinal by the side of my bed. A lot more convenient, but as I discovered when I

(over, please)

1

Fig. 9.14 (letter opening number 43) The letter itself doesn't begin until halfway down the page, which makes this letter a hybrid—advertisement + letter. Assuming the reader absorbs the ad *as an ad*, the "Whether you do this ... or do that" opening performs its rightful function: apparently giving the reader a position of choice and dominance. In this instance, all the choices relate to the headline. Note: Figure 9.17 is a different message from this same source.

SHOOTING SPORTSMAN
The Magazine of Wingshooting & Fine Guns

P.O. Box 1357, Camden, ME 04843

> *Join us. We have a FREE TRIAL ISSUE reserved in your name. May we send it to you?*

Dear Sportsman,

Whether it's the sight of mallards pitching in to your decoys, the wash of air through the wings of geese, the the burst to flight of quail, woodcock or grouse that makes your heart race, you'll experience the same excitement on every page of SHOOTING SPORTSMAN.

SHOOTING SPORTSMAN is the premier magazine devoted entirely to wingshooting and fine shotguns. In our pages top writers and photographers bring you the latest and best on topics ranging from upland hunting and waterfowling to gun collecting and sporting clays—and they deliver it with fine prose and breathtaking pictures.

If you're as devoted to wingshooting and fine guns as we think you are, then you'll eagerly await each and every issue. Listen to what our readers say:

> *"The fine gun information is tremendous, and the articles are very entertaining as well as nicely written. I had been searching for a magazine such as yours for some time. Thanks for putting together a great package."*
>   *—T.A. Calabrese*
>   *Elma, NY*

(over, please . . .)

Fig. 9.15   (letter opening number 43) The first sentence is considerably longer than might be comfortable, but it flows well. "Whether you do this … or do that" pulls the reader into the message orbit, by seeming to offer and await a choice.

44.   The classic quotation

For heaven's sake be careful with this one. You're okay, if dull, with "A penny saved is a penny earned," but you're out of the reader's depth (and acceptance range) with "Poetry fettered, fetters the human race."

We've all transgressed, but let's take the vow: no more rushing to *Bartlett's Familiar Quotations* to find a quotation we can use as our opening shot. Why not? Because if we have to lean on *Bartlett's* we risk alienating readers who feel—correctly, as it turns out—we're trying to lord it over them.

I like quotations dipped in acid because the reader feels comfortable joining us in satire or disdain. Can't you see the reader staying with you when you open with something like these?

———————————

Was Alexandre Dumas right when he said, "I prefer the wicked to the foolish, because the wicked sometimes rest"?

———————————

Or . . .

———————————

You probably feel the way Mary Buckley does: "Husbands are awkward things to deal with; even keeping them in hot water doesn't make them tender."

———————————

Lots of these around. They're grabbers. So why did the writer of this letter start by showing off?

———————————

Dear Friends:

"Great things are done when men and mountains meet." William Blake wrote these words, words that resonate today. I'd like to invite you to join me in proving this concept, in exploring the high landscapes, and in being a part of a chronicle of special places and times.

———————————

Don't you get the feeling that joining this guy will result not in special times but in torpid times? Aside from the plural greeting ("Dear Friends") and the unindented paragraphs, quoting William Blake to start a letter symbolizes another Blake quotation: "Every night and every morn/Some to misery are born."

45.   I have to tell you the truth.

Name somebody who isn't fascinated with soul-baring and you've named somebody who probably is a poor prospect for a sales letter. After the startling episodes of Bill Clinton's presidency, "I have to tell you the truth" has taken on some sardonic overtones . . . which actually helps this opening.

"I have to tell you the truth" suggests we're going to read something private or slightly naughty or wayward, a self-immolating tale told out of school. Usually it doesn't materialize, but meanwhile we're temporarily hooked.

An excellent and persuasive example of this opening:

Dear Herschell & Margo:

I'd be lying to you if I suggested that the reason for my letter today is wholly selfless. But to some extent it is.

That extent is a charitable trust I have set up for Meals-on-Wheels. . . .

My first move, reading the greeting, was to look for the signature to see who's calling us by our first names. By gum, it *was* a friend, as spokesperson for a not-for-profit organization.

I'd have put that second sentence in parentheses, but the letter has to succeed because it combines genuine personalization with self-revelation.

46. YOU'RE IMPORTANT TO US.

Can you "overstroke" (see opening number 18) a customer or a client or even a prospect? Only if you slather so heavily you dribble rhetorical saliva onto the reader's hands.

Stroking isn't the same as claiming importance. You *can* destroy budding rapport by misuse of the word *important*. And therein lies the danger of substituting "You're important to us" for "We love you."

The standard recommendation applies: After making a declarative statement, then quickly, quickly explain why. You've avoided the hit-and-run syndrome that leaves the reader sitting as reader, not participant; and you've forced yourself to shovel some rapport fertilizer into the mix.

An example of "You're important to us" is a subscription renewal letter from a controlled-circulation magazine whose subscribers are computer dealers.

The letter begins:

Dear Executive,

Your business is important to us and that's why we're extending this limited time FREE offer especially to you. A full year's subscription to *COMPUTER RESELLER NEWS*—the Newspaper for Value Added Reselling—is being offered to you absolutely FREE. Chances are you've already heard of *CRN*. For over a decade, *CRN* has been the leading publication for resellers—bringing you late-breaking industry news, as well as in-depth analyses on emerging technologies and hot, new products.

Suppose you're a value-added reseller, a VAR. Would you accept this offer?

Probably . . . but not because "Your business is important to us"; no, you'd go for it only because it's free.

What happened here is a standard dereliction in letter writing, the whole point behind this listing of openings: The writer begins with a concept and then forgets or ignores that concept. Why do that? You chose an opening for a reason.

Not one word after the first six justifies the claim, "Your business is important to us." Instead, we sense a growing frenzy. What's going on here, since the magazine is free?

The publication could handle this in either of two ways:

1. Any one of ten or twelve other openings already described might have been a better lead-in—such as numbers 17, 19, 20, 25, 32, 36, 38, or 39.
2. Justify the first six words.

47.   Now you can . . . *or* At last!

"Now you can" and "At last!" are close enough to warrant a single entry, although they aren't identical. "Now you can" is narrative, while "At last!" is exclamatory.

"At last!" is an old dependable in many a space ad because it's an automatic statement of superiority. "At last!" says both "This didn't exist before" and "You need it." For most business letters "Now you can" is probably safer because this *seems* to be more the result of thought or investigation.

A letter for a "religious epics" video library, after a three-color Johnson box, begins:

Dear Friend,

Now you can own the best of Hollywood's grand and glorious spectaculars—inspired by the most powerful stories of all time.

Academy Award®-winning actors and directors . . . stunning costumes and casts of thousands . . . striking locations and panoramic photography . . . scenes of passion, greed, terror, and salvation.

For me, that "®" maims the poetry, but can you see the mismatch? "Now you can" demands a payoff. What's strange is that this letter is

SPANISH! FRENCH! GERMAN! ITALIAN! PORTUGUESE! HEBREW! JAPANESE! CHINESE! KOREAN! INDONESIAN! ENGLISH!

TL:1450

Finally! A Fun, *New Way* For Kids 6 & Up To Learn a Second Language.

Give Your Children A Gift They'll Use For Life!

Try It RISK-FREE for 60 Days!

Dear Fellow Parent,

You're having a party. All the relatives are over. All of a sudden <u>your child</u> surprises, astonishes and impresses everyone by...

Speaking perfectly in a foreign language!

And, it won't take many months or years for your children to express themselves in another language. With *KidSpeak*, you'll notice results on the very first day!

You see, with its colorful animation, games, puzzles and songs, *KidSpeak* is an innovative, completely interactive way for your children to learn a second language <u>on their own</u> using your Mac or PC.

Because it's interactive, your children will be entertained as they're educated. Plus, it's so fun, kids don't even realize they're learning.

But, here's the most exciting news!

Save nearly 80%
As part of a marketing test, we're offering
***KidSpeak* to you and a small number of others at just**
$29.95 for the next 30 days!

At this price I can't think of a better investment you can make in your child's future. Using state-of-the-art multimedia CD-ROM technology, *KidSpeak* is many times more interesting, involving and effective than nationally advertised children's video language courses selling for as much as $180.

With *KidSpeak*, your children will <u>play</u> in a variety of simple (but challenging) games, puzzles and activities that capture their attention, stimulate their minds and keep them interested for many hours.

Plus, not only will your children have fun with this exciting, new way of language learning, you'll find that their feelings of

(Go To Page 2)

Fig. 9.16 (letter opening number 47) "Now you can," "At last!," and "Finally" all suggest a breakthrough. To some creative communicators, "At last!" seems more breakthroughish than "Finally" because it suggests the reader has been waiting for whatever it is. This letter uses "Finally!" and makes its point the way this type of opening should—with an absolute statement unhampered by "if" qualifiers.

FROM THE DESK OF DR. LEONARD HAIMES, M.D.

Finally, the Medical Establishment Confirms What We've Known All Along — There is a Way To Make Your Heart Incredibly Strong and Healthy!

Dear Friend,

Although the alternative medical press has been reporting it for years, most people have never heard the true facts about heart disease. In fact, so much misinformation and disinformation has been in the press that even doctors and cardiologists don't know.

I'm talking about a discovery that was made nearly 30 years ago...a finding so important that it promises to revolutionize our most basic understanding and treatment of coronary disease. It's an amazing story that anyone who fears heart disease should pay close attention to....

It's A Story of Brilliant Research, Great Hope...and Wasted Time

Back in the late 1960s, I read a Harvard-published medical paper that identified the most insidious and single-most dangerous cause of coronary disease ever revealed — *and how absolutely easy it was to treat.*

It was one of the most startling medical breakthroughs of this century! But strangely, the brilliant young medical detective who broke the research, Dr. Kilmer S. McCully, was fired from Harvard for proposing his "daring" theory....

You see, back then (and still today) the mainstream medical establishment had begun riding the cholesterol bandwagon. Anti-cholesterol medications would grow into a multibillion-dollar industry, so the mainstream had a huge stake in fanning the flames of the cholesterol mission.

So despite the compelling nature of Dr. McCully's research, greed simply won out...and perhaps millions of lives were lost over the years as a result.

Fortunately, the truth about heart disease and the deadly molecule homocysteine is finally coming out, in volumes of new medical evidence.

Homocysteine (pronounced HO-MO-SIS-TEEN) is an amino acid produced naturally in the body when metabolizing protein. When left to multiply in the blood unchecked, this molecule becomes a deadly killer — destroying arteries and promoting life-threatening blood clots.

Today, we're finally discovering how dangerous homocysteine actually is. A blizzard of new medical research from many of the world's most eminent scientists is showing that

(over, please)

Fig. 9.17 (letter opening number 47) Figure 9.14, from this same source, uses opening number 43, a more explanatory opening than this one, which begins "Finally." Which has greater impact? The products aren't identical but the aim is parallel. Might this heading, part of the first sentence, be more energetic than the semi-specific "Finally" opener? "Most people have never heard the true facts about heart disease. How about you?"

loaded with payoff lines, but they're buried. For example, the letter could have borrowed some text from a few paragraphs down:

Now you can see internationally-renowned actor Max Von Sydow as Jesus, Charlton Heston as John the Baptist, Jose Ferrer as King Herod, Telly Savalas as Pontius Pilate ... all right in your own living room.

Take a look at just a few of the spectacular adventures that await you....

"You're important to us" and "Now you can" share a challenge: They demand a payoff. Hit-and-run will damage response.

48. THEY THINK I'M NUTS!

"They think I'm nuts" or "I must be nuts" has two advantages over many types of letter openings: First, it's 100 percent informal, which means the seeds of rapport have already half-germinated. Second, it's disarming because it's self-denigrating, and it doesn't demand a specific follow-up.

A fund-raising letter begins:

Dear Ms. Nelson,

When we began sending out these free calendars, people said we were crazy!

We mailed these beautiful calendars absolutely free to good, caring people like yourself.

"You can't do it—the Veterans of Foreign Wars will go broke!" many doubters said. "People will use their calendars, but you'll never hear from them again."

But, it didn't turn out that way at all. In fact, thousands of people like you....

Except for the unnecessary underlining of "you'll" and the comma after "But," I admire this letter, especially since it came from an organization usually regarded as stuffy and humorless.

Suppose the letter had begun, "We owe our veterans something. They fought for our freedom." Would this approach, even accompanied by a free calendar, have generated the immediate bond the "They think we're nuts!" approach accomplishes?

49. BEFORE YOU DO THAT, DO THIS.

This opening makes sense for many business-to-business communications. The writer preestablishes a favorable-to-vendor relationship between the parties. "Before you do that, do this" suggests writer superiority and reader inferiority without saying so, by imprinting an acceptable direction without being imperative.

An example, from a mailing-list company:

Dear Business to Business Marketer . . .

Before you look at your new Penton Lists Catalog, there's a few things you might want to know about your customers . . .

Research shows: More than $11 trillion in goods and services are sold each year in the U.S. It is business and government, NOT individual consumers that account for two thirds of this spending.

What does it mean to you? Business and government markets offer far greater sales potential for many companies than consumer markets.

For this analysis let's ignore the grammar of "there's a few things" and the looseness of "It is business and government that account" and focus on the use of "Before you do that, do this." Does this example maximize the function of this opening?

No. The opening *is* provocative and pulls the reader into the letter; it then takes a strange turn, suggesting the reader doesn't really know his or her customers . . . which isn't the intention. What if the opening had been more letterlike, without boldface and with indented paragraphs, and had begun:

Before you look at your new Penton Lists Catalog, take just one moment to consider:

Does it mean anything to you that two-thirds of all spending in the U.S. is by business and government, not by consumers?

I cheerfully admit I'm not a fan of research as a selling tool. In my Book of Doom, researchers join lawyers and accountants as people so strangled by self-importance they're unable to sell. But that's a prejudice, not a researched fact.

50.   WOULDN'T IT BE LOVELY IF . . .

I like this one for three reasons: First, it suggests hope in a troubled world. The psychology of this opening is unassailable—it suggests with gracious mildness that the world is imperfect but not impossible. Second, it has the reader pondering the better life just around the corner, if we'll only look.

The third reason delights the copywriter's own troubled world. This is one of those magical openings that always seems to work. Somehow, those first few words steer the message on an inoffensive but impressive course.

A letter for computer software begins:

_____

Dear Word Processor User:

Wouldn't it be great if your word processor had built-in macros to help you work faster ...

... if you could control the way your screen looked—without leaving your document ...

... if you could work *exactly* the way you liked best—keyboard, mouse, pull-down menus, buttons or dialog boxes....

_____

See how effortlessly the text influences the reader? The writer isn't preaching, isn't selling, isn't demanding. The "if" factor disarms skepticism and antagonism. (I don't know why this wording moved into the less motivational past tense.)

That's the batch for this chapter. Openings 51 to 75 are in chapter 10.

10

25 More Ways to Start a Letter– Openings 51 to 75

In this chapter:

(An asterisk means applicable to e-mail.)

51. *The best just got better.*

52. *If I can show you how to . . . will you . . .**

53. *Let's face it.*

54. *It's late and I'm tired, but I have to tell you this.**

55. *We've chosen you* or *You have been chosen.**

56. *I'm surprised I haven't heard from you.**

57. *How would you like to . . .**

58. *It gives me great pleasure to . . .*

59. *I used to think that, but now I think this.*

60. *Does this sound [seem] familiar?*

61. *I'll tell you what pleases me.*

62. *This is what happens when they [you] do it wrong.**

63. *Looking for . . .*

64. *The cry of "Wolf!"**

65. *Here's the deal.**

66. *We can do it where others can't.*

67. *Remember when . . .*

68. *Isn't it sad?**

69. *Ouch!*

70. *Chances are . . .*

71. *Take just two minutes.**

72. *Things were going great. Then all hell broke loose.**

73. *I'm going to make your day.**

74. *Am I right about you?**

75. *When was the last time you . . .*

The third twenty-five include grabber and competitive-comparative openings, some of which can startle as well as challenge. They direct the reader, which means intelligent targeting becomes a major ingredient of the marketing mix.

51.   THE BEST JUST GOT BETTER.

This is a solid, serviceable boilerplate opening which incorporates a major advantage: It's comparative without stating a specific comparison because it's an implicit statement of superiority.

Where this old dependable can fall flat isn't in the statement itself; rather, it's in failure to follow up the statement with specific ostensible proof: The best just got better *in this way.* . . .

Now, what if you can't generate such a follow-up? No problem. You've just proved "The best just got better" is the wrong opening for the message at hand. Try a different start.

An example of "The best just got better" is a letter which does follow up the claim, but the example is flawed by presenting a generality as a specific:

The best value in the computer industry has just gotten even better. Every new Modemaster system you buy (V line and above) includes a complete package of free hardware, software, and service designed to insure more than your machine . . . it insures your productivity!

A couple of questions here. First—and I offer this as opinion, not fact—"has just gotten even better" is considerably more ponderous than "just got even better." Second, the parentheses make the statement before them a

AT&T
AT&T Universal Platinum Business
Post Office Box 44177
Jacksonville, Florida 32231-4177

5.9%

Variable APR on purchases

One card delivers savings plus Platinum-level benefits of special value to small business.

Dear Herschell Lewis,

You'd expect a credit card from AT&T Universal Card not to charge an annual fee. But with the new AT&T Universal Platinum Business Card, that's just the beginning.

Now you can get this MasterCard BusinessCard® card with a low variable **Annual Percentage Rate**, currently **5.9%** (based on the prime rate minus 2.6%), on purchases. This great rate will remain in effect through your April billing statement. After that, a variable APR (based on the prime rate plus 7.4%), currently 15.9%, will apply to purchases.

Created especially for the needs of small business, the AT&T Universal Platinum Business Card gives you credit, cash, calling and control all in one, to help you manage your business more productively.

- Credit line up to $25,000 gives you access to capital whenever you need it.
- No annual fee. Some cards charge as much as $300 per year. You pay $0.
- Worldwide acceptance. Use it for travel, purchases or emergency cash at more than 14 million MasterCard® merchant locations and 580,000 ATMs and financial institutions worldwide.
- $500,000 Travel Accident Insurance protects you and your additional cardholders when you travel on business.[†]
- Dedicated Customer Care associates understand the unique needs of Platinum-level small businesses. They're available all day, every day, to help you.
- Annual Activity Report plus detailed monthly statements and optional quarterly reports help you track expenses, plan budgets.
- AT&T Calling Card feature with 10% savings built in. Use it to save on eligible calls from phones virtually anywhere in the world.

To get the AT&T Universal Platinum Business Card, and a low variable **APR**, currently **5.9%**, on purchases, apply before 09/11. Just complete and return the Invitation Certificate below or call 1 800 68-APPLY. Please note, this Invitation Certificate must be signed by an Authorized Officer of your company. Thank you.

Sincerely,

Daniel R. DeMeo

Daniel R. DeMeo
President and CEO
Universal Card Services Corp.

P.S. Apply today to save on interest with the AT&T Universal Platinum Business

Margin notes:
Credit line up to $25,000

Free of annual fees

$500,000 Travel Accident Insurance

Worldwide acceptance

10% savings on eligible calling card calls

Assign credit lines for additional cardholders

Secure online account information

Fig. 10.1   (letter opening number 51) "The best just got better" has a benefit over many other openings: It suggests *comparative* superiority without actually making a comparative claim. This letter opens with a statement of superiority and then reinforces the claim with flat fact.

weasel rather than a fact. Using commas in this instance would have solved that problem.

If you're asking why this letter opens with generalities instead of specifics, this replication of the text cheats. Specifics do appear in a typed Johnson Box effect before the greeting.

Regardless, I'd have chosen a more inspirational overline and saved the meat for the first paragraph. You decide: Is that opening better than this suggested revision?

The best value in the computer industry just got even better. Every new Modemaster system you buy, V line and above, *includes* an internal modem, two-year on-site service, one-year toll-free software helpline, and a whole bunch of other goodies—all free.

If your next question is, "What about the software the original letter mentioned? *What* software?" Beats me. The letter never tells us.

But none of this detracts from the dependability of this venerable opening.

52.   IF I CAN SHOW YOU HOW TO . . . WILL YOU . . .

Here's another "If" opening, joining all-time favorite number 1, "If you're like me," number 3, "What if," and number 42, "If you like that, you'll love this." It's the distant relative of one yet to come, number 98, "If you're worried, here's the solution."

I'm a fan of "If" openings because they're a nonthreatening provocative. The assumptive attitude attached to "When" doesn't apply to "If" and readers become involved in the "If" just as they would become involved in a question.

The one huge caution about this opening is the relevance requirement. Suppose I say to you, "If I can show you how to poach an Albanian cockroach, will you agree to try my exclusive Albanian Cockroach Poacher?" Chances are I'm aiming at a nonexistent target. Any "If . . . then" statement needs relevance to survive.

Does this example survive?

Dear Mr. Lewis,

If we could show you a way to increase your sales potential, generate higher income, and reduce your overall Marketing costs . . . would you be interested?

It's borderline. The thought is a mild cliché, and eliminating any one element would make it stronger: "If I could show you a way to generate higher income while reducing your marketing costs . . . would you be interested?"

I would eliminate "increase your sales potential" because it's the most generalized of the three components; as long as we are in the operating room I would also lowercase "marketing." And I'd change first-person plural to first-person singular because, although you can't see it, the letter is signed by the company president.

Keep up the silent three-word scream as you write a letter opening: "Relevance and specificity!" Your response doesn't have any choice—it has to go up.

53.   LET'S FACE IT.

I admit, I don't like this opening. It always strikes me as being too smug to establish reader rapport. But some writers I respect use "Let's face it," so it deserves inclusion among the Hallowed Hundred.

I offer a single caution for "Let's face it": Whatever follows has to be a problem-solver, an approach differing from number 32, "We're solving your tough problem." The difference between number 32 and number 53 is the potential of this one to establish immediate rapport and the ugly uncoupling if it doesn't. Here are two recent examples which exemplify how this opening can connect or disconnect. The first:

———————

Dear Herschell Lewis,

Let's face it: if you want *real* tax reform, you'll just have to do it yourself. Now you can—simply by using TurboTax®, America's #1 tax preparation software.

———————

This one does qualify under our empirical set of standards. I wouldn't have used the weak word *simply*, and I'm not sold on that "®" symbol in mid-text when other solutions to the legal requirement exist; but these are picky objections.

Now let's look at the second example:

———————

Dear Creator:

Let's face it. Your job is unique. Unlike your friend, the accountant, you have to do more than put numbers in little squares all day long.

———————

Any opening that has me asking, "Huh?" isn't a barn burner. I enjoy being called the "Creator" (Oh, all right—Let there be light), but what does the assumed uniqueness of my job have to do with "Let's face it"? Does this use establish rapport or damage it?

54. IT'S LATE AND I'M TIRED, BUT I HAVE TO TELL YOU THIS.

This one is a favorite of fund-raisers, and you can see why: The touch of martyrdom reaches out to the best prospects. Number 54 and the forthcoming number 58 are the only openings in this group of one hundred beginning with "It's" because under most circumstances the word *it* doesn't hack it as an opening; the word works here because of its quick tie to emotion.

This opening is underused by commercial mailers, many of whom feel they're taking off their pants in public. In that objection is the nucleus of why number 54 can work when no other opening can grab and shake your target. If you seem to be firing blanks, that's the time to strip down for action.

A fund-raising letter is an archetype of "It's late and I'm tired, but I have to tell you this":

It's 11:30 P.M. on a Tuesday night and I'm tired, I need a shower, and I want to go to bed.

But I can't sleep . . . not until I finish this letter and pray that God will fill your heart with compassion for the poor of Appalachia—as he did mine in 1967.

See how the writer's agony coats the reader's attitude? Try it the next time you're mounting a *commercial* letter test.

55. WE'VE CHOSEN YOU *OR* YOU HAVE BEEN CHOSEN.

This is the cousin of two other openings, number 17, "Because you are who you are, you may get special attention," and number 18 "Stroke, stroke—You're a rare bird." The difference between this one and the other two is that number 55 puts the writer, or the organization the writer represents, in a parental position.

The obvious determinant of whether to use number 55 in place of numbers 17 or 18 is *who* is sending the letter. If the recipient accepts the sender as a superior, then this is the preferred opening: If God walks among mankind, He's less godlike—which would be the impression numbers 17 or 18 would transmit in this circumstance.

A subscription letter begins:

Each year we invite selected candidates to join the largest private nonprofit scientific and educational organization in the world.

> Your name has been selected as a candidate for membership in the
> National Geographic Society.

Notice that word *candidate*. It's in key with the posture the writer takes.

STATUS: Pre-Selected

COST: No Annual Fee

MONEY BACK: Up to 1%[†]

OFFER: 6.9% until May 1

Get your
Discover® Card
and choose your
Free Gift!

Limited Time Offer
Apply for your card now!

S417 P1 **AUTO******5-DIGIT 33317
Peggy J. Nelson
340 N Fig Tree Ln
Fort Lauderdale, FL 33317-2561

Dear Peggy J. Nelson:

You have been pre-selected to apply for the No-Annual-Fee Discover® Card. Apply for your card now, and you'll receive a low 6.9%* Fixed APR on all of your purchases until **May 1**! After that, the APR is Prime + 8.99 percentage points.* Once approved, you'll also receive one of four **free gifts**. Use the free gift selection form below to choose the gift you want.

In addition, you'll get all of these great benefits:

• **No Annual Fee.** Why pay $20, $30 or more?

• **Money Back on Purchases.** You get a Cashback Bonus® award of up to 1%, paid yearly based on your annual level of purchases. That's money back directly to you!

• **Interest-Free Cash Advances.** Simply pay your balance in full each month, and for only a small transaction fee,* your cash advances are interest-free.

To take advantage of this offer, we must receive your reply by November 1. So mail your completed application in the enclosed postage-paid envelope today!

Sincerely,

L. Lampert

L. Lampert
Vice President, Marketing
NOVUS Services, Inc.

* See Important Information on back of application.
† Up to 1% paid yearly, based on your annual level of purchases.
C8F S04

it pays to DISCOVER®

http://www.discovercard.com

Fig. 10.2   (letter opening number 55) Literally millions of credit card offers have used a version of this opening, usually "You've been pre-approved." Here we have "You have been pre-selected," but "to apply for" destroys the "selected" image.

Nomination

To: Herschell G. Lewis
President
COMMUNICOMP
340 N Fig Tree Ln
Fort Lauderdale, FL 33317-2561

From: John Counter, Chairman, SME-International

Herschell, it is my privilege to announce that you have been nominated for membership in Sales and Marketing Executives of Ft. Laud./W. Palm. This nomination was based on your leadership role in marketing and your unique background and work experience.

SME is a group of CEOs and top executives meeting regularly to discuss tactics and learn the latest trends and ideas in marketing, and most importantly, how to implement these ideas within your own company. When you join SME, you will have access to the Ft. Laud./W. Palm area's leaders in sales and marketing management.

Enclosed you will find some additional information about SME. Several membership options are available including direct and corporate, however, I do encourage you to apply for membership in the local chapter, SME - South Florida. I am sure you will find the lifetime professional alliances, friends and ideas gained from your involvement as worthwhile as I have.

Herschell, congratulations again on your nomination, and we look forward to meeting you in person!

P.S. *Please return your application right away to allow the SME - South Florida board time to make a final decision and approval at the next board meeting!*

Sales & Marketing Executives   *"SME - The Worldwide Association of Sales & Marketing Management."*
Chapters Worldwide • Home Office: Sales & Marketing Executives-International • 5500 Interstate North Parkway, Ste 545 • Atlanta • GA 30328 USA
• Web: www.sell.org • Fax: (800) 385-9178 • E-mail: membership@smei.org • Telephone: (770) 661-8500 (National and International) •

Fig. 10.3   (letter opening number 55) The first paragraph, pure stroking, is also a pure example of "We've chosen you" or "You have been chosen." Why letters such as this one use "apply for membership" instead of the less denigrating "accept membership" is a mystery.

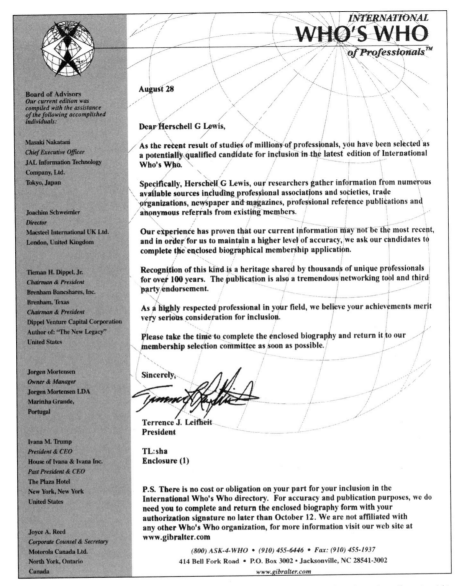

Fig. 10.4   (letter opening number 55) Here is another standard example of the "You have been chosen" opening. A bit of hyperbole ("studies of millions of professionals") plus considerable hedging ("potentially qualified candidate") intend to reinforce the exclusivity of the invitation.

56. I'M SURPRISED I HAVEN'T HEARD FROM YOU.

Danger signals explode in every direction from this supercharged opening. Because "I'm surprised I haven't heard from you" can make you a hero or a bum, think of it as dynamite with a short fuse. If you don't get out of the way it'll demolish you instead of your reader's apathy.

A better comparison: it's the old "Frankly, I'm puzzled," laced with strychnine. The question you have to answer *in the very next sentence*: "Who is this person and what right does he or she have to expect a response from me?"

The clarity and persuasiveness with which you answer that question determines who gets wiped out by the dynamite. And this adds another caution, a universal rule of force-communication:

> ✐ Don't use dynamite to kill a butterfly.

A letter to my wife from a company pitching a refrigerator service contract begins:

Dear Margo E. Lewis:

We are surprised we haven't heard from you about our recent offer of Extended Service coverage. Maybe one of the following applies:

- You haven't received our previous letters

- We did not sufficiently cover the benefits of our Asure™ program

- You are not interested in the extended protection

. . . and some more bullets, followed by a warning that the first year's warranty is about to expire.

See the hole here? Who the devil is the woman who signed this letter to try to nail us with the nasty mantle of causing an unpleasant surprise? Who is she to draw *any* supposition?

That's the key: We've never had any relationship. In this nonrelationship, the writer had a plethora of alternative openings that would not have been abrasive—for example, numbers 22, 9, 3, 32, 41, or others not yet covered; or on a lesser plane numbers 1, 10, or 23. If you can see the usefulness of each and the risk of this one or numbers 40, 45, 49, 15, or 6, you are getting as much effectiveness from this list of one hundred letter openings as I am.

SOUTH PLAINS MORTGAGE COMPANY

Expect more from the Nations Leader

3101 Maguire, Suite 259
Orlando, Florida 32803
407-898-1501 • 1-888-550-NOTE(6683)

Mr. Herschell Lewis
340 N Fig Tree Ln
Ft Lauderdale, FL 33317

Dear Mr. Lewis:

A short time ago, I sent you the attached letter explaining all the benefits of letting South Plains Mortgage Company buy the real estate note you are carrying for $180,000 in Florida. With your busy schedule, you may have put the letter aside, so I wanted to give you another opportunity to take advantage of this lucrative offer.

Why should you sell your note? Well, for one thing, you'll lose the burden of taking care of **all the tiring chores** that come with it--<u>collecting payments, keeping tabs on taxes and insurance, and filing government forms</u>. Most of all, you won't have to ever worry again about whether payments are made.

Instead, you will have a **generous, lump sum payment** right in your pocket. A payment you can use to supplement your pension, take a dream vacation, pay bills or do anything else you would like to do **if only you had the money**!

Now, you may be tempted to wait, thinking that your note is as good as money in the bank. But, if you read the papers or watch TV, you know that residential mortgage rates are creeping back up. And each **increase in interest rates** means that your note loses value as an investment. To put it simply, **the longer you wait, the less money you will be able to get for your note**.

And with South Plains Mortgage Company, you will get that money quickly! We handle all the paperwork and even purchase notes where the payments are behind.

So, please reread my first letter now. Then call me **toll free** at **1(888) 550-NOTE(6683)**. I will be happy to give you a quote on your note's value if you have the information ready when you call. And the sooner you call, the sooner you will have cash--**free and clear**!

Yours for greater financial security,

Joe DiLuzio

Joe DiLuzio
Regional Vice President

P.S.   If you would like a quote on the value of your note, call in Orlando **(407) 898-1501** or toll free at **1 (888) 550-NOTE (6683)**. There is no cost or obligation, and we can give it to you over the phone.

©South Plains Mortgage Company. 1993 "MET FL 5-11-98 26613"

Fig. 10.5   (letter opening number 56) The first appeal from this company is shown as figure 8.3. This follow-up is a variation on the "I'm surprised I haven't heard from you" theme. Follow-up letters should *never* assume the reader recalls the original communication. Recapitulating the offer, as this letter does, is the proper approach.

57.   HOW WOULD YOU LIKE TO . . .

"How would you like to" is a more personable cousin of number 3, "What if." The difference is that this one implicitly suggests you *can*; no "if" factor exists.

So the very natural follow-up to "How would you like to" is, "It's as easy as. . . ."

What the writer has to consider is whether the reader actually wants to accomplish or enjoy whatever the offer includes. This is a classic example of the benefit of demographic-psychographic-creative matchup.

An eight-page letter begins with a printed headline and a ten-line explanation of what the letter contains (a technique with which I don't agree), then launches into high gear:

Dear Friend:

How would you like to earn $1,000 a day—every day?

Imagine! Making more money in one day than most people do in a week. You can do it! (You'll even earn big profits while you sleep!)

Cash in on the most profitable field in the modern world.

How? By publishing information.

To many, that last four-word paragraph is a letdown because it doesn't seem to validate the claim and doesn't seem easy to do. I would have used a comma, not a colon, after the greeting, and would have softened the apparent letdown with "How? Believe it or not, by being a respected publisher." Still, I understand this letter has been successful; and anyway, what matters is the choice of opening, not any particular use.

58.   IT GIVES ME GREAT PLEASURE TO . . .

Unless it's tied to an emotional hook—"It's late and I'm tired, but . . ."— "It" is a weak opener because it's the most unspecific of all pronouns. But who has the guts (or the folly) of making this a blanket condemnation? "It gives me great pleasure to" is a logical enough opening for a pleasant offering.

That's the key: What follows has to be pleasant for the message recipient. If you're writing, "It gives me great pleasure to tell you that your account has been assigned to me," you are losing stature by being recipient of the assignment instead of its instigator and you're announcing a nonevent that brings pleasure to you, not to your target.

So focus your pleasure on a tight beam aimed outward.

An example of this opening:

Dear CorelDRAW Registered User:

It's with great pleasure that I advise you of a brand new CorelDRAW User's Group that is forming in your region!

If this collection had a different theme you and I might attack the double use of "that" in the same sentence, the standoffish "advise," and the overencompassing "region" instead of "area." Instead, let's reach agreement on the value of suggesting pleasure.

Suppose this letter opened, "A brand-new CorelDRAW User's Group is forming in your area. Don't you want to be part of it from the word go?" Would that be stronger or weaker? If you're undecided, *don't* use the "pleasure" approach. Save "pleasure" for more obvious pleasure.

59.   I USED TO THINK THAT, BUT NOW I THINK THIS.

Once again we have a double-edged opening. If what you now think is immediately beneficial for the reader, you've established rapport on a level comparable to opening number 1, "If you're like me." In fact, the rapport could be stronger because the ploy isn't as transparent.

But if your reference is abstruse or inconsequential—not to you but to your reader—ugh. It's too late for the caution flag because you've already wrecked your vehicle.

As you read this example of opening number 59, ask yourself, "What might I have done to use this same device more effectively, with parallel wording . . . and what's the tip-off that the writer is unsure of the device?"

Dear Fellow Executive:

I used to think that less was more when it came to managing people.

I believed, in other words, that the less management interfered with the daily routine, the happier and more productive their people would be.

Perhaps you once felt the same way. Perhaps, too....

The tip-off is "in other words." Whenever you see that string of words, feel free to conclude the writer realizes he or she wasn't clear enough or emphatic enough or convincing enough the first time around.

So we knock off the obscuring first sentence and the message becomes clearer, more emphatic, and more convincing:

Dear Fellow Executive:

I used to think that the less management interfered with the daily routine, the happier and more productive their people would be.

Perhaps you once felt the same way. Perhaps, too. . . .

Okay, it's no barnburner, but we've stifled the impulse to tamper with individual words, such as substituting "maybe" for "perhaps"; we're using the same basic words to drive closer to a point. And one of the Great Rules of Force-Communication is:

> ✏ Get to the point!

If you can master this opening by being both relevant and pointed, you'll be well under way with a strong selling argument.

60.   Does this sound [seem] familiar?

Properly used, this one can't miss.

What does "properly used" mean? Simple: It means matching whatever sounds familiar to an individual to whom it *should* sound familiar. This opening should find increasing favor as databases refine themselves and enable communicators to achieve near perfect pinpointing.

(I'm using "sound familiar" instead of "seem familiar" because even though letters don't usually talk, *sound* is closer to actual conversation than the dreamier *seem*.)

A highly targeted letter selling a newsletter subscription begins, after the usual display type at the top of the page:

Dear Network Administrator:

C-R-A-S-H.

Panic rages. Confusion reigns. Voices scream: "The network's down!"

Sound familiar?

Network Administrators like yourself face this nightmare every day. You're the one they turn to when. . . .

Yeah, whoever sent this might have handwritten the "C-R-A-S-H" and cleaned up that muddy "they" reference, but this opening has terrific guts.

Now, suppose I'm *not* a network administrator and I get this letter? Then the company should take issue with the mailing-list company or the database compiler, not the writer . . . who came up with a dynamic and readable opening.

61.   I'LL TELL YOU WHAT PLEASES ME.

This gentle opening has a benefit that doesn't exist in revelatory first-person openings such as number 45, "I have to tell you the truth": The reader of number 61 knows that whatever follows won't be abrasive or heavily challenging. It has a benefit that doesn't exist in first-person openings such as number 54, "It's late and I'm tired, but I have to tell you this," which can carry the seeds of intrusion: The reader of number 61 knows that whatever follows will be upbeat.

Effective writers even before the legendary John Caples ("They laughed when I sat down at the piano") have known how *I* as surrogate for *you* side-steps hostility. Who can object to another person blabbing what he or she is doing?

By its nature, "I'll tell you what pleases me" has implicit limits on its use. This opening is a delicate tap on the shoulder, not an elephant gun. Consider it when your target or what you're hawking has overtones of quiet, civilized pleasure.

A letter from a gardening publication begins:

———————————

Dear Gardening Friend:

Beautiful gardens are inspiring to me. Whenever I see one, I immediately want to get in close to find out everything I can from the garden itself and from the gardeners who created it—how did they get that delphinium to grow so well in such terrible conditions . . . how did they come up with such an ingenious way of landscaping that steep slope in the backyard . . . how did they. . . .

———————————

And on it goes. The opening paragraph is nine lines long, with some eighty-eight words. As intolerable as I find a first paragraph of this length, the comfortable "I'll tell you what pleases me" opening is considerably better than it would have been if the writer had lapsed into a standard "you" opening:

———————————

Dear Gardening Friend:

Aren't beautiful gardens inspiring to you? Whenever you see one, don't you immediately want to get in close to find out everything you can from the garden itself and from the gardeners who created it—how did they get that delphinium to. . . .

———————————

Simplest suggestion for reader tranquility: Let the first sentence be the entire first paragraph.

Incidentally, if you're a wordsmith you never would write, "how did they get that delphinium to grow so well *in* such terrible conditions." You'd replace "in" with "under," wouldn't you?

62. THIS IS WHAT HAPPENS WHEN THEY (YOU) DO IT WRONG.

Talk about power! Number 62 couldn't be further from number 61 in its demand for an immediate red-hot emotional response.

We all know The Inside-Out Power Rule:

> ✏ The more powerful the wording, the more dangerous the wording.

From the rule we quickly extrapolate the decision-making mechanism: "This is what happens when *they* do it wrong" has less power—ergo, less danger—than "This is what happens when *you* do it wrong." The reader can join the attack on *them*, but not so easily on him or herself.

If you love comparative advertising (as I do), then this opening is dear to your heart. You recognize, going into the arena, a basic truth of both bullfighting and bull-*throwing*: Your performance will bring some flowers and some brickbats.

But you won't be ignored.

A letter using this device begins:

Dear Friend:

The fastest indicator of a poorly designed vacuum cleaner is when somebody sneezes whenever you run it. You are most certainly recycling dirt and even molds from the floor right back into the air!

Clever. The writer has sneaked "you" into the mixture without your recognizing the inclusion. So *you* as victim are glued to *you* as observer.

In this use, an introductory sentence might have added a dimension of receptivity the immediate "vacuum cleaner" reference is too specific to permit.

An example:

Dear Friend,

Here's what happens when they do it wrong:

The fastest indicator of a poorly designed vacuum cleaner....

FROM THE DESK OF BOB NELSON
Author, *1001 Ways to Reward Employees*

Dear Colleague:

How many employee incentive programs have you tried over the years?

How many of those approaches <u>really worked</u> to fire up your employees and achieve tangible results *over the long term*?

If you're like most managers, you've discovered firsthand that *old ways* of motivating employees--either with carrots or sticks--no longer work in today's business environment.

Yet I want to tell you: I've met *hundreds* of smart managers who are <u>succeeding wildly</u> in energizing and motivating their employees--and they're achieving truly *spectacular increases* in profit and productivity!

What 'secret' techniques do they know that you don't?

Over nearly 20 years, as a management consultant and author, I've discovered how the world's most effective managers get their people energized--and <u>keep</u> them inspired day in and day out.

The best news is, most of the breakthrough techniques that are <u>really working</u> today to motivate people *cost little or nothing*! It's not about money!

That's why I originally wrote the best-seller *1001 Ways to Reward Employees*--and why I want you to see *Bob Nelson's Rewarding Employees* newsletter.

Every month *Bob Nelson's Rewarding Employees* arrives to <u>remind you</u>--to keep you and your fellow managers focused on your most important job: *motivating people.*

To show you how *Bob Nelson's Rewarding Employees* can help, on the following pages I want to give you a taste--with dozens of specific examples--of the kinds of breakthrough motivational approaches I'll be sharing with you over the coming months.

But first, let me tell you what this newsletter <u>won't</u> do.

BOB NELSON'S REWARDING EMPLOYEES <u>WON'T</u> GIVE YOU IVORY TOWER ANALYSIS . . .
AND IT <u>WON'T</u> WASTE A MINUTE OF YOUR TIME

If you're busy, you'll like this newsletter. It's terse. It's tight. It's written crisply, with plenty of bulleted points.

In fact, *Bob Nelson's Rewarding Employees* is written so concisely--and at such a high level--that you'll speed through each issue in <u>just minutes</u> a month. Most importantly, *Bob Nelson's Rewarding Employees* is focused on <u>action</u>--what you can do *right now*, the minute you arrive at work in the morning, to achieve better results that day.

(over, please . . .)

BNL

Fig. 10.6   (letter opening number 62) When you tell a target reader "This is what happens when you do it wrong," you then explain: (a) doing it wrong is normal; (b) more people do it wrong than do it right; (c) here's how easy it is to do it right. This letter benefits from following the classic sequence, using short paragraphs.

Yeah, while I was at it I substituted a comma for the standoffish colon after "Dear Friend," and I indented the paragraph. Mechanics aside, can you see how adding that opening brings universality to the sales argument?

63. LOOKING FOR . . .

Ever since Diogenes, we've all been looking for something or other. So this opening has two advantages: It touches an archetypical nerve and it asks a question.

Certainly you've spotted the obvious caution: Whatever follows shouldn't be stupid or irrelevant. If you open a letter with "Looking for a new type of wall covering?" you'd better have the world's best database as your mailing list. (If you aren't sure, why not use number 61, "I'll tell you what pleases me"? Self-examination is less intrusive and therefore less likely to seem stupid or irrelevant than the always externally aimed "you.")

Here's a use of number 63 which, because it includes an "If" beginning, relates to number 52, "If I can show you how to . . . will you." Ask yourself, "Does the nature of 'Looking for' make this approach stronger without an 'If' filter?"

———————

Dear Investor:

If low CD and money market rates have you looking for higher yields, there is an important step you need to take before moving your money: decide how much you want to keep in savings and how much you want to invest for higher longer-term returns.

———————

What's your decision? I vote for staying with the purified version of number 63. It would read something like this:

———————

Dear Investor,

Looking for higher yields?

Who isn't?

Let's assume you *are* looking for higher yields, as any sane investor should during this period of low CD and money market rates....

———————

Understand, I'm not militating against expanding any of these openings. Every one of them can profit from experimentation and tweaking. But adding an "If" clause to a positive question is dilution, not expansion.

64.   THE CRY OF "WOLF!"

In the last decade of the twentieth century "The cry of 'Wolf!'" came into its own. We now use it as stick-on notes affixed to letters or printer-faked on envelopes. We use it as rubber stamps. We use it as handwritten overlines.

It works.

Prediction: Its form also has to mutate constantly or it will have a short happy life because its message is both volatile and eventually recognizable. We all know the story of the boy who cried, "Wolf!" When a wolf actually appeared, the message had lost its impact.

While it lasts, let's use it . . . with one eye cocked open to watch for signs of flagging impact. Right now, as long as our targets think there's a wolf out there, let's bay at them.

A business letter begins:

Dear Executive:

Hiring workers as independent contractors instead of employees is getting much more risky.

The revenue-hungry IRS is on a nationwide campaign to collect taxes and penalties from employers who pay workers as independent contractors when the IRS considers them employees.

A suggestion if you're crying "Wolf!": Stay in character. This letter says, "The revenue-hungry IRS is on a nationwide campaign to collect taxes and penalties from employers. . . ." A consummate wolf-cryer knows how to keep his victims ever nervous. You or I would have written, "The IRS is hungry for more money. They're out to nail employers like you for more taxes and (slather) more penalties. . . ."

See the difference? You're supposed to *cry* "Wolf!" not whisper the word. But you can see, too, how reader-involving any opening of this type instantly becomes.

65.   HERE'S THE DEAL.

This approach is similar to number 39, "I'll get right to the point," but it's more positive. It's not as close to number 33, "This is short and sweet," because this one makes a hard promise.

Need I point out that if you say, "Here's the deal," you then *immediately* offer a deal? No nonsense, no puffery, no "Here's who we are." Offer a deal fast, or else choose another opening.

A communication from a printing company has "500 for $19.95" in a sunburst at the right edge. The letter itself begins (see page 236):

Dear Friend:

The great thing about our Mini-Sweeps is that
you actually have a decent chance to win.

I mean, we're not sending this offer to a
zillion people all over the universe. So don't
look for the PCH Prize Patrol or Ed McMahon to
come knocking on your door -- but don't be too
surprised to get a prize in the mail next month.

Anyway, I wish you luck.

        *   *   *   *   *

Now, let's get down to business.

Serious business.

I have a deal for you that will save you money
and bring you long-lasting benefits. (I admit,
it will be okay for us, too.)

Along with your enclosed RAFFLE TICKETS you will
also find LIST RENTAL TICKETS -- each entitling
you to a free 5,000 test of our lists -- CONSUMERS
DIGEST and YOUR MONEY active subscribers -- plus,
if you wish, a combined Masterfile of both lists.
Almost 2,000,000 unduplicated active names are
available. That's a pretty serious number. Right?

In other words, you can get up to 15,000 free names.

        *   *   *   *   *

In addition, these people are 100% mail-sold,
and furthermore, they have money to spend.

How do I know that? Well, consider this.

People buy CONSUMERS DIGEST because we advise
them about health, travel, retirement, investing and
money management plus other things that
affect their quality of life -- but primarily
they buy it because they want our Buying Guides.

Our Buying Guides (inserted in every issue) have

Fig. 10.7   (letter opening number 65) A "Here's the deal" opening should use verbalisms, as though the writer were *talking* to the reader instead of writing. That's what this one, in an odd booklet form, does.

-2-

Best Buys and best prices on TVs, VCRs, stereos, cars, trucks, tools, cameras, kitchen appliances, gardening equipment, and almost anything a person may need. I don't have to be a genius to know our readers have money to spend. They read CONSUMERS DIGEST <u>because</u> they have money to spend.

No wonder they respond to all kinds of mailings. It just makes sense, doesn't it?

<u>It's the same thing with YOUR MONEY</u>.

People read YOUR MONEY because they're looking for help in handling their money. They want information about mutual funds, stocks, bonds, insurance, interest rates, mortgages, and ways to save on taxes -- things like that.

These are solid citizens with money to spend -- and mail buyers as well -- the kind of people you look for. It's as plain as day.

          *   *   *   *   *

To top it all, the lists can be segmented into individual groups of people with special interests -- such as fitness, golf, health foods, sports, collectibles, charitable causes, self-improvement, travel, home decorating and many more. You'll find a complete index of all Lifestyle Selectivity segments on the back of the enclosed cards.

This segmentation allows you to zero in on your best prospects, and I recommend that you try it. It works. It will give you a lower cost per order. For quantities and other information, call me at (847) 763-9200, ext. 7121. Or you may fax me at (847) 763-0200.

                    <u>HOW SWEET CAN IT GET?</u>

                    <u>SWEETER THAN YOU MAY THINK</u>.

BECAUSE THESE LISTS KEEP GROWING WITH A STEADY

INFLOW OF FRESH NEW NAMES, YOU'LL BE ABLE TO

Fig. 10.7   Continued

Amsterdam's Special Introductory Envelope Offer is a great time to cash in on a real value. Naturally, our envelopes are constructed from the finest quality 24 lb. white wove stock, and are die cut to ensure easy insertion.

We ask ourselves, mightn't this have had considerably more wallop if the writer had actually written, "Here's the deal"? After all, it worked (temporarily) for Ross Perot. Compare our suggested version with the original:

Here's the deal: 500 envelopes for $19.95.

These aren't "schlock" envelopes. They're our finest-quality 24-lb. white wove stock, die-cut so you'll never have an insertion problem with them.

As is true of so many examples we've dissected, a principal barrier to effectiveness seems to be *staying in character*. If you make a deliberate choice of an opening, staying in character should be easy. In the words of number 65: Here's the deal. Choose an approach and just stick with it. Okay?

66.   WE CAN DO IT WHERE OTHERS CAN'T.

This one suggests instant problem-solving, and the combination of absolute competence and absolute relevance has terrific impact. Consider it for two circumstances: business-to-business problem-solving and consumer mailings in which a direct competitive comparison isn't feasible.

Improperly used, "We can do it where others can't" generates a negative impression rather than a positive one. And what's an improper use? Inability to make good on the claim.

Does this opening make good on its claim?

Dear Reader,

The Literary Guild is the one book club that can change your mind about book clubs forever.

For over 65 years, The Literary Guild has worked to provide selective, discerning, demanding readers like you with the *best variety of all the best books* you could wish for, the cream of the crop from all publishers.

We're the club that makes this unrivaled array of books available to you in a way that's *convenient, uncomplicated* and *very affordable*....

What's your opinion? Mine is based on the whole concept of this series of openings: Nothing after the first sentence makes good on the claim. The writer should have asked after writing the first sentence, "Okay, *how* does this club change their minds about book clubs forever?" That would have been the way to get the reader to think, "Yeah . . . they *can* do it where others can't." (Capitalizing "Club" would add stature.)

67.   REMEMBER WHEN . . .

This is quiet nostalgia at work. Don't equate it with number 37, "Historical buildup," which recounts an action to which the reader wasn't privy. Don't equate it with a dangerous ("If you'd done that then, you'd be in this position now,") which is half scolding.

"Remember when" has a huge benefit when used properly: It instantly establishes rapport, because whatever it recounts cements a common experience shared by writer and reader.

Use this opening with two cautions:

1. When you say "Remember when," be sure the episode is one the reader *will remember*, fondly.
2. Follow up with "We're bringing it back for you," or you've wasted the opening.

A health magazine opens its letter with three indented bullets, really a pre-opening. The message itself starts out in fine fettle:

Remember when eating well was so simple? The days when we could savor a juicy shrimp without thinking twice about *cholesterol* . . . when we could tuck into a prime steak and not worry about *growth hormones* . . . the times when an apple a day wasn't clouded with concerns about *pesticides* . . . the good old days when all the *salt* in chicken soup meant nothing to us. . . .

Altogether, a pretty good opening, isn't it? Heads nod, "Yes, that's how it was"; and the intention of this opening is fulfilled.

(This letter, in its move toward complying with caution 2, for no good reason quickly turns cold and pitchy; but we're concerned only with the opening.)

68.   ISN'T IT SAD?

Peril lurks in this opening. I see two totally different uses for it—either a fund-raising letter basing its appeal on episode . . . or a tongue-in-cheek easygoing and humorous sales pitch.

Oh, does peril lurk! For fund-raising, if you don't have the communicative power to convince the reader this *is* sad, you've struck a wrong chord; for tongue-in-cheek humor, if the reader isn't in sync with the satire, you've lost a possible sale.

Oh, but if you do connect, you can raise funds and make sales where no other approach cracks the barrier of apathy.

An example of "Isn't it sad?":

Dear Friend,

A commercial whale hunt is a sad, bloody scene: Explosive-tipped harpoons shot from cannons on the "catcher" boats . . . the whales butchered right at sea in factory ships. . . .

Good, serviceable opening, isn't it? I think the writer could have gone even farther down the gory road, eliminating the nondescript "catcher" boats:

A commercial whale hunt is a sad, bloody scene: Laughing, jeering "cannoneers" shoot explosive-tipped harpoons that tear great holes in the whale's flesh. Unbearable agony! The bleeding, tormented whale is hauled aboard, still alive . . . then butchered with no thought that a few minutes ago this was a majestic creature, one of the last of a vanishing species. . . .

My point: in for a penny, in for a pound. The benefit of choosing *any* opening—whether it's "Isn't it sad?" or "Congratulations!"—is lost in direct ratio to the amount of water in the rhetorical soup.

69.   OUCH!

I've seen business-to-business mailings actually crack the impenetrable Secretarial Barrier with a one-word exclamation. I've seen astounding results in consumer mailings to people who seem to be impervious to more standard openings. (My usual preference for single-word exclamations opening a letter is handwriting.)

To me, the biggest benefit of this type of opening is that it promises easy reading. An example:

Dear Business Owner:

Yeoww! Running a small business can mean a lot of aches and pains. But we don't need to remind you about the kind of unbearable pressure that pounds and throbs from the top of your overhead all the way down to your bottom line. You suffer from it everyday.

Well, the second sentence doesn't really grab us because it loses specificity and abandons the quickness of "Yeoww!" by lapsing into the nonspecific "a lot of aches and pains"; and "everyday" should be two words. But you certainly can see how a one-word grabber jump-starts a letter.

70.   CHANCES ARE . . .

Here's an easy, low-key way to swing into a selling posture the reader implicitly accepts.

You aren't making a claim the reader can reject, you aren't establishing a position the reader can regard as adversarial, and you aren't being stiff-necked and distant. So this is a serviceable opening, a welcome friend on those days when your imagination and Alzheimer's are engaged in a great civil war inside your brain.

An example of this opening:

Hi, there, and top of the morning to you . . .

Chances are you really aren't in the mood for a sales pitch this morning.

Okay, neither am I. . . .

Irritation, if any, stems from "Okay, neither am I," not from the opening sentence. A more-in-keeping second sentence would be, "Boy, do I understand that." It's an opinion, not an edict.

Good thing, too. Chances are you'd resent an edict.

71.   TAKE JUST TWO MINUTES.

If you don't see the difference between "Take just two minutes" and "It'll take you just two minutes," you'd better send out a letter of your own, using opening number 5—"I need help."

"Take two minutes" is an imperative. Letters are the imperative component of a mailing, and by lapsing into the declarative with the neutral "It" opening, your letter puts water on the flame instead of giving it a shot of gasoline.

A letter from Handgun Control, signed by Sarah Brady, begins:

Dear Friend,

Please take two minutes to answer the National Public Safety Survey I've enclosed and return it to me today.

Your completed survey will help Handgun Control, Inc., the largest national organization devoted exclusively to *keeping guns out of the wrong hands*, convince the new Congress. . . .

Imperfect? Darn it, yeah. Why in heaven's name did whoever wrote this put that "Inc." after "Handgun Control," immediately creating a corporate impression? And sure, many of the best potential donors have long since passed the point where they're surprised to find a request for donations hooked to the survey.

But in this ambience, what if, instead of the polite imperative "Please take two minutes," the letter had opened in an immeasurably weaker neutral gear . . .

Dear Friend,

It'll take you just two minutes to answer the National Public Safety Survey I've enclosed. . . .

See how much more anemic "It" makes this opening? Opening number 71 is an imperative. Use it when you aren't afraid your demand will prompt an "Oh, no, I won't" reaction.

72.   THINGS WERE GOING GREAT. THEN ALL HELL BROKE LOOSE.

This type of confessional requires high professionalism or it comes off as stupidly self-serving. We see it in fund-raising, but if you sell self-help courses or get-rich-quick concepts you might test "Things were going great" against a straightforward "Have I got a deal for you" approach, or against numbers 1, 3, 6, 10, 47, and 52—which may be too transparent through overuse by competitors.

The power of "Things were going great" is the human desire to spy on somebody else's misfortune. No, not to share it; asking a reader to share misfortune is wastebasket bait. We want to be voyeurs, not participants, when reading personal negatives.

A letter headed "An Important Message from Annette Funicello" begins:

Hello, Ms. Lewis . . .

I've always lived a kind of charmed life . . . starting with those years I had on the *Mickey Mouse Club* as a little girl . . . the great times I had making those "zany" beach movies in the 60's . . . and the wonderful years I've had with my family.

I guess I thought nothing bad would ever happen to me—but then multiple sclerosis struck.

The concept is 100 percent sound. The heading, "An Important Message from Annette Funicello" (which many might regard as an outlandish concept), isn't as potent as opening directly with "I've always led a kind of charmed life."

AMERICAN *Sales Leads*
a division of American Business Information, Inc.*

1350 Linton Blvd, Ste A2
Delray Beach, FL 33444-1147
Phone: (561) 265-1141
Fax: (561) 265-1366

|..||...||...||....|||.|.|.|.|.|.|.|.|.|..|.|.|.|..|||.|.|
•••••••••••••••••••••3 DIGIT 333
Margo Lewis
Communicomp
PO Box 15725
Plantation FL 33318-5725

*FREE SALES LEADS**
for one ZIP Code
from our database of
10 million businesses.

It happens to almost every business… things are rolling along just fine and then WHAM! It's like your sales have hit a brick wall. New customers are harder and harder to find. You want to expand into new markets, but how? Well, help is on the way!

American Sales Leads will help you track down your best prospects, generate great leads and find profitable new customers. I'd like to prove it to you with a fantastic offer… ***FREE SALES LEADS**** for one ZIP Code area. That's right — absolutely ***FREE!***

First, let me highlight why you can expect your best results when you use our lists:

- **You'll find prospects you didn't think existed.** We can help you identify all the potential customers in your market area so you won't miss any opportunities.

- **You can select exactly the right prospects.** Choose by Type of Business, Yellow Page Heading, Number of Employees, Estimated Sales Volume, Years in Business, Credit Rating Score , and other criteria that will help you maximize your marketing efficiency.

- **Pick the most convenient formats for you.** We can provide:
  Prospect Lists for your distributors, *Mailing Labels* for direct mail campaigns,
  Sales Lead Cards for your salespeople, *Maps* to pinpoint your prospects,
  or *Diskettes* to set up a "Sales Automation" database system on your PC.

- **You'll get the best quality information available.** Our database of 10 million businesses is the finest in the industry… because we use the best sources and verify our information with 16 million phone calls each year. That's 65,000 phone calls *every day!*

Over 1 million businesses across the country use our database to find new customers and grow their sales. You can, too! Call me at (561) 265-1141 to arrange a time when we can talk about your sales and marketing challenges.

Sincerely,

Michael E. Harvey

Michael Harvey
General Manager

P.S. Even if you sell to <u>*consumers*</u> . . . our offer still applies. Select households by age, income, or other factors, and get ***FREE SALES LEADS**** for one ZIP Code.

† Our Credit Rating Scores are indicators of probable ability to pay. They are based on business demographic factors such as number of employees, years in business, industry stability and barriers to entry, and government data. While they do not reflect actual payment history, the ratings are a good starting point. We recommend that these ratings should not be the sole factor used in making a credit decision, especially for larger dollar amounts. You must obtain more information from bank and trade references, local credit bureaus, or other sources before extending credit. We will not be liable for any losses resulting from the use of this information.

Fig. 10.8   (letter opening number 72) Readers love this opening—"Things were going great. Then all hell broke loose." It humanizes the writer … and humanizing the writer helps build rapport. The "FREE SALES LEADS" display type at upper right probably isn't the best wording, and the asterisk positively maims rapport. (The hard-to-find matching asterisk explains that the number of sales leads is 100. Why not simply say "FREE 100 SALES LEADS"?)

73. I'M GOING TO MAKE YOUR DAY.

This is the reverse spin of a Clint Eastwood homily. Because the reader can just as easily interpret its promise as arrogance-based instead of fact-based, handle with care.

"I'm going to make your day," properly reinforced within the next two or three sentences, has considerably more wallop than number 10, "I have something good for you," or number 23, "Good news!" What's perplexing to me is a letter that chooses "I'm going to make your day" and then immediately loses its bravado.

An example is a letter that begins, curiously, with a backed-off approach:

———————

Good Morning!

I want to make your day.

You're one of a very special group of individuals we've chosen to get a *free desktop calculator* when you order a supply of the most elegant, most beautiful bank checks that ever graced anyone's checkbook.

———————

Technically, no problem; it's clear, well written, and to the point. But why take two sidesteps? (1) "I want to make your day" only has about 37 percent of the impact "I'm going to make your day" would have had. (2) Nothing in the following paragraph makes the reader's day.

Opening with number 6, "Congratulations!" or number 23, "Good news!" would have been more in keeping with what follows.

Let's suppose *we're* the creative team. We decide to use number 73 as our opening. Keeping the flavor undiluted is as easy as:

———————

I'm going to make your day.

I'm not only going to give a whole new personality to your bank checks. I'm going to give you a full-function desktop calculator for the privilege of doing it.

———————

My point: Letter openings parallel the opening of a conversation. The first sentence gets attention, or it doesn't. The next few sentences have the other person nodding yes, or they don't.

74. AM I RIGHT ABOUT YOU?

What a blessing for us is the human sense of insecurity! We feel triumph when we watch a TV quiz show and can come up with the answers two seconds before the troglodyte contestants can. We save and even frame such nonsensical throwaways as our high school diploma or a press clipping identifying us as third person from the left. We suck in our stomachs when we're in camera range of a tourist from Latvia shooting a photograph of his fat spouse.

These reactions connect directly to our desire to be loved, to be admired, to warrant applause even by passersby whom we never saw before and who forget us six paces later.

That characteristic is the force underlying "Am I right about you?" It slams into the bull's-eye of the human psyche.

A letter from a business mogul who seems to care more about this country than many of our elected representatives begins:

―――――――

Dear Friend:

I hope that what I've been told about you is true.

I've been told you are one American who understands the dire consequences for your family and our nation if we fail to eliminate the federal deficit.

―――――――

Buddy, as unpatriotic as it may seem, I'm more concerned with eliminating my personal deficit. But, yeah, you have a point . . . except that you're approaching it in too cerebral a manner and you get to the point too fast. *Dire consequences* and *eliminate* aren't knockout terms.

"Am I right about you," in order to build itself to maximum thrust, has to stay in the "you" mode until we've achieved that magical word *rapport*. Then you can bring in God, Abe Lincoln, and motherhood.

75.   WHEN WAS THE LAST TIME YOU . . .

I like this one because it's implicitly reader-involving. Where danger lurks is in a mismatch between this opening and the database from whence the recipient sprung. "When was the last time you" has to match the target or it appears either foolish or insulting.

This isn't a major problem. After all, *every* opening should match the target; but the specificity of this one calls for unusual care.

A mailing from a book club has four printed overlines before the greeting. It begins:

―――――――

GO AHEAD . . . INDULGE YOURSELF!

Sample the exciting *Special Club Magazine* enclosed.

Take 5 books for 99¢ with membership . . . along with valuable extras that make this a terrific deal.

Dear Reader,

When was the last time you <u>really relaxed</u> with a good book?

I'm not talking about sneaking in a few pages between household chores or office meetings. I'm talking about curling up in a favorite chair and....

———————————

Why am I vaguely dissatisfied? Is it because the writer underlined "relaxed" as well as "really?" Is it because the pre-greeting text gave away the play? Is it because the whole concept doesn't quite come off?

No matter. "When was the last time you" does work, if it's soaked in nostalgia.

(Now, when was the last time you read a flat claim like that?)

That's the batch for this chapter. Openings 76 to 100 are in chapter 11.

11

25 More Ways to Start a Letter– Openings 76 to 100

In this chapter:

92. *I won't waste your time.*

93. *Thank you.*

94. *Why do you need this?*

95. *Are you really sure they're giving you the right facts?*

96. *You're in my thoughts today.*

97. *If I'm sure of anything, I'm sure of this.*

98. *If you're worried, here's the solution.*

99. *Test yourself.*

100. *I'm mad as hell.*

The final twenty-five are a potpourri of pleasant, personal, and powerful letter openings. Many of them are so direct they wouldn't have been acceptable a generation ago. Directness—a marker of the last decade of the twentieth century—can bring results where dignity fails. Evaluate these and all letter openings according to one criterion: Is it more likely to bring a positive response?

76.   QUICK: WHAT IF . . .

We're really in the provocative neighborhood with this one, which hurls down an irresistible gauntlet. "Quick: What if" challenges the reader without the dangerous suggestion of superciliousness we see in other challenges.

The reader is forced to reach a *premature* conclusion; the benefit to us is the reader's recognition, even while reaching that conclusion, that we're about to present a better solution.

A computer software company makes good use of this opening:

Quick. What would happen if the power went out right now?...

Would the data on your PC be safe ... or would you have to "start all over?"

Most people don't back up their data every day. I'll admit that I miss a few days here and there—and sort of take my chances. I'm in a hurry, or in the middle of something else—or I just plain forget. So my files sit vulnerable to all kinds of "outrageous electronic fortunes ..."

Yep, this one sags a little after that powerhouse opening sentence. Putting "safe" before "start all over" (question mark should be outside the quotation marks here) is inside-out psychology. (You or I would have bypassed "safe" altogether or written a killer second sentence such as,

"Ugh. There goes that brilliant letter or the four hours you've just spent on a financial projection.") But even with the slight loosening of the reins, it holds the reader long enough for the sales message to kick in.

77. ISN'T IT NICE TO KNOW YOU'RE LOVED?

I'm enamored of this opening because it thrusts deep into the core of human reaction. The difference between "We love you" and "Isn't it nice to know you're loved?" is one of projected apparent sincerity. The second approach is more credible because it's a step beyond the declaration of love. Love is taken for granted, and the writer has moved beyond the statement to invite your reaction. Wonderful!

Why, then, isn't this delightfully effective opening more widely used? Simple: It isn't as universal as so many of the other openings we've discussed, such as number 1, "If you're like me," or number 41, "Visualize this scenario," or even its more mundane cousin number 46, "You're important to us."

A call for volunteers, from a nonprofit organization, makes perfect use of this opening:

_____

Hi! Isn't it always nice to feel you're wanted? Well, you *are* wanted....

_____

I like "Hi!" too. It's much in keeping with the tone of the letter . . . and it doesn't require personalization to be personal. A nice touch.

78. TODAY I FOUND OUT THAT YOU . . .

This opening is highly effective for subscription renewals, fund-raising, and highly targeted follow-up mailings.

Without "Today" or an even tighter "This morning," this opening doesn't work. Here's an example:

_____

Dear Member,

This morning I learned that we have not yet received your annual Membership Renewal.

_____

See how weak this would be if the opening were, "I recently learned that . . ."?

The danger of number 78 is the occasional necessity to include *passive* voice because the letter writer is *re*acting, not acting; action, or lack of it, is on the part of the message recipient. So whenever possible, replace words such as *receive* with harder verbs . . . which are more jarring to the reader.

79. YOU WANT IT. WE HAVE IT.

How assumptive and straightforward can you get? The effectiveness of this opening depends on the validity of the names on the mailing list.

The advantage "You want it. We have it" has over number 66, "We can do it where others can't," is its total reader involvement. That's the key to its potency . . . and to its incredible ability to annoy if you're off target. This is the stuff heavy response, coupled with heavy white mail (letters of complaint or damnation), is made of.

A subscription letter for an adult publication begins:

YOU WANT IT, WE'VE GOT IT!

Dear Reader,

The word is out! *Gallery* magazine is not a secret anymore, and you should know what almost 4 million yearly readers have known for 20 years. *Gallery* is the *hottest men's magazine available anywhere.*

I know, there are hundreds of magazines out there making the same claim, but only *Gallery* delivers, with every issue, 13 times a year.

Yes, it's mildly incoherent. If four million readers have known about this for twenty years it can't be much of a secret. (Is it number juggling? "4 million *yearly* readers" might be a thirteen-issue total, which means just 307,692 readers per issue.)

This writer placed the opening above the greeting. It certainly is strong enough to justify that position. If it had been under the greeting, I'd have retained the capital letters.

If you're hung up on dignity, forget this one. If you're hung up on response, it's a perfect test against a more staid opening.

80. IN THE TIME IT TOOK YOU TO OPEN THIS ENVELOPE . . .

This venerable opening is useful for both positive and negative news. Followed with "you could have," it suggests the time could have been profitable; followed with an ongoing disaster, it's a serviceable way to generate guilt.

A fund-raising letter begins:

Dear Concerned Citizen:

Even as you are reading this, others elsewhere who do not share our easy-to-obtain clean, clear water are imbibing water that may have disease-causing bacteria.

Do you wonder, as I do, why the writer damaged specificity with words such as *others* and *elsewhere*? And *imbibing*? How distancing can a word be? No matter. The opening is automatically reader involving. A proper gauge of the writer's talent is the ability to maintain and expand involvement, once the first few words are on the screen.

81. Even if you . . .

What a serviceable and effective opening this is!

"Even if you" has two variations. The first has *never* as the next word—"Even if you never . . . you'll still. . . ." The intention is to overcome implicit rejection of something readers think isn't an improvement over what they have.

The second use of "Even if you" is for the business-to-business ambience, presenting something to improve on what readers think may be unimprovable.

An example:

———————————

Hello, My Friend!

Even if you regard your market position as unassailable, your attitude, as a top executive, has to be: Is a competitor about to start breathing down the back of my neck?

AT&T, duPont, and IBM proved *any* company can face a sudden hot and nasty competitive breath. Nobody can rest easy in the uneasy millennial era. . . .

———————————

The value of "Even if you" is its unsettling effect, the demand for a second look. If you've been getting a "We don't need this" reaction to your offer, consider it.

82. Repeat a word.

This mechanical gimmick is so easy to implement I'm including it for those who aren't professional letter writers. Repetition, properly handled, is like the Chinese water torture—drops keep dripping until they produce a profound effect.

Do I have to point out that the chosen word should have some guts? Do I have to point out that *three* is the standard number of repetitions? Do I have to point out that whatever follows should be down and dirty, because the thrice-repeated word is supposed to represent drama, not quiet poetry?

An example of the repeated word:

Dear Friend,

LOCATION-LOCATION-LOCATION. The three most important ingredients in a retail business are also the three most important ingredients in choosing where to spend your hard-to-come-by advertising dollars.

The new Colorstick provides the best location for Communicomp to advertise its goods or services....

I'd have used periods instead of hyphens—"LOCATION. LOCATION. LOCATION." Some exponents of this opening add drama by intensifying each repeat: "Location. *Location.* **LOCATION!**"

What else works, other than "Die, die, die!" or "Now, now, now!"? Questions work—"Where? Where? Where?"; exclamations and invented words work—"Ycch. Ycch! YCCH!" and "Yeah, yeah, yeah!"; comparatives work—"Hotter . . . hotter . . . hotter!" which has greater impact than the progressive "Hot, hotter, hottest!"

Note that many of these end with an exclamation point. This, too, is standard dramatic technique for repetitions, whether on stage or in print.

83. You've made us unhappy.

This one is loaded with danger, even for fund-raisers, because today's Me-oriented society is crawling with latent antagonisms waiting to be unleashed. So instead of generating guilt, "You've made us unhappy" is just as likely to generate resentment.

"You've made *me* unhappy" is less likely to create an antagonist because the recipient doesn't feel he or she is battling an army. An example:

Dear Friend,

I am sorry to see that you've allowed your EARTHWATCH Membership to lapse. And I wanted to write you one last time to inquire why.

Because it's hard to imagine you've lost faith in the enterprising, hands-on brand of science that EARTHWATCH so energetically endorses and supports. I'm sure you still value these proven messages of study and personal, individual growth....

Aside from the incomplete second sentence, why not add a qualifier such as "truly" between "I am" and "sorry"? This softener also is reader involving, and "You've made us unhappy" fails without reader involvement.

Too, "And I wanted to write you one last time to inquire why" increases distance instead of diminishing it because past tense isn't called for here and "inquire" is as arm's length as a supposedly personal letter can get. Better: "I really do have to ask why." Then, as an option if this is a longtime supporter, "Have we somehow, some way, let you down?"

A reasonably standard use of "You've made us unhappy" is *deep* in a subscription renewal series. But wherever you use it, don't make the tone accusatory unless it's a last-ditch effort after all other goads have failed.

84. IMAGINE THIS.

"Imagine this" is one of the easier workhorses, which implicitly means it doesn't carry a lot of dynamite. It lacks the punch and vigor of its better-dressed cousins, number 3, "What if," number 26, "Have you ever wished," and number 41, "Visualize this scenario."

That recognition doesn't suggest that "Imagine this" is useless; if it were, it wouldn't be in this group. Rather, we should save this opening for circumstances where our relationship with the reader is so tenuous we're walking on eggs.

Adding an exclamation point—"Imagine this!"—literally doubles its impact; but even doubled, it's a lightweight.

A letter from a publication begins:

Dear Executive:

Imagine the convenience of reaching for a single-source general reference publication that provides you with a wealth of information on demographics, lifestyles, consumer segment profiles, and consumer magazines/direct mail lists to help you successfully market your product or services. Imagine it costing less than the bookshelf it sits on.

This is a loser in every way—too wordy, uses standoffish words such as *provides*, has a cliché in a crucial spot ("a wealth of information"), and no grabber. But the biggest problem is the misuse of "Imagine this." What's the word *imagine* doing here at all?

I'll repeat: Number 84 does work, but only when handled deliberately and professionally.

85. YOUR LIFE IS ABOUT TO CHANGE.

Wow, does number 85 fling a challenge! If you have the moxie to use this one, be sure you have a deal to match.

I've seldom had an offer strong enough or absolutely targeted enough to justify this powerhouse; and every use of it I've seen has been damaged by the writer's desire to use it without having the backup of a proposition the reader regards as a barn burner. An example (see page 253):

NATURAL CHOICE-USA

T. W. SIMMONS
NATIONAL DIRECTOR

Gordon H. Lewis, you CAN have it all...
more <u>money</u> than you've ever dreamed of,
and the <u>time</u> and <u>freedom to enjoy it!</u>

<u>You'll find out how when you accept my invitation...</u>

Mr. Gordon H. Lewis
340 No. Fig Tree Lane
Plantation, FL 33317-2561

Please R.S.V.P. by January 30

Dear Mr. Lewis,

I'd like you to be my guest at a very exciting event coming soon to Fort Lauderdale. Mark your calendar for January 30th, 31st and February 1st. Choose your most convenient day and time, and join us at the Doubletree Oceanfront Hotel.

I'm not exaggerating to say that this meeting can change your life forever. It has already changed the lives of thousands of people like you. Yet it takes just a little of your time, there's absolutely no obligation, and it costs you nothing.

<u>In fact, I'm going to send you a rebate check for</u> $1,150.00!

You'll find out about an amazing money-making opportunity that can give you the personal and financial freedom you want. A business that takes just a few hours a week, and starts <u>filling your pockets with cash</u> in as little as 60 days!

This is not a sales seminar. <u>Don't even bring your</u> <u>checkbook because you can't buy a thing</u>. But you'll come away with information so valuable, it can start you on your way to fortune and freedom!

You'll discover the amazing <u>all cash</u>

(over, please...)

RN011FLH T011 BE8 886 327

5700 BUCKINGHAM PARKWAY, CULVER CITY, CALIFORNIA 90230

Fig. 11.1 (letter opening number 85) Great power beams from a "Your life is about to change" opening if the reader believes the offer. Would the typical reader believe this one? Maybe … because of the clever "Don't even bring your checkbook" line.

SPECIAL NOTICE TO:

Herschel Lewis

Po [sic] Box 15725

Plantation, Fl 33318

Your whole perspective of real estate investing is about to change! I have enclosed a special invitation for you and a partner to be my guest at a unique event ... where you will learn what I consider to be the **most important breakthrough in real estate investor history**.

See what I mean? Oh, I'm not picking it to pieces because of my misspelled name or the "Po Box" or the unindented paragraphs; no, it's because *nothing* has any impact here, including "perspective" when tied to "change."

This writer would have been better off hybridizing this opening with an "If" prelude, something such as:

If you're a serious real estate investor, I'm about to change your life.

I'm not kidding ... and I mean a change *for the better*. No, make that a change for *light-years* better.

(And isn't that—a change for light-years better in our own letter openings, by judicious choices—why this book exists?)

86.   I couldn't wait!

One approach to categorizing divides letter openings into three varieties:

1. aggressive
2. permission asking
3. bubbling over with enthusiasm

"I couldn't wait!" is the archetype of a "bubbling over with enthusiasm" opening. And here's where the whole concept of letter-opening choice comes home to roost: Do you *want* to bubble over with enthusiasm? Do you *want* to risk being thought of as foolish by gushing over a subject your target may regard as trivial?

You're in command of the reader's reaction. *Who are you?*

The *professional* decision to use this opening involves more than the *simple* decision to use this opening. The professional doesn't just say, "I used number 85 last time so this time I'll use number 86." The professional says, "*This* is the right opening for generating a response to *this* offer from *this* recipient."

A letter marked "Personal" (bulk mail) begins:

Dear Linda:

I just couldn't wait to write to you, because I have just learned that in the next few months I believe that some *absolutely fantastic* things could be coming your way. Never before in my career have I seen such powerful signs of good fortune for one individual!

Hilarious? To us jaded marketers, sure it is. This was bulk mail, which meant "Never before in my career have I seen such powerful signs of good fortune for one individual!" is pure hogwash. And "I have just learned that in the next few months I believe that . . ." qualifies for the Department of Utter Confusion.

But before we damn this opening, let's once again go back to our premise—the professional says, "*This* is the right opening for generating a response to *this* offer from *this* recipient."

So the correctness and effectiveness of "I couldn't wait!" should never be linked to what we, the uninvolved, oversophisticated, scornful critics opine; it's tied to the hopes and dreams of the Lindas of this world.

87.   DO ME A FAVOR *OR* I NEED A FAVOR FROM YOU.

Ben Franklin said—well, may have said—"If you want to make a friend, have him do something for you." Old Ben (or whoever) spoke pre-psychiatric wisdom there. The person who does a favor for you is tied to you more closely than the person for whom *you* do a favor.

So why not adapt this to a letter?

A couple of reasons come to mind, pro and con.

Pro:
1. Ben Franklin was right, and affinity is the result.
2. Curiosity forces the reader to read on.

Con:
1. Even a minor misdirection can generate antagonism instead of rapport.
2. If your target feels the "favor" is stupid, out of line, too self-serving, or desperate, instead of impaling a prospect with Cupid's arrow you've shot yourself in the foot.

Golf Digest

5520 Park Avenue ● Trumbull, CT 06611

****

Will You Please Do Us a Favor?

And do something for yourself at the same time? The favor
I'm asking is easy to do...fun...enlightening...and guaranteed to
make you a better golfer. What is it, you're probably wondering?
Well, I'll tell you. Or, I should say, ask you. Will you please
do us a favor and examine 2 issues of GOLF DIGEST risk-free? There
are no strings attached. None at all! And there's a FREE GIFT
waiting for you, just for giving GOLF DIGEST a look-see...

****

Dear Fellow Golfer,

Do you ever find yourself dreaming you can transform your golf game so
you swing like Nick Price, putt like Loren Roberts and chip like Phil
Mickelson? What about mastering the mental game of golf and staying cool
under pressure like Justin Leonard? Well, you can! There's one proven way to
turn your dreams into reality, and **gain the confidence and skills to unlock
your true potential as a golfer**...GOLF DIGEST!

How can one magazine accomplish all that?

I'm glad you asked! Because GOLF DIGEST is NOT just a magazine. It's
more like having a **personal coach** right by your side, all year long, helping
you improve every aspect of your game! You'll have Tiger Woods (a GOLF
DIGEST exclusive!), Phil Mickelson, Judy Rankin and many other pros on your
"coaching staff" dispensing top-shelf advice. All for less than the price of
lunch at the halfway house!

Whether you're a beginner with a 30 handicap...a weekend player...or a
die-hard, 7-day-a-week golfer, **if you're hungry for improvement...if you
truly desire to bring your game to a higher level, GOLF DIGEST will take you
wherever you want to go!**

I kid you not! Get ready to start on a path to a better golf game
the day you receive your first risk-free issue and 3 FREE GIFTS, a 3-guide
collection of 101 Stroke-Saving Golf Tips. GOLF DIGEST's bigger size and
graphic clarity make every tip, every secret easily understandable...
and memorable.

You get all the expert advice you can possibly absorb from the
best of the best. Pros like Ernie Els, Justin Leonard and Tom
Watson. (They're all listed on the envelope — and other playing
editors, advisors and teaching professionals who bring you tips
and techniques from GOLF DIGEST's 500 schools around the country.)
That's where the "demos" that appear in GOLF DIGEST are field-
tested on players of all levels. Pointers only GOLF DIGEST subscribers are privy to. You'll get them FREE with no obligation to
subscribe!

(over, please)

Fig. 11.2   (letter opening number 87) In keeping with Benjamin Franklin's possibly apocryphal comment, "If you want to make a friend, have him do something for you," many target individuals who never respond to an outright pitch feel empathetic toward someone who asks for a favor. Here is a standard subscription offer, aided by the "favor" flavor.

This seems to be the case with the publisher of a directory, who begins a sales letter this way:

Dear Colleague:

I need a small favor from you. If, after reading this message in its entirety, you can think of a reason not to reserve your no-risk examination copy of the new **Card Industry Directory**, please drop me a line.

Sorry, buddy, you're presenting this in a way that makes it seem too big a favor. First, what's the phrase "in its entirety" doing there? This transforms "favor" into "demand"—poor salesmanship. Second, the whole concept is transparent. Third, I still think paragraphs should be indented.

Why didn't the writer, using the same opening, lean toward rapport instead of arrogance by writing something like this?

Dear Colleague,

I need a small favor from you.

The favor is simple for you and means much to me. I'm quite convinced you'll quickly see the benefit of owning the new **Card Industry Directory**. But obviously what matters is what *you* think. So if, after reading my reasons in this letter, you don't agree, will you be my friend and tell me why?

The difference in reader interpretation between the original and our revision is one of *int*ent, not *con*tent.

88.   GET READY!

This bright opening is best used when you're positive of the demographic-psychographic match between your offer and your reader . . . and your offer is manifestly either amusing or vigorous.

A variation of "Get ready!" is "It's coming!"—but you can see the difference: "Get ready!" is loaded with *you*; "It's coming!" leaves *you* as a spectator.

A letter from a rock music source has this overline:

Ready to rock?

This is your special invitation to personally audition the world's greatest guitar bands in your house for 10 days . . . free!

The letter then begins in high gear:

Dear Rocker,

Call your friends … check your fuse box … and get ready to rock … because we're planning to bring the world's loudest, heaviest, most awesome guitar rockers to your house for 10 days … free.

Nice piece of writing. I'd have said "we're bringing" instead of "we're planning to bring"; but the writing is so sprightly it—well, it rocks!

89.   TIME HAS PASSED . . . or IT'S BEEN A WHILE SINCE . . .

This is the sedate second cousin of number 31, "We've missed you," and a first cousin of number 56, "I'm surprised I haven't heard from you."

Number 31 is generic, an all-purpose opening for contacting inactive customers or donors. Numbers 56 and 89 are more specific. Both have a powerful place in fund-raising. The difference is in apparent pressure. Number 56 tries to superimpose guilt; number 89, far gentler, attempts to generate guilt.

The definition itself proves that the writer of "Time has passed" needs greater communicative ability than the more bold approach—"I'm surprised I haven't heard from you." Want proof? Visualize these as telephone openings rather than letters.

A fund-raising letter begins quietly:

Dear Friend and Supporter,

It's been a while since you last sent a gift to Greenpeace. Your past support helped make Greenpeace a unique force on the world scene. You know what I mean … [Ellipsis theirs, ending the paragraph.]

Good writing. I don't agree with the word *gift* in the first sentence of a "Time has passed" letter, and no, I don't know what they mean; but these are the mildest of flaws in an oh-so-gentle reminder.

90.   WE'VE ALL BEEN WAITING [STRIVING] FOR THIS.

In no way is "We've all been waiting for this" parallel to number 23, "Good news!" "Good news!" is aimed *outward*. "We've" says to the reader, "You *and* I."

One problem with this opening—as with many—is the possibility of including outsiders who will scoff. But is it really a problem? This opening is reserved for co-thinkers. And for cold lists (outside names) the writer has every right to depend on respectable list selection to eliminate those who

Herschell Gordon Lewis
Chairman
Bozell, Jacobs, Keyon & Eckhardt
340 North Fig Tree Lane, Box 15725
Plantation, FL 33317-2561

RELEASE 1.0

104 Fifth Avenue, 20th Floor, New York, NY 10011

"Come, I will tell you of my voyage home…"

ULYSSES

Dear Herschell Gordon,

There's never been a business like the one we're part of. Trying to describe it to a friend the other day, it occurred to me that Homer's *Odyssey* might be just the right metaphor. The past two decades have certainly been an amazing adventure, complete with heroes, triumphs, disasters, and incredible war stories. And as I write to you today, our own odyssey has barely begun.

Esther Dyson and **Release 1.0** have been aboard from the start. No publication has chronicled this unfolding adventure with greater insight. And now, with this invitation to subscribe to **Release 1.0**, you have the opportunity to come along for the ride.

A GUIDEBOOK FOR THE ROAD AHEAD

There are a few things you should know about **Release 1.0** at the outset, because it is unlike any newsletter, magazine, newspaper, journal or insider briefing you've seen or subscribed to.

First, Esther has been hip deep in this industry and writing about it for more than 20 years. There is simply no other reporter with her authority, perspective or access to industry leaders. Kevin Werbach, her managing editor, is recognized as a leading analyst of media convergence, next-generation network infrastructure and policy issues affecting the software and Internet industries. Check out both their impressive bios at http://www.edventure.com/.

Their focus in **Release 1.0** is current events with long-term implications. They are utterly practical, and whether you accept or reject the ideas in **Release 1.0**, they cannot be ignored. In an atmosphere of constant change, you need to know what they write about.

"Esther and Kevin bring really important issues to the surface. In our fast-changing ocean of opportunity, you can use them to chart your course."

John Doerr, General Partner, Kleiner Perkins Caufield & Byers

Also worth noting: while our subscribers together wouldn't fill an average sports stadium, they are far and away the most influential and important people in the information industry. They depend on Esther and Kevin for an unvarnished, well-informed view of what is going to be new, what's going to be hot and who's going to make it happen.

One small example: You and I have witnessed a revolution over the past couple of years as the Internet and World Wide Web revolutionized our industry. **Release 1.0** anticipated this change, as it has so many others, well before the changes made headlines.

Fig. 11.3 (letter opening number 91) Who are we? To use the vernacular, beats the hell out of me. This letter, intending to use "Who are we?" as an opener, succeeds only in mystifying. What the offer is supposed to be is too elusive to be pursued. When you pose the rhetorical question "Who are we?" the next step is to explain who you are, in coherent wording the reader can decode.

every right to depend on respectable list selection to eliminate those who automatically snort, "No, I *haven't* been waiting or striving for this."

A more logical problem is using this opening and then being unable to convince your co-thinkers this really is something all of you have been waiting for.

A letter begins:

Dear Friend of Planned Parenthood,

The moment we've all been working for is now at hand: the creation of a national system of healthcare that includes abortion and other essential reproductive health care as a matter of right for *all* American women.

Yes, it's a shade on the intellectual side, but unquestionably the writer of this letter has every right to assume the recipient, a member of the organization, will agree with the premise.

91. WHO ARE WE?

If you'll reread "Who Are We?" in chapter 1, you'll see why this opening requires the ultraprofessional touch. Asking the person who gets your message, "Who are we?" can generate guffaws instead of phone calls: "These guys don't even know who they are."

The easy and obvious test of validity: If the next sentence justifies the question, it's a grabber opening; if it doesn't, steer away from "Who are we?"

A letter from a sweepstakes company:

Dear H.G. Lewis,

Who is Ventura and why are we writing to you? We're the people with a lot of first hand experience working with Direct Response agencies. We help them to help their clients:

• Increase awareness

• Increase response levels

• Increase order size....

Does this use of "Who are we?" work? Yes and no—yes because in an introductory business-to-business communication this opening is a safe choice; no because the answer to "Who are we?" is neither specific nor potent. "We're the people with a lot of first hand experience working with Direct Response agencies" is a claim I've heard from 22,346 sources.

Incidentally, way down in paragraph 8, this company—and it really is a distinguished supplier to our industry—clarifies what it has to offer. The writer should move that paragraph to the top and justify "Who are we?" as a rhetorical question.

92. I WON'T WASTE YOUR TIME.

This is a good expert-to-expert vehicle. We can envision Albert Einstein beginning an explanation this way.

And that's the caution. How many conversations, let alone letters, have you had in which some boor says, "I won't waste your time" . . . then wastes your time?

Terseness is the key to number 92. If you say, "I won't waste your time" and then launch into a historical summary, you've chosen the wrong opening. Einstein has given way to Tolstoy, and the word-glutted reader consciously or unconsciously becomes a resentful "I thought so" outsider.

Overlines are fashionable, but they just don't go with this opening. Here's the printed overline on a subscription letter from a computer publication:

———————————

Announcing an important NEW, LABS-BASED RESOURCE dedicated solely to helping you successfully integrate your multi-platform information systems. One that will cost you nothing whatsoever, now or ever.

———————————

The letter begins:

———————————

Dear IS Expert:

I won't waste your time. The challenge you face now is the most complex, most demanding, most important challenge in information systems today . . .

Now, you must find a way to integrate a wide range of systems into one, incredibly powerful, multi-platform environment that lets your company's technology play in concert.

———————————

Okay, what have we learned? Nothing. So "I won't waste your time" is—well, it's a lie.

I'm not attacking the writing; I'm attacking the use of this opening for this message. It's a mismatch. The letter would have been stronger without the overline. Compare that opening with this possibility:

———————————

Dear IS Expert,

I won't waste your time.

You need us. Simple as that. We're the key to integrating your multi-platform information systems. And incidentally, we're free.

———————————

If you can't be terse, choose another opening.

93.   THANK YOU.

How can you go wrong saying, "Thank you"?

I like *ending* a letter with "Thank you" because to me it's more logical to thank the reader for performing whatever act the letter suggests. Thanking in advance, though, has its own benefit—setting a mood of gratitude.

So the question the writer has to ask is, "What am I thanking this reader for?" If the answer doesn't make sense, the thanks doesn't make sense.

A subscription mailing for a newsletter begins:

Dear Reader:

Thank you for taking the time to open the envelope. Right up front, here are answers to questions you may have....

I wonder about this. Thanking the reader for opening the envelope— well, for-hire communicators know such an act is certainly worthy of thanks. And it does put the reader in a receptive state of mind. So I'm not about to attack this use of the "Thank you" opening.

But this person already *has* opened the envelope. That second sentence has terrific guts to it. Did the mailer test the opening against one which opens in high gear?

94.   WHY DO YOU NEED THIS?

Here we have the third "Why" opening in our one hundred opening listings. The others are number 20, "Why are we doing this?" and number 28, "Why do they . . . *or* Why don't they."

You can see the logic: The first example is first person, "I" or "we." The second example is "he," "her," or "they." Who's left? "*you.*"

Tying "Why"—an implicit reader-involver—with "you"—an explicit reader-involver—should be surefire. "Why do you" is considerably weaker than "Why don't you," but it's also considerably safer because it doesn't engender the "They're trying to sell me something" reaction from skeptical readers.

A mailing for a directory begins:

Dear Marketing Planner:

"Why would I need another print media directory?"

That's what you may be asking yourself as you read this letter.

After all, you've probably already got the directory that you think of as "The Bible" in the media field....

This approach may be a little too cautious. "Would" and "may" are conditional, not straightforward. I have a feeling you or I might have taken a slightly more slam-bang approach:

Dear Marketing Planner,

I'll bet I can guess the question you're about to ask yourself:

"WHY DO I NEED ANOTHER PRINT MEDIA DIRECTORY?"

If that question is on target, it's because you're used to that other directory—the one most planners use as their "Media Bible"....

"Why" tied to "you" has an edge over many of the other openings we've discussed: It's never a terrible way to start out.

95. ARE YOU REALLY SURE THEY'RE GIVING YOU THE RIGHT FACTS?

A principal value of this opening is its inference—"You're smart, but the people who are feeding you information may be neither smart nor honorable"—without making an open accusation.

Note the crucial difference between "Are you sure they're giving you the right facts?" and "Are you sure you're getting the right facts?" The first statement assigns responsibility to an outsider; the second assigns responsibility to the reader.

Note, too, the edge this opening has over a simpler but less reader-involving "Are they giving you the right facts?"

So *after* the letter establishes competitive positioning, switch to a statement saying something such as "Now you'll get the right facts about Whatever." The compromise opening, "Now you can get the right facts about Whatever," is unrelated (see opening number 47) because it subordinates "they" to the reader's sudden capability.

An example of "Are you really sure they're giving you the right facts?":

Dear Publishing Executive:

Are you comfortable—really comfortable—about the information you're using to make today's tricky business decisions?

You're not you say? That's not surprising.

The omitted comma in the second sentence is the writer's error, not mine, and as the letter continues into the third paragraph it becomes bookish; but the tone of this letter is moderately on target. "They" aren't feeding you the right information. The competitive challenge has an extra arrow in its quiver.

96.　You're in my thoughts today.

Careful with this one! Yes, it's highly emotional. But it's *so* personal you really can tick off the recipient. If you're not fund-raising, save it for genuine relationships. For fund-raising, be sure whoever signs the letter is someone who *might* have the recipient in his or her thoughts. (It's especially valuable for milking prior donors.)

A respected fund-raising organization mailed this holiday message:

———————

Dear Mr. Lewis,

I often ask myself what The Salvation Army would do without good friends like you.

The men, women and children you've helped are living, breathing proof of the good you have done for this community. You've given those in need food, clothing and shelter. And, you've brought hope into their lives.

That's why you are in my thoughts today as we approach the Christmas season. Because hunger knows no season....

———————

Altogether, completely professional.
But . . .
What if the writer had *opened* with number 96? The letter might have read . . .

———————

You're in my thoughts today. I'll tell you why:

It's because I often ask myself what The Salvation Army would do without good friends like you.

The men, women and children you've helped are living, breathing proof of the good you have done for this community. You've given those in need food, clothing and shelter. And, you've brought hope into their lives....

———————

Isn't the message more powerful when "You're in my thoughts today" is the opener rather than an ancillary?

97.　If I'm sure of anything, I'm sure of this.

This opening is valuable for immediate emphasis of the writer's sincerity, openness, or integrity.

Dear Friend,

    I write this letter as a Jew ... as a Holocaust survivor ... and as a partisan.

    Despite what may seem to be a parochial viewpoint, I know one thing for certain. The Nazis persecuted everyone they hated.

    Although Jews were the primary victims, non-Jews were also targeted by the Nazis. It happened to the handicapped, to Roma and Sinti (Gypsies), to Polish intellectuals and priests. And it also happened to homosexuals.

    In concentration camps throughout Nazi Germany and other countries under Hitler's dictatorship, homosexuals were forced to wear identifying signs like the Jews. But instead of armbands, these were pink triangles worn on their pockets. And in the terrible atmosphere of the camps, homosexuals were treated very cruelly.

    They were singled out for brutality not only by concentration camp guards, but by other inmates as well. And when the long-awaited "liberation" finally came, these victims of Nazi oppression were not released ... but were forced instead to serve out the rest of their terms in prison.

    The reason for my letter today is to ask for your help in honoring the memory of thousands of homosexuals who suffered in the Nazi regime ... and in educating millions of Americans about what can happen when hatred and bigotry become law.

    As I'm sure you know, the United States Holocaust Memorial Museum is one of the largest and most important museums in the world dedicated to telling the story of the Holocaust.

    Since it opened in 1993 — and despite controversy and objections by some — this Museum has never shied away from examining the experience of homosexuals during this period of history.

    With films, seminars, lectures, publications, and special exhibitions, the United States Holocaust Memorial Museum — perhaps more so than any other Holocaust museum in the world — has worked hard to educate the public about the treatment of homosexuals by the Nazis.

                       over, please

Fig. 11.4   (letter opening number 97) The recipient of a letter which says "If I'm sure of anything, I'm sure of this" (here worded "I know one thing for certain") either shares the writer's philosophy or rejects it ...no middle ground. This fund-raising letter could generate hate mail from those who claim the Holocaust never happened. If it does, the letter is a success because it also will generate contributions from those who know it did.

Dr. Andrew Weil's

Self Healing

CREATING **NATURAL HEALTH** FOR **YOUR BODY** AND **MIND**

P.O. Box 1969 • Marion, OH • 43306

"TAKE TWO ASPIRIN... AND THROW THEM AWAY."

"Who said that?"

"MY DOCTOR SAID THAT."

"Is he a real M.D.?"

"REAL? HIS M.D. IS FROM THE HARVARD MEDICAL SCHOOL."

"I want to know more about this doctor."

"GOOD IDEA. JUST READ THIS LETTER."

Good Morning!

I really believe the next 4 1/2 minutes — the time it will take you to read this letter — can make a whopping big difference in your life.

I'm serious... and I'm confident, too, because I'm about to describe the most unusual, the most useful, and the most personal Newsletter you ever heard or read of: Dr. Andrew Weil's Self Healing letter, written and edited by the celebrated Dr. Andrew Weil.

Certainly you know Dr. Weil's reputation. You may have seen him on ABC's "Prime Time Live." You may have read one of his books... or one of his many articles, whose titles range from "Margarine vs. Butter" to "Eleven Medical Practices to Avoid." Your family doctor may have warned you, "This guy practices a different type of medicine. He thinks natural healing is as good as synthetic prescription chemicals."

I'm about to offer you the opportunity to judge for yourself whether Andrew Weil, M.D., is a genius or an eccentric. And it won't cost you even a dime to find out.

"HEALING IS FUNDAMENTALLY A NATURAL PROCESS."

As his picture in the brochure I've enclosed certainly proves, Andrew Weil isn't your typical doctor — although he's a <u>very</u> respected member of the faculty at the

Fig. 11.5 (letter opening number 97) With a slightly different text, this letter might be listed under opening number 71, "Take just two minutes." But as structured, it is an elegant example of number 97. The confidence is contagious. You can see the structure building and building, which makes this, the final example reprinted in these pages, an appropriate model.

This is a highly useful, dynamic opening, but just one caution: Don't let it disintegrate into a used-car dealer's arm-around-the-shoulder "I'll be honest with ya" pitch.

A letter from a computer software company begins:

Dear Registered User:

I know one thing for sure about my computer's memory ... it's a pain in the neck. Frankly, I don't want to worry about memory. I want enough room to do my work and that's it. I want my system's memory to be handled automatically! Just take care of it and don't bother me!

It works, but number 1, "If you're like me," might work just as well or better. "Frankly" damages the pitch, as does the exclamation mark after "automatically" because the message becomes shrill and car dealer-like. Are these objections? Nope. They're suggestions, proof that what each of us does best is criticize the creative work of others.

98.   IF YOU'RE WORRIED, HERE'S THE SOLUTION.

Openings like this become more and more valid as computers and snooping give us greater and greater ability to pinpoint our targets.

A second value of this opening is its ability to generate a worry that may not have existed. The target thinks, "Hey, I really should be worried about this."

A letter with a big, black, printed overline—"Why hasn't your broker told you about today's most overlooked, misunderstood and *profitably secure* investments?"—begins:

Dear Investor:

If you're worried about your financial future ... worried about increasing your investment income and looking for sound diversification ... then I ask you to consider subscribing to *The Laird Letter*.

I have a feeling half a sentence is missing here. The writer brings in *"The Laird Letter"* as a solution without justifying it as a solution. Too, worry "about your financial future" is a generalized worry. Specifics outpull generalizations. So "If you're worried that your investments won't increase and aren't diversified enough" changes no fact but moves toward specificity.

Those are comments about *this* letter, but they don't affect the worth of the opening.

99. TEST YOURSELF.

This one can't miss. People are suckers for self-testing. They try to outguess the contestants on quiz shows; they look for trivia questions in the in-flight magazines; they'll spend money for a by-mail IQ test.

The key is to have them test themselves. They resent testing from the outside. So if you use this opening, the test has to be logical, relevant, one the reader can pass with pride or fail without dishonor, and above all, *clear*.

A letter to business executives begins:

_____

Dear Friend,

According to management consultants, the single most important asset a busy executive can possess is skill in managing time.

> Test yourself: Do you know how to free your mind for important decisions? How to guarantee that you get top priority projects finished first? Is your work organized?...

_____

Okay, what's your opinion? Does this "test" qualify on grounds of logic, relevance, pass with pride or fail without dishonor, and clarity? I don't think so. Asking someone, "Do you know how to free your mind for important decisions?" is an unanswerable question. A muzzy question begets a muzzy answer, if any. The *second* question qualifies on all counts: "How to guarantee that you get top priority projects finished first?" Why not use that one as the key test, or even the only test?

(What is that first limp sentence doing there at all? If the writer had a mad urge to include a management consultant reference, a better lead-in to "Test yourself" might have been: "Management consultants agree. Do you? Managing time is *the* key executive ability.")

100.   I'M MAD AS HELL.

This opening has a colossal benefit: It's contagious. Like some of the other openings we've discussed, ranging from numbers 9, 26, 67, 68, and 74 right up to number 98, "I'm mad as hell" has the power to generate a state of mind.

Being mad as hell is obvious for fund-raisers, but astute business marketers can get results with it when all ninety-nine other openings don't seem to work. Obviously, the anger has to be directed at "them," not you.

In this instance, the actual words aren't necessary. What's necessary is transmitting the flavor of righteous outrage. Do that by using emotional words. Attack with fire and flame, not matchsticks.

What a way to end a series! The example is from the Nationwide Campaign to Halt Advertising Abuse. A Johnson Box is headed:

SICK AND TIRED OF ADVERTISING CONSTANTLY JUNKING UP YOUR LIFE? HERE IS YOUR CHANCE TO FIGHT BACK AND STOP IT!

The letter proper begins:

Dear Citizen,

I believe America stands for far more important values than "shop 'til you drop" and "when the going gets tough, the tough go shopping!"

And right now, it's high time to *stop* Madison Avenue from defining *our* core values for ourselves and our families. We are far more valuable as human beings than *what we consume*—and we must choose and fight for an American culture of responsibility and community over runaway commercialism....

Uh-oh. He's lost it. I got as only far as "defining our core values" before dropping out. The signer is "Michael Jacobson, Ph.D.," and the letter has too much of the Ph.D. in it to carry the contagion we need. Remember that key—emotional words. What could be less emotional than *defining* (I hate that word in selling copy) and *core values* and *consume* and *choose*?

If you're mad as hell, be mad as hell. Don't be as angry as Hades.

. . . Which I'd like to think you are to see this listing of one hundred ways to begin a business letter come to an end.

12

A Concluding Thought

As we drive the golden spike into this communication railbed, smoke has to clear away so the Master Key to effective letter-writing can become clear.

The Master Key isn't cleverness. It isn't a massive vocabulary. It isn't thorough product knowledge.

In fact, those three elements can *suppress* response.

Cleverness too often becomes the end instead of the means . . . and in this Age of Skepticism we all know that cleverness for the sake of cleverness may well be a liability rather than an asset.

Massive vocabulary? Bosh. Effective letter-writing often depends on vocabulary *suppression*. People who know the big words usually know the smaller, clearer words, too. If I write here and now that big words can be obfuscatory, many readers will have to look up that word—*if they choose to*.

What have I proved? That I know a big word? Bully for me! But better for me if I'd skipped *obfuscatory* and relied on a more dependable term, *confusing* . . . or said that many people aren't sure what some big words actually mean and subliminally resent the arrogance of a writer who uses them to show off.

Thorough product knowledge too often brings results skewed 180 degrees from the effect we're after, because regurgitating product knowledge is 180 degrees skewed from the Master Key to effective letter-writing. I, as prospective buyer or inquirer or donor, care far less about what something is than about what it will do for me. Letters loaded with product knowledge usually are also loaded with corporate arrogance, a Me-centered message which leaves the reader as reader, not as an involved participant.

So by using one of the one hundred ways to begin a letter—and using it properly—at once we eliminate such openings as . . .

- "We have developed a wide variety of interlocking marketing services ranging from [SNORE] . . ."

- "If your business demands reliable communication and you demand value . . . choose [NAME OF COMPANY]."
- "You have better things to think about than your busy schedule."
- "DON'T PAY TAXES ON MONEY YOU AREN'T USING."
- "[NAME OF COMPANY] shops the world to find the finest quality designer jewelry."

See how easy it is to write a lousy opening?

The Master Key:

> ✏ Write in a style and mode that matches the reader's demographic, psychological, and attitudinal position of the moment.

Not easy, you say? Wonderful. If it were easy, anybody could do what we do.